Pockets of Freedom

"Pockets of Freedom," by Jacek Jachimowicz. ISBN 978-1-60264-722-0.

Second Edition

Copyright for all editions of Pockets of Freedom, A Portrait of My Mother by Jacek Jachimowicz

Editor: Jason Warshof

Photo inserts: All photo inserts courtesy of the author

Manufactured in the United States of America.

To Norah, Maia, Tami, and Adi—
Adela's blood runs in your veins

Jacek Jachimowicz

POCKETS OF FREEDOM

A Portrait of My Mother

Rankiem, 28 stycznia 1998 roku,
zmarła we Frankfurcie nad Menem,
a nazajutrz została pochowana na tamtejszym Cmentarzu Żydowskim

IRENA JACHIMOWICZOWA

30 lat temu zmuszona do opuszczenia ojczystej Polski
Osierociła i pogrążyła w bólu dwóch synów,
kilkoro wnucząt i liczne grono przyjaciół.
Była pięknym Człowiekiem:
dobrym, ciepłym, wielkodusznym
i wyrozumiałym dla ułomności ludzkiej natury.
Była również Człowiekiem szczodrym,
bo chociaż na obczyźnie borykała się często
z niedostatkiem, wspomagała wielu rozbitków życiowych,
nie zważając na ich przynależność etniczną,
narodową czy wyznaniową.
Darzyła mnie przyjaźnią,
co poczytuję sobie za zaszczyt
Elwira Milewska-Zonn

GAZETA WYBORCZA *Sobota–niedziela 31 stycznia–1 lutego 1998*

In the morning of January 28, in 1998
died in Frankfurt am Main

IRENA JACHIMOWICZ

and was buried there in the Jewish cemetery.
30 years ago, she was forced to leave behind Poland, her fatherland.
She orphaned and plunged into pain her two sons, along with
her grandchildren and a large circle of friends.
She was a beautiful human being:
good, warm, magnanimous,
and forbearing of the infirmity of human nature.
She was also a generous person, for even when
on foreign soil, often struggling with her own privation,
she helped many human shipwrecks,
regardless of their ethnicity, or their
national or religious affiliation.
She bestowed her friendship upon me,
which I consider to be an honor
Elwira Milewska-Zonn

Warsaw, Saturday-Sunday 31 January–1 February 1998

It is by his freedom that a man knows himself, by his sovereignty over his own life that a man measures himself. To violate that freedom, to flout that sovereignty, is to deny man the right to live his life, to take responsibility for himself with dignity.

—*Elie Wiesel*

Introduction

FOR EACH PERIOD IN her life, my mother acquired a distinct name: Adela Guterman until 1939; Irena Siekańska during World War II, until her imprisonment in Auschwitz; 74721 at the death mill of Auschwitz-Birkenau; and Irena Jachimowicz for her years in Poland after the war. A fifth name comes to mind: Frau Jachimowicz, or Frau Irene, which fits the last part of her life, when she lived in Frankfurt.

These names suggest a life frequently interrupted, and this is largely how Adela's years unfolded. Several times she was compelled to reinvent her persona and to rebuild everything from scratch: throughout the war, in postwar Poland, during her short stay in Israel, and in Frankfurt from the 1970s onward. In spirit and character, though, Adela's story is one of unity. For all the dismal cards she was handed, she remained above the fray: adhering to her principles, coming to the aid of others when a situation demanded it, never allowing her decency to waver, and above all, creating her own pockets of freedom, however oppressive the climate around her.

Nowhere is the unity of my mother's life more evident than in her actions and behavior throughout the Holocaust—or Shoah, the Hebrew word for "calamity"—and the Second World War. When the war began, she was barely a young woman, two and a half months from turning seventeen. By her twenty-third birthday, not only her world but also the face of humanity had been overturned. The events of the Second World War shaped me as well to a large extent, even though I was born years after it ended.

Humankind has filled the last six decades with genocide, war crimes, and other atrocities, but the Holocaust remains unprecedented in modern history, and unsurpassed in its horror. This is so for many reasons, among them the national scale of participation in Nazi aims; the hatred directed toward Jews and others of "impure" ethnicity; and the detachment of the operators and executioners in their pursuit of annihilation. Those gears of death, it seems to me—meticulously designed, constructed, and brought to effect—could only have been the product of legendary German engineering. Even the methodology was impeccable, with bookkeeping and archiving planned out in advance and with frightening precision. But for all I have just mentioned, nothing about the Holocaust is more chilling than the success of Adolf Hitler and his men in convincing the German nation that finding, exposing, and ultimately murdering a Jew was not only a necessary step in the purification—or "Aryanization"—of a people but a fundamental civic duty, a matter of public health supported by "scientific" claims. This act was placed on the same level as voting or sitting on a jury, and only the compliance of Germany's citizens allowed the machine to churn ahead as it did. I therefore think it fitting that author and historian Christopher Browning refers to Hitler's agents and executioners as "ordinary men."

Auschwitz has come to represent the Holocaust as a whole, the face of its evil. Günter Grass, Germany's unofficial literary spokesman of the post–World War II era—who in 2006 sparked debate about his credibility by admitting to his own involvement in the Waffen-SS as a teenager—has referred to Auschwitz as the greatest tragedy of his life. I myself am not alone in thinking of the Auschwitz death camp as humanity's lowest point in modern history. And it was at Auschwitz that my mother spent her most harrowing period under Nazism. The camp's design and construction were not the work of a few Nazi "monsters," as some might assume today. The plan involved architects, engineers, urban planners, administrators, accountants, and many other professionals at all levels. The industries employed in operating the camp were even more numerous, and special legislation was passed to facilitate the rounding up and the global resettlement of Jews. This systemic complexity combined with the use of technology to add a new dimension to genocide, insofar as the world recognized the concept at that time—that of "industrial killings," according to Omer Bartov, a professor of European history, in his book *Mirrors of Destruction*—not to mention industrious killings.

But while the smokestacks of Auschwitz's crematoria seemed only to howl death, in many ways the camp was also about life. In order to remain among the living, the accepted protocol was to mind one's own business and absolutely nothing else. "Every man for himself," was the motto that led each prisoner. Ka-Tzetnik,[1] the pen name of a survivor who sharpened our understanding of the Holocaust by writing about the camp for almost four decades, called Auschwitz "another planet," a world inhabited by creatures where the usual codes, customs, and rules of humanity did not apply. Bartov writes about Ka-Tzetnik in *Mirrors of Destruction:*

---

[1] The name denoted a concentration camp prisoner during the Holocaust. The writer's real name was Yehiel Dinur, and his work documented Nazi horrors during the war; 135633 was the prisoner number tattooed onto his forearm.

His attention is focused more on the disintegration of even the most basic human relationships and moral codes among the inmates, the cruelty to which hunger, deprivation, and humiliation give rise, the fall of those who under other circumstances would have been the most admired members of a community. Few figures retain their humanity for long … and the isolated figures that do so are quickly destroyed precisely because of their failure to adapt to the new and for them unacceptable world…. Even if rarely asserted is the assumption that only those who adapted by shedding their humanity, forsaking their loved ones, their faith, indeed leaving their old selves behind in the crematoria, had even the faintest chance of surviving.

Shmuel Ron was Adela's longtime friend, as well as her sometime coconspirator in the resistance movement and fellow Auschwitz prisoner (No. 176467). Of Auschwitz, he writes as follows in his memoir, *Die Erinnerungen haben mich nie losgelassen* (*The Memories Never Let Go of Me*):

I will never forget the lessons I learned from Yankele [Shmuel's bunkmate]: people can be turned into beasts of prey if that is the price of survival, and even that mentality lasts only for a short while.

For my mother, such a process of dehumanization never occurred, and this is part of what makes her story exceptional. At Auschwitz and throughout her life, Adela refused to compromise her humanity, no matter the circumstances. This earned her immense respect from her fellow prisoners. Rivka Ledor, a survivor who participated with Adela in the camp's underground resistance, began with these words when I met her for the first time in 1986: "Your mother brought me a large piece of cake when I was lying on my bunk so sick and hungry I was sure I wouldn't make it through the night." A formal introduction came later. "Without options, without hope, and against all odds, moral resistance was a more difficult order than armed resistance," says author and Shoah survivor Henryk Grynberg.

Of Adela's altogether distinctive features, two stood out: her eyes and her smile. People who knew my mother said that her eyes reflected the events and stories of her past, and virtually anybody could read them. I certainly noticed this. Shmuel Ron went a step farther in a letter of September 1991: "Have you ever noticed that your mother's eyes immortalize the entire history of the Jews?"

In pictures, my mother seldom smiled. Most photographs of her show tightly closed lips as if to say, "Too much has happened; maybe we can talk some other time." Yet these photographs belie the essence of Adela's character. She was neither overly serious nor incapable of experiencing joy, and in person Adela smiled often enough to show her defining traits: warmth, kindness, and expansive acceptance of others.

I was born in Poland, five years after the end of the Second World War. My older brother, Felek, and I were very fortunate. By the time we came around, my parents were already well-situated professionals in the new government. My family and our friends enjoyed the usual comforts of a governing class in any country, although our lives were less privileged than what may come to mind for Western officials. (My parents never tolerated material extravagance, and there wasn't much money around to begin with.) Still, my brother and I had a mainly worry-free youth surrounded by warmth, love, and a live-in housekeeper an unthinkable luxury for an ordinary Polish citizen. We attended schools with children of influential people both inside the government and out. Our political education, of course, followed the spirit of communism, and to that we had no objection.

But this lifestyle, pleasant as it was, hid the legacy of World War II and the Holocaust. To speak of those years, for every reason that you can imagine, was taboo. And we did not ask. As a rule, people in communist countries such as Poland were taught not to ask questions. And yet it was impossible to live in postwar Poland and ignore the invisible footprints that marked so much of our youth. Though we didn't know the details of what had happened to our parents, almost to the point of ignorance, we still sensed something colossal in their past, something devastating. Of the years from their childhood up through early adulthood, especially the period of the war, my brother and I knew almost nothing, and we grew detached from people, places, and times that ordinarily become an extension of one's roots, a continuation of one's family legacy. Without a doubt, it was Hitler and his henchmen who, by killing my grandparents, aunts, uncles, and cousins, bear responsibility for this detachment. Even today, at almost age sixty, I consider this erasure of the roots from which we all build an identity my greatest personal loss. At times, it still fills me with a sense of confusion and abandonment.

Perhaps not surprisingly, the first obstacle to writing this book came when I was looking for stories of my mother's youth. As I learned about her life in the 1920s and 1930s, I realized I was not prepared to face a certain truth. By this I do not mean the threat posed by Nazi Germany but instead the atmosphere of dividedness and mutual resentment that existed between gentiles and Jews in Poland. It is not my nature to be part of a segregated culture, nor, apart from a few incidents, has it ever been my immediate experience. But it was my mother's. On my visits to Upper Silesia, the Polish region where Adela grew up, this fact came to be a heavy burden. And I started to suspect that my mother's silence about the first decade and a half of her life had in part been her protest against a society divided according to religious, social, and economic lines. Even if I am wrong, and she had not intended to deal with her feelings in this way, at least this book enables me to break the silence.

This book also allows me to tell the story of my mother's role during the war. Had Adela not resisted the Nazi occupiers, had she allowed herself to become dehumanized like millions of others, the outcome of the Holocaust would not have been any different. Adhering to high standards of humanity earns a person no rewards. She knew that. But, according to the Jewish saying, saving one life equates to saving a whole world. Sometimes it seems to me that this phrase was invented especially for Adela.

Of the scores of biographies, memoirs, and documentaries that portray Holocaust survivors, a few contain chapters about my mother, including Joseph Goldkorn's *Unbelievable but True* and Shmuel Ron's memoir, noted earlier. So my mother's life, on some small level, has been documented as historically significant. My own concern is obviously not that of a historian but of a son. I am driven by force of emotion, by the duty to show my children who they are and where they come from, and by the urge to document the life of a person who is important to me, and who made a difference in the lives of at least a few fellow human beings. I owe it to my mother, to her family, to her compatriots and friends, and to all those who helped her stay alive during the years of the Holocaust. It sustains me to know that this book will enable her to stand taller, looking down at the once-untouchable, cold-blooded tormentors who tried but failed to destroy her.

One more issue still needs to be dealt with, namely memory. The following text is a documentary of my mother's life—a biography. It has been composed based on my direct recordings of her story, interviews with eyewitnesses, and written accounts. I verified almost all accounts with at least two sources, but a handful remain Adela's recollections of events that took place two, three, and even four decades before I started recording her story. I wasn't able to find archived documents, witnesses, or written accounts to confirm all such recollections. It must also be mentioned that the years can have a distorting effect on people's memory, especially those who have survived traumatic experiences.

One

Piłsudski Street

ADELA GUTERMAN WAS BORN on December 15, 1922, in her parents' home in the small industrial town of Niwka, Poland. The youngest of four siblings, she was delivered at home with the help of a midwife, the custom in those times. The three other children of Rózia and Fishel Guterman were Chaim, born in 1911; Hala, born two years later; and Moniek, seven years older than Adela and later to be her role model and companion. The Gutermans rented an apartment in a two-story building on 7 Piłsudski[2] Street. At the front of the building was their fabric shop, Sklep Tekstylny-Guterman; at the back were the living quarters. In the same building lived the Mandelbaums,

[2]Józef Piłsudski (1867–1935) is known for his efforts to restore Poland's statehood before and after World War I. Having earned national reverence for defeating the Red Army in 1920 in a battle on the banks of the Vistula, he seized power in 1926. During Adela's youth, Piłsudski was the most prominent figure in Poland's political life. In every classroom in Adela's school, a portrait of Piłsudski was affixed to the wall. Government buildings and many retail establishments also displayed his photograph.

1

relatives of the Gutermans, along with several other families whose finances ranged from comfort to outright poverty. This contrast in wealth became clear in my own mind when I learned that the less fortunate tenants would sometimes come to borrow Fishel's hat on formal occasions. In the backyard of the building, storage sheds were lined up on one side—one unit for each family—with individual compartments for coal storage on the other side. Children played in the yard as well as in the garden, located at the rear.

Inside the apartment, the Gutermans had two bedrooms, a kitchen, and an eating-living area. Adela slept in the second bedroom with her three siblings, two to a bed. Compared to other Jewish families in Niwka, the Gutermans had a small brood. According to former Niwka resident Salomon Goldman, most families had six to nine children, which usually meant a crowded bedroom. Yet a tight sleeping arrangement, large family or small, was standard in places like Niwka and in no way a reflection of poverty. In fact, the Gutermans were quite well-off. Their textile shop netted ample income to support a family, even to provide the children with a few luxuries: money for clothing, occasional travel, and, when the time came, generous wedding dowries.

To enter the textile shop from the street, you rang a bell and then pushed open a heavy door, which was seldom locked. Inside to the right you would find a wide counter, behind which Rózia or Hala would be serving customers. The wooden floor planks shifted and squeaked under customers' feet. A little deeper into the shop, shelves reached to the ceiling, overburdened with rolls of fabric. Through a small square window in the door at the back of the shop, you could peer into the Gutermans' living room.

A town of 1,600, Niwka was located in Zagłębie,[3] a region in Polish Upper Silesia known for its mineral resources and dotted with coal and zinc mines, steel mills,

---

[3] Zagłębie Dombrowskie, in full.

and enormous brick kilns. Though Niwka had been settled in the early eighteenth century, the town itself had been transformed in the nineteenth century into an industrial settlement for coal miners who worked at the local mine, Maurycy. The cities of Sosnowiec and Katowice lay a few kilometers to the southwest, Kraków about eighty kilometers to the east. At the time Adela was growing up, Jews made up about a third of Niwka's population, with the other segment consisting of gentile Poles and a handful of French industrialists who ran the area coal mining operations. Those same industrialists, residing on the outskirts of town near the mines, were the fabric shop's best and richest clients.

In appearance, Niwka was drab and unadorned with two- and three-story buildings closely spaced and constructed of brick and mortar or cement blocks. Only the main street was paved (with bricks), and after the first autumn rain the side roads would turn into a mire. There were no sidewalks, not even wooden boards placed over a puddle or a sinkhole. I imagine groups of children on their way to school hopping between the puddles, trying to keep their shoes dry. Drivers of horse-drawn wagons would struggle to deliver goods on time, their carts bogging down in the sodden ground. Like many small towns in Zagłębie in the early twentieth century, Niwka had electricity but no indoor plumbing, and coal was the main source for heating and cooking. Daily supplies of fresh water—stored in a large barrel that usually sat on a sturdy kitchen table—were lugged into town in buckets by a few rather robust young women who were hired by a local water distributor. Under the barrel, Rózia would store the herring, purchased every Friday, until she was ready to prepare it for the Sabbath meal.

The First of May Street was the town's main commercial thoroughfare, connecting Niwka with nearby communities. Along it, shops offered all the basic necessities, including a few kosher butchers frequented by Poles as

3

well as Jews, a tailor or two, a shoe-and-leather shop owned by the Goldmans, and their competition, the Landaus' shoe shop, not too far down the road. There were shops owned by Poles as well, but they were clustered separately from the Jewish merchants. Within the town limits, in addition to the sizable coal mine, there was a steel mill and a factory that produced heavy mining equipment.

One of Niwka's few charms was Kościuszko Park.[4] Located on the way to Modrzejów, a neighboring town with which Niwka shared utilities, social services, and the Jewish cemetery, the park consisted of a monument to Tadeusz Kościuszko and a large grassy area for recreation. In the space around the monument, parades, public gatherings, and funerals for coal miners killed in accidents took place. In their free time, young people visited the park to kick a soccer ball or spend time with members of the opposite sex without having to worry about parents breathing down their necks. On warm summer days they might take along a picnic.

It is clear that Rózia was the practical-minded figure of the Guterman couple. Though afflicted with a heart condition at a relatively young age, she still managed to run the family textile shop, all the while tending to her four children and husband. A man of impressive intellect, Fishel focused his attention on abstract matters. He was a devout Jew in the old sense of the term, deeply respected as an authority on religious subjects. "A Groysse Fishel"—the Great Fishel—everyone called him, in recognition of the range and depth of his knowledge. Regarded just as highly for his honesty as for his capacious mind, he would on occasion be summoned to guard people's savings. At

---

[4] Tadeusz Kościuszko was a famous and brilliant military leader, known principally for leading a revolt in 1794 against Russia. He also took part in the American Revolution. In Poland, many streets, parks, and monuments are named after him.

weddings and circumcisions, hosts would feel honored by his presence.

The dynamic between husband and wife was starkest in the handling of the fabric shop, which prospered under Rózia's direction. She would work daily behind the counter, offering advice on materials and balancing the account books. She also made regular trips to Łódź, Poland's center for textiles, to select and purchase materials. As Rózia carried the family's welfare on her shoulders, her husband spent his days praying, poring over the ancient texts, giving counsel to members of the community, and mediating in disputes—with this last role reflecting the reality that Jews in Poland did not often take advantage of the legal system, while the legal system did not encourage its use by the Jewish community. Instead many Jews used what is called a *din Torah,* an informal body that operated according to the laws of the Torah, or else the arbiters' understanding of right and wrong. In Niwka, Fishel served as the undisputed judge of this body.

Sometimes, while studying in the back room, Fishel would peer into the shop from the window in the living area to make sure all was well. If Rózia went out to purchase fabrics or during periods of heavy business, he would take over behind the counter. When he did so, however, he harbored a discomfort about charging customers above cost. He felt profit was indecent in its nature. Rózia would joke that if she were to leave her husband alone in the shop for too long, he'd give away all the merchandise for free.

In discussing Adela's siblings, the fact that the eldest, Chaim, was a boy should not be understated. As the locals of Niwka might have said, God must have taken a stroll along Piłsudski Street to make it happen. A girl, even the smartest and most attractive in town, would never approach the honor of studying Torah or inquiring into God's wisdom. And who would say Kaddish, the prayer for deceased parents—and, according to Jewish law, a tradition

5

reserved for sons—for Rózia and Fishel when the time came?

From a young age, Chaim was serious, studious, devoted to religion—a tireless disciple of his father. As he grew older, he stuck closely to this path, and Adela recalled the not uncommon scene of A Groysse Fishel and his son, Chaim, studying at the kitchen table, books spread in every direction, the only sound the occasional rustle from a page turning. Fishel's first-born child's commitment to religion would end up being even more fervent than his own. People who knew Chaim claimed he was a Hasid even though he wore no traditional black garb, and covered his head with a *kippa* only on Shabbat and Jewish festival days.

In 1929, shortly after his eighteenth birthday, Chaim received his draft letter, with eight weeks to prepare for the physical. From the start, he knew he would never serve a day in the Polish army, or any other army for that matter. Not only did he espouse pacifism as a philosophy, but he would have no chance of upholding kosher life or halakhic restrictions while dwelling in military barracks. Immediately after receiving the draft letter, Chaim went on a starvation diet—water and a few matzos per day. To disfigure his posture, he slept on the kitchen table. After a few weeks of this regimen, his skin turned jaundiced and his eyes sank, causing his cheekbones to protrude alarmingly. Though Fishel and Rózia fretted about their son's condition, soon enough the draft commission representative showed up and pronounced him classify-cation D—unfit to serve. The ripple effect was impressive. Into Sosnowiec, Katowice, and Dąbrowa Górnicza, Chaim's strong will was the subject of admiration and envy among young Jewish men like himself. And I am sure many emulated his tactic with similar results.

On the opposite side of the spectrum was Moniek: pragmatic, entrepreneurial, and infused with joie de vivre. Though he would never dare object aloud to the strictures of observant Judaism, Moniek must have quietly rued those weekly Sabbath eve trips to the *shtibel* (prayer house) with his brother and father. He would have preferred to be thinking up business ideas, attending Zionist meetings, or gallivanting around Sosnowiec, where he might have listened to American jazz (which had infiltrated clubs in central Europe's larger cities), watched a silent film, or visited a café. Though Sosnowiec and Katowice weren't Warsaw or Vienna by any stretch of the imagination, the cultural life of the two cities was relatively rich and thriving. (Niwkaites of Moniek's generation were known to spend an evening at Katowice's Café Bagatela, dancing swing and foxtrot until the early morning hours.) Today people associate Sosnowiec with the famous tenor and actor Jan Kiepura, the Hollywood star Pola Negri, the pianist Władysław Szpilman, and the violinist and composer Paul Godwin, all of them adored by audiences worldwide. Moniek was also the first hobby photographer in Niwka. He would take his camera around town, searching out friends, acquaintances, and young women to arrange in amusing poses. And on occasion he drove a car, though never in Niwka. Tradition-minded Jews would have viewed the act as a betrayal of one's birthright. "If you live like the goyim," Fishel would say, "you will disgrace your childhood, and you will become one of them."

Apart from my mother, the only member of the Guterman family I had a chance to know personally was Hala, whom I met for the first time at Ben Gurion Airport, in Tel Aviv, where my mother, my brother, and I had flown after our unceremonious departure from Poland in the summer of 1968. Israel was to be our new home. At the time, Hala was fifty-five years old, already a grandmother, and married to her second husband, Bernard Salomon. From the moment I met Hala, I knew that she wasn't going through the motions as a dutiful aunt. She intended for Adela, my brother, and me to become a part of her immediate family. With every cell in her body, she was

7

determined to make our life in Israel as comfortable as it could be.

In the following year or so, I would often crash at Hala's apartment in Tel Aviv on weekend breaks from my army training. To an eighteen-year-old city kid from Warsaw, training in the Israeli army was no cinch, and it placed demands on my physical strength that I could scarcely have been prepared for. On those breaks I was so exhausted, I'd virtually sleep for twenty-four hours, waking up only to eat or use the bathroom. Finally, I'd rouse myself just in time to catch a bus back to the base. Though I slept through most of those visits with Hala, I had the feeling she was worrying about me the whole time— wondering if I was hungry, having nightmares, was perhaps somehow unwell, concerned about what Adela would say if she knew I was sleeping so much. Though it may have only been in my head, I was certain I could hear her breathing from behind my door.

Hala was a gentle and soft-spoken woman, though serious, and I think she was that way in her youth. She could also be timid to the point that people might try to exploit her—though not always. Outside the home, my clearest memory of my aunt Hala is in a fabric shop that we'd sometimes visit together. From her experience assisting Rózia at the shop in Niwka, she could tell the type and the quality of a fabric by feel alone. And when it came to bargaining for what she considered a fair price, this quiet, unassuming woman would turn into a lion. Her arguments were crisp, and always yielded a favorable outcome. In looking back on those fabric-shop visits, I do not think it was so much her bargaining skills that made her successful but rather the respect the owners had for her expertise.

A handful of yellowed photographs survive from my mother's youth in Niwka. One is a family portrait circa 1934 (included at the close of this chapter), with the six family members posed in what appears to be the living room. Adela, Fishel, Rózia, and Hala are seated on the sofa, with Chaim and Moniek standing a bit in the background. Hala and Moniek smile, and Rózia's face beams. "Look at my beautiful family," she seems to say. In line with their character, Fishel and Chaim wear stern expressions, and Fishel's beard and clothing are typical of a religious Jew. The rest of the family also is well dressed. Other pictures I have located include small portraits of Adela's aunts Bela Diamant, a woman of inner strength; Lejcia Apfelbaum, on the shy side; and Hala Mandelbaum, known for her personal dignity.

Another photograph, taken at Chaim's engagement party in 1937, provides the only surviving image of my great-grandfather Paltiel, who sits at the table to the left of Chaim. My grandfather Fishel sits to Paltiel's right. Moniek is also pictured along with several other family members, all males. The vodka bottles, at least two in number, indicate the event was a celebration in earnest.

Central to the experience of growing up Jewish in Poland in the early twentieth century was extended family. Adela's relatives on her mother's side lived both in Niwka and en route from Niwka to Sosnowiec at a negligible distance. Her Guterman relatives lived in Dąbrowa Górnicza, a larger town about eight kilometers away. At a time when train and horse-drawn carriage were the main modes of transportation, eight kilometers was a long way, and it prevented Adela from being as close to her father's side of the family as she was to her mother's.

Paltiel and Henka (aka Pesa) Czapelski, Adela's maternal grandparents, lived in Niwka and ran a produce shop. Like Rózia at the fabric shop, Henka, a tall, handsome woman, kept her family's business afloat. Though the shop specialized in fruits and vegetables, local youngsters valued the place for its assortment of sweets. According to Gucia Mandelbaum, the Czapelski grandchildren had a ritual of dropping by the store after school and racing straight for the corner cabinet filled with *landrynki*—hard candies of various flavors. "It was often the best part of the day," Gucia recalled. As for Grandfather Paltiel, he lived in a way not different from Fishel, and was known for his obsession with cleanliness. It was not typical in those times to bathe daily, but Paltiel did so anyway—every morning. And he would wash his eyes with hot water. Paltiel also groomed himself meticulously. During winter, he would dress so warmly that a joke made the rounds in the family that he would be well prepared if the Jews were exiled to Siberia.

Around holiday times, particularly Chanukah, Paltiel would give out money to his grandchildren in his singular way. Before handing the appropriate-size coin to each child (amount according to age), he would reach so deep into his pocket that his arm would disappear past the elbow. This spectacle would captivate his grandchildren. He would search for that coin for what seemed an eternity, and, as he did, he would never take his eyes off the child's face, as though evaluating it for patience or some quality that he alone could recognize. And then—at long last—he would remove the coin, always the correct denomination.

One Saturday morning, Henka was stricken by a heart attack and died instantly. Her death wrecked Paltiel's inner peace. Unable to cope on his own, he would sleep at each of his five daughters' homes in succession—one night at a time. To Rózia, then Hala, then Zelda, Lejcia, Bela, and finally back to Rózia, initiating the cycle anew. On the days when Paltiel returned to his apartment, Salomon Goldman and his brother Iciek—Paltiel's neighbors as well as close family friends to the Gutermans—would spend the night with him, to alleviate his fear of being alone.

For young people, growing up in Niwka in the 1920s and 1930s entailed a conflict between the old and the new. Niwka represented the old. It was small and provincial, dreary and segregated. Unlike Jews in Kraków and Warsaw, and even some smaller cities around Eastern Europe, all Niwka Jews of the older generation were religious. Anyone who attempted to live a secular life was considered a goy. Observance of Sabbath and other holidays was the cornerstone of Jewish life—year in, year out.

The scene on a Friday evening at the Gutermans' may give some idea of the traditional mores that prevailed. After praying at the *shtibel*, Fishel and his two sons would return home to Rózia, Adela, and Hala, who had prepared the dining room for the Sabbath meal. The men would gather around the table to gaze at and inhale the tantalizing aroma of the food, hungry after all that praying. But they would never think of eating until the last lines of the Kiddush had been recited and the embroidered challah cover was lifted to reveal the fresh, sweet bread. Then, the elaborate Friday evening meal would proceed: gefilte fish with raisins (for a sweet Sabbath), marinated herring, hot *yiowoch* (a stew of chicken or beef), a baked goose, perhaps a plate of prune-filled pierogies, a dessert of apple or some other fruit compote, and finally tea. Fishel and Chaim, because of their religious inclinations, might have taken a *glasele* (of vodka) to toast the sanctity of the Sabbath.

Strict religious observance aside, the experience of community among Jews in Niwka could be confining. Everyone knew everyone else's business. For this reason, many young people felt restless. According to Salomon Goldman, they countered this restlessness through intellectual engagement. Modern society stirred their imaginations. Though almost everyone eventually attended trade schools, and not *gymnasium* (high school), this simply reflected the practical realities of their lives. They were well read, progressive, and keenly aware of the world beyond Niwka. *"Dobra, inteligentna młodzież"* (good, intelligent youth), Gucia Mandelbaum repeated a few times during one of our numerous conversations. Young people's allegiance typically fell into one of three camps: Zionism, socialism, or Jewish orthodoxy. Of these, Zionism was the most popular. Moniek Guterman himself was an active member of the Zionist youth organizations Bnei Akiva and HaNoar HaTzioni, and he seriously considered emigrating to Palestine. He also gave much time to the popular Akhshara movement, which provided agricultural training to young people before they emigrated.

In most cases the Zionist outlook alarmed the older generation, though more enlightened parents could not help empathizing with their children's impulses. Makeshift and uncivilized as Palestine might have appeared in the Jewish-European mind, it represented a feasible alternative to the deteriorating situation in Poland and throughout Europe. Alongside anti-Semitism, which provided the most convincing argument for emigration to Palestine, a Zionist infrastructure was in place, making it possible for those considering the option to be part of a momentous nationalist venture: the leaders, local branch organizations, means of transport to Palestine, opportunities for work. Not to mention the mythology that arose around the formation of the Jewish state through the manifestos, songs, and poetry by the likes of Saul Tchernikhowsky and Chaim Nachman Bialik. This aura turned Palestine into not just a chance to improve one's lot, but also a call to action. Many young Jews knew in their guts that it was foolish to negate this possibility for a brighter future.

In his memoir, *A Tale of Love and Darkness,* Amos Oz paints a vivid picture of Polish sentiment toward Jews in the interwar period through a monologue by his great-aunt Sonia:

The Polish attitude toward the Jews was one of disgust, like someone who has bitten into a piece of bad fish and can neither swallow it nor spit it out. They didn't feel like spewing us forth in the presence of the Versailles nations, in the atmosphere of minority rights, in front of Woodrow Wilson, the League of Nations: in the 1920s, the Poles still had some shame, they were keen to look good. Like a drunk trying to walk straight, so that no one can see he's weaving. They hoped to appear outwardly more or less like other countries. But under the table they oppressed and humiliated us, so that we would gradually all go off to Palestine and they wouldn't have to see us anymore.

This humiliation came in the form of state- and church-sponsored anti-Semitism, with help from an easily excitable media. Between the two world wars, anti-Semitism penetrated every crevice of Poland's political, social, and commercial life. By the early 1930s, the Polish government had already instituted policies that blocked Jews from participating in higher education, forcing those who wanted to attend university—and could afford the expense—to travel to Prague, Paris, or London.

Anti-Semitic measures picked up momentum through the next decade. In 1937, the Synod of Polish bishops adopted a resolution calling for the isolation of Jewish students from gentile students in schools—a practice that would come to be associated with "seating ghettos" and showed the symbiotic relationship that flourished between church and state in the interwar years. The Synod also called for a nationwide ban on Jewish teachers instructing Polish children. Equally ominous were the anti-Semitic pamphlets disseminated by Catholic priests such as Józef Kruszyński and Stanisław Trzeciak, and the hate-filled sermons of Cardinal Hlond, which were rife with fabrications.

As early as 1936, in its official publication, *Dziennik Ustaw Rzeczypospolitej Polskiej*,[5] Poland's Ministry of

---

[5] *The Journal of Law of the Commonwealth of Poland.*

Commerce openly endorsed a boycott of Jewish businesses. According to Celia Heller's book *On the Edge of Destruction*, Commerce Ministry officials ordered all "estab-lishments to carry the names of the owners as they appeared on their birth certificates." Largely as a result of such policies, organized terror and abuse targeting Jews escalated steadily in the years before the Nazi invasion. When in 1939 the German Wehrmacht entered Poland, much of the local gentile population already embraced—or at least accepted—Hitler's ideology of anti-Semitism. For Adela and so many Polish Jews of her generation, life was so tightly tied up with anti-Semitism that perhaps only they could truly understand Salomon Goldman's assertion, "We were born already conditioned to living under hatred." Celia Heller elaborates on the situation:

> Most of the governmental measures that were squeezing Jews out of their traditional economic pursuits without providing them with other ways of making a living were preceded by militant anti-Jewish activities, including boycotts and terror. Terror was unleashed with special bravado by the young radical splinter groups from the nationalist *Endecja* movement.
>
> The anti-Semitic climate of opinion that crystallized in interwar Poland had many ingredients. The basic component was the widespread traditional anti-Semitism, which had persisted for centuries. It was marked by religious beliefs and medieval myths of the evil Jew as Christ killer, the devil, who used Christian blood. Superimposed upon the traditional beliefs were the nationalistic stereotypes of the Jew as the antithesis of everything Polish: the enemy and corrupter of Polish values, the underminer of Polish nationhood, the Communist.

By excluding Jews from commerce, the government sought ostensibly to stabilize the deteriorating economy, but the measure fostered open hatred. Several pogroms took place in Poland in the late 1930s. In addition to emigration to Palestine, Jews responded to the various fronts of Polish anti-Semitism through attempts to assimilate, submissiveness, conversion to Catholicism, and even militancy, though this last response took place mainly as rhetoric alone.[6]

Even before Adela had reached her teenage years, Moniek would bring her along to all sorts of activities, including meetings of the Zionist organizations. She'd follow him virtually anywhere. As Adela grew into young adulthood, she and her brother took part in more and more activities. Together they attended summer camps and parties, and traveled alone to the resort towns of Zakopane and Krynica. In those times, such a level of freedom was unheard of for young people, and perhaps it says something about Rózia and Fishel's permissiveness relative to the rest of the community.

For Adela and her peers, life in Niwka would never have been as full as it was without the *ken* (Hebrew for "nest"), a meeting place where young people would socialize, discuss issues in the Polish and Jewish press, and listen to talks by representatives of Zionist organizations. The *ken* also gave them the chance to experiment, and rebel a little against their parents' orthodox ways.

In her teenage years, Adela's best friend was Gutka Piotrkowska, who sometimes also played the part of an accomplice. At that time, relations between young men and women were quite chaste compared with how they are now. As such, a girl would need to be accompanied by an older sibling in order to attend the *ken*, or to meet with someone of the opposite sex. Adela—not always a saint— would occasionally tell her parents she was attending a *ken* meeting, when in reality she would be socializing without

---

[6] See Celia Heller's book for documentation of such responses, both through narrative and statistics.

the presence of an adult or an older sibling. To clear her path, she often invoked Gutka, who willingly stood in as a decoy. Eventually, Adela's assignations developed into a connection between herself and David Glejcer, who was also from Niwka and, at least according to a surviving photograph, quite handsome. As the horizon in Poland darkened, their relationship became increasingly close.

Historic records place Jews in Poland since the twelfth century, in Niwka dating back to at least 1713. Records show further that the early Niwka Jewish community had organized a *kahal*—a self-governing body—as well as a synagogue, cemetery, and *mikvah,* a Jewish ritual bath. On the headstones in the Niwka Jewish cemetery—which were ripped out by the Nazis for use as paving stones, and replaced arbitrarily after the war—all inscriptions are in Yiddish. In Adela's youth, her family and the other Jews of Niwka spoke Yiddish at home, Polish in business transactions with gentiles. Many in the older generation spoke Polish poorly, suggesting how insular the Jewish community could be. On this count, it also bears remembering that Poland had only regained its national sovereignty in 1918. Among siblings and friends, Yiddish and Polish were spoken interchangeably. (After the Second World War, whenever my mother met with survivors of her generation from Niwka-Modrzejów, they conversed in Polish.)

Though Niwka and other places like it were implicitly segregated, Jews did not live in a ghetto. Instead they settled in loose concentrations around the town. According to Salomon Goldman, in a Jewish-owned building of twelve apartments, ten might be occupied by Jews and the other two by gentiles; in a gentile-owned building, the figures would likely be reversed. In the Gutermans' section of the building on Piłsudski Street, there lived a single Catholic family, the Sielągs. A clan of eight, their apartment had just two rooms, and parents and children all slept in the sole bedroom. From ages nine to twelve, Adela considered one of the family's daughters, Janka, to be her dearest friend. The two were close enough that Janka learned to speak Yiddish quite well. When they would play the card game Twenty-one, Janka would show off by reciting all the numbers in Yiddish.

Out of necessity, Jews and gentile Poles interacted in a number of venues. In public schools, for example, Jewish children learned alongside Poles, the same curriculum with the exception of religious studies. During lessons on religion, Jewish students would leave the room for separate instruction from a teacher of Jewish material who was employed by the state. Jews and Poles also met in less common circumstances, sometimes out of mutual sympathy. In a coal-mining town like Niwka, miners were respected by their neighbors. They wore sleek uniforms, not unlike those worn by police officers or firefighters, black and replete with brass buttons. A few times a year, the mining companies would stage mass memorial events for employees killed in the line of work. These memorials were more like celebrations, with plentiful drink and food and a marching band. If Jews knew the miners killed in the accidents, or did business with their families, they would pay their respects by attending.

But by no means was all well between Jews and gentiles in Niwka. Relations were characterized by suspicion and frequent hostility, and the communities rarely intermixed in situations of their own choosing. Fistfights between Jewish and Polish schoolchildren were a common event. And then there was the storied epithet, "*Kaminienice wasze a ulice nasze*" (The buildings are yours but the streets are ours), which coal miners would hurl forth as they passed Jewish families sitting out on the front stoops on summer evenings after the Sabbath meal.

This scene didn't occur only on Sabbath, though, nor did it occur in a vacuum. The early shift at the Niwka coal mine would end sometime in the afternoon, and the miners' route home led down Piłsudski Street. There Fishel and three or four neighbors would be relaxing on a bench, having just enjoyed a sumptuous lunch: gefilte fish and a dish of baked onions, then *yiowoch, choolent,* meat or goose, and, for dessert, compote. As they sat and conversed, the men's body language bespoke their sated, languorous state. They wore fine pocket watches that peeked out from their vests. So it was undoubtedly envy, and a swell of resentment, that prompted the miners to snarl their remark about the buildings and the streets of Niwka. Their faces would be covered in black soot from their day in the mines, and their blackened carbide lamps would clank noisily as they swung from their belts. The whites of their eyes and their teeth, the lore went, would glower wolflike.

Aside from such flare-ups, what Jews feared most was the possibility of mob violence. This was evident during the major Catholic festivals, when Poles would parade through the main streets of town carrying posters of the Catholic saints and usually a crude replica of Jesus on the Cross. Leading the procession would be a priest, surrounded by four altar boys who held up the *baldachim* (canopy) that offered him symbolic protection. On parade days, the town's Jews would lock themselves in their rooms so as not to present any cause for belligerence. Recollected Salomon Goldman: "One of the largest processions was held on All Saints' Day. Jews would retreat to their apartments, lock the doors, and draw the shutters. We did not want to be seen. Our clothing, the hats in particular, would give our faith away. It may have been seen as a provocation to gentiles. We knew it would take only one instigator to turn the mob against us all." Gucia Mandelbaum added, "We defended ourselves in silence." On one occasion, Gucia did watch a procession from the sidewalk, and as she stood very near to the action, two paraders stepped from the group, grabbed her by the shoulders, and forced her into a kneeling position. The

Catholics watching the parade from the sidelines would already be kneeling in reverence, but for a Jew to kneel was forbidden, if not a sin.

In Poland at the time, the military units were also known for their anti-Semitic tirades: heckling, spitting at Jews, and the occasional gratuitous beating. Sometimes a regiment would pass through town, congregating at a local bar or restaurant. Then, too, Jews knew to keep away: remain indoors, keep a low profile.

Jews weren't the only target of the authorities' wrath. Each year on May 1, International Workers' Day, clandestine Marxist-Leninist organizations feted the occasion with street demonstrations. Though some Jews in Silesia were active in communist and socialist groups, the main participants in these events were proletarian gentiles. Around Niwka, that meant a high concentration of miners. The Polish authorities looked upon these demonstrators with bitterness comparable to their sentiments toward Jews, and in the days before May Day, they would arrest any known organizers and activists and jail them until the hated day had passed. A Niwka anecdote shows how sensitive Polish law enforcement agents could be in this regard. One May Day, a Jewish tenant of Adela's building carelessly hung a red towel from the window to dry. No sooner did the police spot the towel than they stormed the building arresting the tenant for subversive (read communist) activities. The tenant had to go to great lengths to explain to the police that she merely owned a red towel, and wished to advance no political agenda.

Because Zagłębie's economy rested almost wholly on its vast mineral resources, the region largely avoided the financial devastation that ravaged the rest of Europe in the 1930s: massive job loss, stratospheric inflation, widespread breakdown of morale. Up until the start of the war, miners continued their work. The Vienna-Sosnowiec railroad continued transporting raw materials in a timely way

19

between supplier and client. Capital, to some extent, flowed.

But that didn't mean Zagłębie—and Niwka, in particular—was immune to the nationalistic fervor then sweeping through Europe. Hitler wasn't only a racist, he was also the era's nationalist par excellence. His monomania regarding the so-called Aryan race filled Germans with a sense of self-respect that they hadn't felt since their humiliation following World War I. Citizens of other nations—Lithuania, Poland, Ukraine—who felt threatened by drastic economic conditions took Hitler's message to heart. They too wanted to feel self-worth and a sense of purpose, and many therefore subscribed to an increasingly vicious brand of nationalism. They also wanted to feel the intoxicating strength that had propelled the Nazis from an obscure fringe group to a paragon of leadership. It is no exaggeration to say that Adolf Hitler gave rise to innumerable little Hitlers.

By the time World War II broke out in 1939, each of Adela's three siblings had married and moved away from home. In line with tradition at the time, Chaim met his wife-to-be, Rivka (Regia) Werdyger, by *shiduch*—or setup. Hala wedded Israel Wajcman in a lavish ceremony held in the Gutermans' backyard. And Moniek—the only sibling not to be set up—married Gitla Bursztyn of Sosnowiec.

With war imminent, and anti-Semitism at a boiling point, these were hardly joyous times in which to marry and raise children. But young Jewish families still tried as best they could to conduct their lives on a normal plane. Running a curtain shop out of her apartment in Sosnowiec, Hala gave birth in November 1939 to a daughter, whom she named Henia after her grandmother Henka. And two years later Moniek's wife, Gitla, had the couple's only child, Estera (Tusia). Only Chaim—for whom the frivolous, theater- and cinema-going Rivka was a poor match—would have no children. In response to their flawed—perhaps even failed—marriage, he withdrew deeper into solitude and Jewish learning. During Chaim's eventual internment at Auschwitz, his adherence to Jewish law was strict enough that he refused to eat the tiny meat rations that, on rare occasions, were given to prisoners; to prevent the possibility that another prisoner would devour the meat, he would bury the morsels in the ground.

Moniek faced the war with his characteristic independence. After the German invasion of Poland in 1939, he consistently broke the curfew imposed by the Nazis, counting on his not typically Jewish features to shield him. Wearing the garb of a Polish landowner, he would ride the train from Miechów to visit his parents and Adela in Niwka. At the time, Jews were denied the right to use public transportation. Disregarding this rule or breaking curfew would earn the offender a sound punishment from the Gestapo:[7] beatings, imprisonment, or banishment to a labor camp either in Germany or on the Eastern Front. But Moniek preferred to act righteously than not to act at all. And never while riding a train did he attract the Gestapo's attention.

One day, probably in late 1941, when Moniek and his family were already confined to the Miechów ghetto, he sneaked out to visit Rózia and Fishel in Modrzejów, where another ghetto had been established. On this particular visit, he was not his usual jovial self. Instead he was nervous and appeared to be holding something back. During a moment of privacy with Adela, he shared his secret: he had procured cyanide pills and was prepared to take them if and when the time came. To be murdered by the Nazis was not in Moniek's plans—nor would he accept such a fate for his wife and little Estera. The clearest remaining option for survival, an escape to the Aryan side (gentile areas outside the ghetto where Jews were not allowed to live), struck him as impossible for a family of

---

[7] The secret state police in Nazi Germany.

21

three. He could not imagine putting them through the wandering from place to place—and the inevitable humiliation.

I visited Niwka-Modrzejów in February and October of 2003. Both towns are now incorporated into nearby Sosnowiec, a city of over 400,000. I went looking for traces of the Czapelski and Guterman families. Because the paper records of the area synagogues went up in flames together with the buildings, few of Niwka's current residents remember where the Jews had been buried. The cemetery headstones no longer sit in their original spots. Though I recognized the poorly maintained area as the Jewish graveyard, I found many stones to be missing and others to have faded beyond recognition. I know for certain that my great-grandparents were buried there. Yet I walked the area yard by yard and could find no evidence of their burial sites. Although disappointed I did not feel alone in that graveyard, because I knew my ancestors, and my history, were located there. In a way, I sensed they knew I was there, too.

In her adult years, my mother never spoke of her hometown with nostalgia or sentimental longing. She thought of the place as archaic, backward, and pitiable, agreeing with writer Roman Frister's recollection of the "poverty...filth...and backwardness" of such settlements. On my two visits to Niwka, except for the abandoned-looking Jewish cemetery, I found no remnant of Jewish life. A once-thriving community had been extinguished, and today, not one Jew lives in either Niwka or Modrzejów. When I searched for 7 Piłsudski Street, I found no sign of my mother's old home. Symbolic of the complete erasure of Jewish life in Zagłębie that began in autumn of 1939, what is left is an empty nameless lot.

The Gutermans, circa 1934

Chaim's engagement party, circa 1937

Moniek, Adela's brother

Aunts Bela and Lejcia

NIWKA.

Osada fabryczna, Colonie ouvrière,
pow. Będzin, distr. de Będzin,
sąd pok. i sąd just. de paix
okr. Sosnowiec, et trib. d'arr-t
5038mieszk.▨× Sosnowiec, 5038
(2 km) Dandów- habit. ▨×(2 km)
ka ♥♁ Modrze Dandówka ♥♁
jów ♣ Niwka. Modrzejów ♣
Urząd gminny. Niwka. Office
1 ☒ kat. 2 szko- communal, 1 ☒
ły powsz.Ambu- cath. 2 écoles pri-
latorjum Kasy maires.Ambulan-
Chorych. Zwią- ce de la Caisse de
zek drobnych malades.Assoc.des
kupców i rze- potits commerç,
mieślników, zw. et assoc. des mi-
górników. Ko- neurs. Mine de
palnie węgla, houille, fondu-
odlewnia żelaza, rie de fer, mou-
młyny. lins.

Lekarze (médecins): Krupiński H.
dr. — Reis Miecz. dr.
Ostachowski St. dr.
Akuszerki (sages-femmes): Hajkie-
wicz S. — Krosta S. — Kubicka L.
— Kun H. — Lolo — Rodzik M. —
Siwankowska A. — Wieczorkow-
ska.
Apteki (pharmacies): Wojmer E.
Bławaty (tissus): Erlich J.— Gut-
terman M. — Zemlewicz H.
Cegielnie (briqueteries): Glejcer A.
— Gorczyński F. — ×„Halina" —
Karon.
Felczerzy (barbiers-chirurgiens): Ja-
godziński E.
Fryzjerzy (coiffeurs): Jabłoński J.
— Lubina St. — Szeftel A. —
Kinematografy (cinémas): „Nowo-
ści", wł. Zapała S.
Kooperatywy (coopératives): ×„Spo-
łem", Spółdzielnia Spożywców.
Kowale (forgerons): Czornik J. —
Pęciklewicz R. — Szumera T.
Krawcy (tailleurs): Saper I. —
Trajb S.

Księgarnie (librairies): Rode M.
*Mechaniczne warsztaty (mécani-
ciens):* „Travail", wł. Fiedoruk.
Mleczarnie (crémeries): Koniecz-
niak B.
Młyny (moulins): Wola F. (wod).
Obuwie (chaussures): Landau S. —
Ruta J. — Zelinger M.
Owoce (fruits): Heliszowicz G.
Piekarnie (boulangers): Neuer M.
— Rej S. — Rozpondek H.
Restauracje (restaurants): Ziółkow-
ska A.
Rzeźnicy (bouchers): Akerfeld L.
— Brenner Sz. — Fryszer F. — Spo-
kojny J. — Szpicman W. —
Zaporowski H.
Skóry (cuirs): Goldman Ch.
Spirytualja (spiritueux): Wojtowicz.
Spożywcze artykuły (comestibles):
Apfelbaum R. — ×Bajer F. —
Broner T. — Burzyński K. —
Czapelski P. — Fogiel L. — Fry-
szer J. — Głodny Ch. —
Herbert — Koźmiński — Krzy-
wda F. — Margules Ch. —
— Rozenfarb Ch. — Sztajnheler
L. — Urbanik A. — Zapała S.
— Zajgler M.
Szewcy (cordonniers): Kordeusz F.
— Kula W. — Oczkowski Sz. —
Ruta J. — Wójcik S.
Tytoniowe wyroby (tabacs): Bajer
F. — Białkowski M. — Burzyński
K. — Rode M. — Smyczyński K.
— Zapała S.
Wędliny (charcutiers): Placek J. —
Winter Z.
*Węgiel — kopalnie (mins de houil-
le):* ×„Halina", wł. Zawadzki i Ska
— ×„Jerzy", Sosnow. Tow. Kop.
Węgla i Zakł. Hutnicz. —„Orion",
wł. Moitlis M.—Tropka J. i Ska.
×„Modrzejów", Sosnowieckie Tow.
Zegarmistrze (horlogers): Fuks I.
— Kestenborg A.

Excerpt from 1929 Polish business directory

Top and bottom: Niwka, 2003

27

Niwka-Modrzejów cemetery, 2003

Courage was to be able to feed your children
Courage was to protect your loved ones
Courage was to leave your home in the morning
and return safely by sunset
Courage was to stay alive one more day

—*Salomon Goldman, Adela's cousin*

Two

Germans

ON THE FIRST DAY of September 1939, the Germans invaded
Poland. Wehrmacht and Gestapo units tore through the
landscape, while the German air force attacked Poland's major
cities from above. Just five days into the invasion, Silesia and
Zagłębie were under German control. Though vastly
outnumbered in defending their country, many Polish units
fought valiantly if desperately, inflicting as many as fifty
thousand casualties on their Wehrmacht opponents. (On
September 17, compounding the Poles' woes, the Russians
invaded from the east.) The Poles kept up their defense of
Warsaw until September 27, when military leaders abandoned
the city, which by then was in flames. The last Polish holdouts,
on the Hel Peninsula, capitulated on October 2. Poland never
formally surrendered and underground resistance formed in the
first weeks of the attacks. In justifying the invasion, Hitler
communicated that his goal was not to oppress the Poles but
rather to rid Poland of its Jews; but the Germans' intent, or at

least desire, to exterminate Jews and other groups not to their liking was evident from the start of the occupation. The Poles, and to a lesser extent other Slavs, were among those considered subhuman in Nazi ideology, and even if they were not destined for annihilation after the Jews, they almost surely would have been enslaved.

With the Wehrmacht came jarring sounds. The once quiet streets of Sosnowiec, Niwka, and Modrzejów now throbbed with engines, barking dogs (all German shepherds), and the commands of the Gestapo, which competed vocally with their canine enforcers. The soldiers hollered orders to their subordinates; to the local citizens; and to anyone and anything that displeased them at any given moment. At their side the dogs, trained to attack, trembled visibly, poised to tear any human being to pieces. The deployment of dogs as a tool of terror against civilians was an effective component of German occupation for the duration of the war.

Other unfamiliar noises disturbed the streets of the area: gunshots and the thump of bodies hitting the ground, the screams of women being raped, and the sobbing of residents being driven from their homes. Once Polish army resistance had fallen, a few citizens' groups tried to slow the rapidly advancing German forces by erecting barricades or shooting at German soldiers, but to no lasting effect. In the early days of the occupation, the Germans displayed a ruthless determination that would set the tone for the next six years. On September 4, 1939, on entering Sosnowiec proper, the Gestapo killed two hundred civilians, including government officials, teachers, business owners, and intellectuals, many of them Jews. The following testimony from eyewitness Samuel Brechner and a summary by Leib Shpeizman tell about that specific day. Both are taken from a collection of testimonies posted on PolishJews.org:

> On Chłodna Street…and Mysłowice Road, Jews tried to build barricades [out] of fences…As a result of this resistance, the Germans after arriving from the road from Mysłowice shot all the men from Chłodna Street. On the same day, at 4:00 p.m…the Germans called upon the

population to leave their homes. They chose Jewish men and set them five in a row and [chased] them…to the [cellar] of the City Hall…. During the night between Monday and Tuesday, the Germans demanded [that] the…victims…deliver their Rabbi under [the] penalty of executing ten Jews. There wasn't a Rabbi among them, but to save ten Jews…Abram Sztyglic, 65 years of age [and] a religious Jew, posed as a rabbi. The Germans took him and after [ripping] out half of his beard threw him [back] into the cellar.

—Samuel Brechner

The first German action started in Sosnowiec, on the 4th of September 1939, about 5 p.m. There the German soldiers passed from house to house, ordering the people to gather in the marketplace. From among the assembled people they chose 25–30 men, nearly all of them Jewish, and shot them on the spot. Those who still showed signs of life were given a final shot from a Nazi-officer's pistol. The dead bodies, watched by a mass of people, were left there…for a couple of hours, and then thrown into a common grave. The execution constituted a reprisal-act for the four [killed] German soldiers…. In Bendin [Będzin] the Jews were told to assemble in the synagogue, which was then set on fire. Many of the assembled [died in the] fire, and those who succeeded in getting out were being shot…while they were trying to escape.

—Leib Shpeizman

On September 5, the Gestapo took control of Niwka and Modrzejów, and four days later they burned the Great Synagogue of Sosnowiec, located on 16 Dekert Street. About fifty homes surrounding the synagogue, and inhabited exclusively by Jews, also went up in flames, with many people trapped inside. The SS, Hitler's defense echelon also known as the Blackshirts, encircled the buildings and prevented anyone from leaving. Those who tried were shot at their own doorstep. The flames rose so high that even people in Niwka could see them clearly. The Great Synagogue burned for hours and the black smoke rose from the building for the next several days. Two other synagogues were set on fire immediately thereafter.

The process of expropriating Jewish possessions and businesses was implemented with remarkable brutality, efficiency, and speed, and in October the Germans ordered all Jews to wear the Shield of David on their left sleeve. Noncompliance was punishable by death.

In Niwka and the surrounding localities, people like the Gutermans attempted to cope with the realities of the day, while the occupying soldiers intensified their assaults. They rounded up young people and sent them to forced-labor camps in Germany. They conducted daily street shootings and public executions by hanging. This growing menace made Jews restless, depleted of hope, exhausted, and frightened. Below is a partial transcript of the deposition of a witness, Masia, questioned by Judge Halevi during the trial of Adolf Eichmann, which allows additional insight into the German program in the early days of the invasion:

Q. Do you remember executions by hanging in Sosnowiec?
A. Yes.

Q. How many times?
A. Twice.

Q. How many people were hanged?
A. Once two were hanged, and once four were hanged, including a father and his son.

Q. Did you witness it?
A. The Germans insisted that the Jews should watch this "show," but many tried to avoid it. At our home the shutters were closed and we did not leave the house, but they left the bodies in the center of the town (the distance from our home was six to seven large houses)—in the central square in the town area.

Q. How long were the victims left hanging?
A. Two or three days. We had to go out of the house, and it was impossible to leave the house without seeing them.

Q. What was the reason for hanging them; what did the Germans say?
A. Concerning the four, they said that they were hanged because of transactions on the black market. But the black market—that was an egg, one egg they found in the possession of a mother who had obtained it from a Pole for her little girl so that she [wouldn't] die of hunger... The two were hanged because of assistance they rendered to people who had returned to us from occupied areas, who managed to cross over to us... They were in the zone of the *Generalgouvernement*,[8] and we were annexed to the Reich. They crossed the border and were illegally with us, and those helping them were executed.

Apart from the killings and rapes, and the burning of synagogues, Jewish homes, and institutions, the invading Germans plundered and looted Jewish shops and homes. They even seized possessions of little value, such as clothing and linens.

Immediately after the Germans took control of the region, they unleashed a torrent of decrees intended to restrict Jewish life, counterparts to Nazi policy enacted in Germany in the thirties. Almost every day a new decree was issued: general prohibition of food stamp distribution to Jews, restrictions on food purchases to a few designated shops, the mandatory shaving of beards and wearing of a yellow patch of fabric in the shape of the Star of David, and the ban on Jews using public transportation. Jews were forced to perform public works jobs—street cleaning and removal of city refuse were

---

[8] German for the administrative sphere of influence encompassing whatever parts of Poland had not been incorporated into the Third Reich. It included five districts: Galicia, Kraków, Lublin, Radom, and Warsaw.

common—and their movement was restricted to a few areas of town. In parks, they could sit only on designated benches and were denied public assembly, defined as two persons talking to each other in a public space. One of the decrees, "Ban on Changes of Place of Residence by Jews within the Area of the Government-General," is included in the reference section of this book as an example.

Later, decrees were directed at gentiles to whom it might occur to help Jews. One was a penalty of death for not only any individual who sheltered Jews but also that individual's entire family. This decree remained in effect until the end of the war.

At first the Germans focused on larger municipalities, such as Kraków, Katowice, Bielsko, and Sosnowiec. A more comprehensive effort was needed to traumatize and gain control over these cities, compared to that for a small town like Niwka, where the SS never even bothered to set up a police station. In Niwka, they satisfied themselves with a small outpost on the main street, which also serviced Modrzejów. Yet one should not gather from this situation that Niwka was unaffected by the SS presence. To the contrary, SS officials would harass, threaten, and abuse the Jews of Niwka daily. It was only in scale and intensity that the actions were greater in larger municipal areas.

The emphasis on larger cities lasted until the second half of 1941. For roughly the first two years after the German invasion, the Jews of Niwka-Modrzejów had been allowed to operate their businesses and, provided they followed all decrees, rules, and regulations, they could exist in relative peace. Despite being spared direct atrocities in the first months of occupation, the sheer proximity to Katowice and Sosnowiec paralyzed them with fear. Every Jewish family in town had at least one relative in those two cities. Living under this continuous threat, the Gutermans and other families prepared for bad times in whatever ways they could. They stocked extra flour, sugar, canned goods, and other necessities. Some even filled up the bathtub with water for drinking, just in case of a shortage.

34

Every day brought news of horrifying deeds, and no one truly felt equipped to deal with the worsening reality. Nor could they know what would come next. The shock of German tactics unnerved them. The indifference of their Polish neighbors left them feeling adrift and isolated. The fear of death and destruction debilitated them. Questions to which there were no answers assailed them from every direction. How could they save the life of a loved one? How could they save their own lives? Should they stay in Niwka? Should they try to go east, toward Soviet Russia? Should parents send their children to "safer" places? Or should the children flee, leaving their parents behind to face almost certain death?

Indeed, a few families from Niwka organized a *beriha*—a flight. They loaded a few belongings on carts and marched east toward the Soviet Union. After a journey of approximately ten days, they arrived at the banks of the Bug River, which marked the border between Poland and Ukraine. But German units, notified of the exodus or perhaps in position by coincidence, cut off the passage across the river, and the fugitives were forced to return. In most cases, an attempt to escape meant leaving behind anyone who didn't wish to make the journey—along with anyone who lacked the discipline, physical strength, or agility to hide in the forest or in basements or to ford rivers at night. That usually included one's parents, grandparents, and younger siblings. According to Antony Polonsky's *From Shtetl to Socialism*, during the first years of the war, 15 to 20 percent of all Jews from the German-occupied territories fled to the Soviet Union.

As far as the Guterman family was concerned, neighbors' plans for escape prompted a wilting uncertainty. In the evenings, the family—only Rózia, Fishel, and Adela remained in the Niwka apartment—gathered around the table with little idea of how to proceed. There was a feeling of hesitancy and much silence. Though the family could communicate with Moniek, Chaim, and Hala, living in Miechów and Sosnowiec, the daily hearsay and the clutter of one's thoughts made the experience of occupation a constant torment.

The Gutermans were perfectly aware of the sentiments of the Germans toward Jews. They had seen an abundance of anti-Semitic pamphlets, analyses in local Jewish papers such as the *Haint, Moment*, and *Dos Yiddishe Wochenblatt*, as well as on street posters with caricatures depicting Jews as impure, false-hearted, and altogether loathsome. Long before the Germans invaded, the Gutermans had listened daily to radio news programs and knew about Kristallnacht. They knew the content of Hitler's speeches and of countless other anti-Semitic gatherings. The 1935 Nüremberg Laws, no secret to Polish Jews, laid the foundation for the policy of anti-Semitism in Germany, and later in its occupied lands. A few Polish organizations, such as the rightist Obóz Narodowo-Radykalny, which was anti-Semitic, anticommunist, and anticapitalist, announced they would work in tandem with the Nazis to solve the "Jewish question" in their own fatherland. But in the end, it was the violence, the dimension, and the madness of the Nazi machine that caught the Gutermans and every other family by surprise, stunning Jewish and gentile Poles alike.

On the day the German army crossed the Polish border, the year on the Hebrew calendar was 5699.

David, my love![9]   *March 1941, Niwka*

By the time you receive this letter, you should already be on the other side of the Bug. You have left only a few weeks ago, but I already miss you very much. Things haven't changed much here since our last evening together. The Germans are terrorizing us as before and, frankly, nobody sees any end to these terrible days anytime soon. We are frightened and don't know what to do. Some people say that going to Soviet Russia was the right thing to do. As you already know, my father does not share this view. For him the Bolsheviks are not any better than the Germans, maybe even worse. Some people believe that the British and the

---

[9]The following letter was reconstructed based on anecdote alone.

French will put a quick end to this, but I am not sure. Nobody expected that the world would tumble down on us like this. Not one day passes without hearing some terrible news about deportations or executions, and the plundering never stops. In comparison to Sosnowiec or Katowice, Niwka is still peaceful, and as long as one does not have to deal with the SS, we can take it.

I am convinced that you and your brother Chamek did the right thing by going to Soviet Russia. It is not easy for me to write to you when I think about the situation that we are in. Soon you will go deep into Ukraine, where you will have to cope with a whole new world. David, my love, what I am about to say brings me great sadness, and I say it with a very heavy heart. Nothing would make me happier than spending the rest of my life together with you, but this situation offers no room for dreams. And dreams should not cloud our reality. Who knows if any of us will be alive after this terrible war is over. So in all fairness to you, I feel obliged to release you from the vows you made to me the last evening we met. Given the circumstances we are in, I think that this is the right thing to do. I am not sure if you agree, but to believe otherwise is just a dream, nothing else.

Always yours,
Adela

P.S. I am giving this letter to Iziek, who is leaving tomorrow morning to follow your same route. I hope that he will catch up with you soon. I also hope that you and Chamek are doing well, and wish you both luck. I love you very much.

It was David Glejcer's idea to go east toward the Bug River. Staying in Niwka and waiting for matters to deteriorate did not feel right and in fact felt suicidal. Crossing to Soviet Russia and from there perhaps traveling to Palestine struck him as feasible, at least for the time being. Anything was better than waiting for the Germans. Yet David loved Adela and would have married her had she been old enough. But she was still just eighteen. He therefore tried his second-best tack before

37

leaving: to persuade Adela to join him. But all his attempts to convince Fishel and Rózia to let their daughter accompany him failed. Even the intervention of David's father, influential among Niwka's Jews, left Fishel unmoved.

An evening before his departure, David met Adela in a meadow near the Biała Przemsza River, which flowed through town. He explained that he would try to cross over to Soviet Russia, to a more hopeful world. The weather was improving, and if not now, then when? As they parted, Adela was in tears, and she returned home crushed. From that moment on, the Germans not only overshadowed her daily routine, they also threatened her most tender feeling yet as a young woman—her love for David.

David Glejcer, his brother Chamek, and a few other people from Niwka set out on their way early the next morning. Israel (Iziek) Goldman, who carried Adela's letter to David, described the trip east in a 2003 interview:

> Many groups of people set off toward the East. Carts loaded with their most precious possessions would roll noisily on dusty dirt roads. On the way, we would often meet and sometimes join together with families from other towns. Groups of Jews and Poles were escaping, entire villages. We would sleep in houses abandoned by people who'd left before us. We arrived at the river Bug safely, but the Germans were faster, much faster, and they would not let anybody cross. We returned to Niwka.

David and Chamek were somewhat luckier. In fact, David received Adela's letter after he'd already crossed into Ukraine. But the letter itself distressed him profoundly. He simply could not imagine his future without her. "I have to return to Adela," David apparently told his brother. "Leaving Poland hasn't made me love her any less. From now on you're on your own." He followed through on this intention. Having endured daily peril in trekking toward Soviet Russia, David reversed course and headed back to Niwka—to his beloved Adela. After a journey of a few weeks, he arrived to learn his father had died only a few days before. Adela happened not to be home when he stopped by, having accompanied Rózia by train to Kraków for a doctor's appointment.

It was a Friday evening, and David had been back in Niwka for two days when he took part in the minyan for his father. The apartment on First of May Street was packed with people who had come to pay their respects. Suddenly, in the middle of the prayer, the door was kicked open and several SS men stormed into the room: "*Ihr Scheißjuden! Was ist das? Eine Bolschewikenversammlung?*" (You shit Jews! What is this? A Bolshevik gathering?) Without awaiting a response, the SS opened fire and let loose a dog to attack the group. David went down first. When the shooting was over, three young men lay dead on the floor, and a number of others were wounded. Blood covered the walls and the floor, and had spattered on the faces of everybody still standing. The *Aktion* lasted about one minute.

David's assassin was an SS captain stationed in the area with the surname Mates, who had earned his reputation for sophisticated sadism and his German shepherd, which could kill a human swiftly. He had been on patrol that day, driving down First of May Street with his guards, when a passerby had alerted him to a "secret meeting" taking place in one of the Jewish homes.

Unusual for late March, a blizzard hit Niwka the day of David's funeral. It was difficult to be outdoors, and only a few people attended. Also, because of the decree prohibiting the assembly of Jews, it was safer to keep the number of mourners to a minimum. The murder of David and the two other men marked the first direct Nazi assault on the people of Niwka. Word of the tragedy spread quickly to neighboring communities. Everybody knew about the horrors committed in Sosnowiec and Katowice, but until now Niwka had been spared. If anyone in town still harbored illusions about German plans for the Jews, these three deaths caused those illusions to evaporate into the air. In the months to come, attacks like the one that claimed the life of David Glejcer were numerous, yet in a broader sense they were recognized as isolated incidents. The Jews of Poland and across Eastern Europe at this point could never have fathomed the plan that would be put in motion when the Nazis issued their first order to liquidate the ghettos.

Naturally, in putting together this book, I became curious about my mother's reaction to David's return and his subsequent death. Yet after carefully reviewing all my recorded interviews with her, I found no reference to this incident whatsoever. In fact, she mentioned David Glejcer just once in a casual way, and only because I had referred to him in one of my questions. What she said was unrelated to his tragic death. Years had passed until one day, when looking inside a heavy envelope where my mother kept old pictures, I found his photograph, and later pieced together his story through interviews with family and friends.

The shattered social fabric of the Jewish community, a sudden void in leadership (both political and spiritual), the overall poverty of ghetto life, and scarcity of food necessitated all possible measures to keep a family going. This meant young people, including children who were able to work, no longer stayed home with their parents. They did whatever they could to earn extra income. At the same time, the sense of doom strengthened young people's desires—for friendship, places to congregate, participation in Jewish organizations, and romance. After all, it was not only life that was at stake but also the act of living.

A related effect of living under German occupation, in close proximity to looming destruction, was that young people encountered fewer restrictions in their personal lives. Parents no longer offered guidance to their children as they had in the past, nor could they hope for their children's obedience or, in many cases, respect. The early phases of the Nazi program produced a new family order—or disorder, one might say. Shmuel Ron writes:

> The ways of the world had changed. Adults no longer showed the way, and there were many examples—rabbis lost their authority, writers' voices were stilled, noted politicians and leaders disappeared, all that had been known and familiar in public life was erased and the masses were left adrift… Hundreds of thousands of people were left to a situation of spiritual paralysis.

In early 1941, the Germans transferred all Niwka's Jews to Modrzejów, where a Jewish ghetto had been created. After learning of the transfer decree, and fearing rough treatment from the SS, many families moved to their new "home" on their own initiative, but the Gestapo was not about to count on anyone's cooperation. They rounded up Jews on the streets and herded them into the ghetto. Many were sent to forced-labor camps in Germany. By German standards, the Modrzejów ghetto was a rather crude one, lacking a physical barrier of barbed wire or brick. Each of its units housed a number of families, with Adela and her parents squeezing into a single room.

About a year later, on an early spring night in 1942, the Gutermans experienced their first personal encounter with the SS. Heavily armed SS men on trucks rolled into the Modrzejów ghetto in order to collect a transport to be sent to Auschwitz. They brought along their dogs and were aided by the Jewish police,[10] who came on foot. As usual, the *Aktion* took place after dark. The Jewish policemen swarmed into the buildings and within seconds had kicked open hundreds of doors. Their verbal assaults set off screams and sobs from the victims. The din filled the air. Streams of panicked people

---

[10] Unarmed units set up by Jewish Councils (*Judenräte*) throughout the occupied territories. On German orders, Jewish police were to aid in the occupation by policing their fellow Jews and, later, by helping with deportations.

emptied down the staircases; into the streets they coalesced into rivers all tumbling toward a massive turbulent lake, the *Umschlagplatz*. This was a collection point for transports to concentration camps, usually a large building or an open area strategically located for quick transfer from the ghetto to the railroad. Once the people had assembled at the *Umschlagplatz*, the SS took over, shrieking orders, pushing, cursing, striking, hitting people with the butts of their weapons, and shooting. Whoever was too slow or who otherwise displeased them would end up dead, facedown on the pavement. Nobody dared move the corpses to the side of the street.

Within an hour, a thousand people stood at the *Umschlagplatz*, Adela and her parents among them. The assembled Jews were ordered to march forward, and the SS packed them into the *shtibel*—the only house of prayer left intact in the area. It was a freestanding building constructed to accommodate two hundred people at the most. Shoulder to shoulder, the prisoners stood gasping for air as they heard the SS guards slam the doors behind them. In little time, the air became thick and still, and as sweat rolled off the detainees' faces, their bodies produced a stifling heat, nearly debilitating even the strongest among them. Hour after hour they stood, face to face, body to body, unable to lift an arm or to change position. The room filled with the repulsive odor of urine. Trying to escape into the yard appeared hopeless.

Adela stayed beside her parents. Though the Gutermans had heard secondhand of events like this roundup, prior knowledge of horrors did not make the reality any easier to tolerate. As Adela stood there, she asked herself whether the Germans were planning to burn them alive as they had done in neighboring communities. Or would they send the whole group to Auschwitz? She also wondered if her brothers and sister were suffering a similar fate. If not, did they know what was happening in Modrzejów? The sobbing in the room eventually died down, the panicked conversations stopped, and everyone stood in silence. From time to time, the Jewish police opened the doors for a quick examination of the crowd but closed them again when the stench reached their noses.

A few hours had passed when Rózia began to show alarming symptoms. "What are those white caps? What are they doing here?" she muttered. (The Jewish police wore white caps to distinguish themselves in crowds.) Adela tried talking with her mother to distract her. But the more she heard her mother say, the more she realized the seriousness of her condition. Rózia was incoherent. "Who is Chaim?" she asked when Adela attempted to comfort her by suggesting Chaim might be waiting outside to get them from the *shtibel.* Adela turned to her father, but he was in a daze himself, unable to acknowledge the situation around him.

Frantically, she tried to understand her mother's condition. Had Rózia taken too much of her heart medication or did she need another dosage? Had her blood pressure risen because of the stress? Or was she simply disoriented from lack of oxygen? In those few moments, the traditional roles of parent and child swung around by a full 180 degrees. For the first time, Adela understood the premature role reversal that had been forced by the German occupation—on her family and every other Jewish family. The welfare, perhaps even the lives, of Rózia and Fishel depended entirely on her.

Adela grabbed Rózia's hand and elbowed her way through the crowd. She was determined to reach the door and shoved against the unmoving clusters of people, stirring just enough movement to enable passage. When they got to the door, Adela pounded on it until finally it opened a crack. She wedged her body into the space and pulled her mother out into the fresh air. After a brief shouting exchange with the Jewish policemen, she and her mother gained permission to wait outside. A few of the policemen knew the Guterman family. Some came from the same town.

It was late at night. Adela persuaded her mother to lie on a bench in the yard, thinking the air might help. But Rózia showed no signs of improving, and Adela became more frightened. She asked her mother not to move from the bench, and slipped through the police line and out of the compound.

By the time Adela got to Dr. Kozłowski's, she was once again standing on her feet. But that hadn't been the case for much of the journey. The strain that came with confinement, the stress of fleeing at night when Germans could be anywhere, and the knowledge of her mother's condition all had combined to incapacitate her. In sneaking past the guards, she had wanted to run, but her legs simply refused to cooperate, as if she were in a dream in which she could only move in slow motion. Adela had made it to the doctor's house by crawling on all fours. Forty-two years later, she remembered a few details: "I made it. I remember the staircase, which I had to crawl my way up. Tiny windows admitted a soft light from the street. Only the landings were visible. The steps were still in total darkness."

David Glejcer, Adela's boyfriend

Three

Dr. Kozłowski

DR. KOZŁOWSKI HAD A medical practice in Modrzejów. Mainly because he lived on the side of town opposite the Jewish ghetto, he would probably not have known about the Gestapo action until the morning after. Nevertheless he felt a bit frightened when his bell rang before sunrise, and he lay in bed a full minute before deciding to open the door. Because the stairwell outside his flat was quiet—no dogs barked, no one shouted or kicked in doors—he knew it could not be the Gestapo. Yet he was relieved to ind a young woman waiting at the door. Soon enough he recognized Adela from the times she had accompanied her mother to his office for treatment of Rózia's heart condition. In their short exchange, Adela spoke so rapidly that the doctor could barely understand her. Recalled Adela: "I told him about my mother and asked him to accompany me back to the *shtibel*. At first he absolutely refused, but later he promised to come.

He told me to return to the compound and that he would come later."

Before Adela left for the compound, the doctor noticed her knees were bleeding and asked what had happened. Surprised by the sight when she looked down, Adela told the doctor she didn't know. Without elaborating, she turned around and raced back in the other direction. Dr. Kozłowski kept his word. Later that morning he arrived in the yard of the compound, where he examined Rózia and administered an injection before returning home. For the next few hours, Adela stayed with her mother on the bench. The two of them looked on as the SS pulled open the *shtibel* doors and ordered everybody out. Slurs once again filled the air. *"Raus! Raus mit Euch! Dreckige Juden!"* (Out! Out with you! Dirty Jews!) The prisoners, stumbling one by one into the yard, were too shell-shocked to protest.

In the crowd, Adela eventually spotted her father. He seemed lost to the world as he shuffled toward the gate, following along with the bedraggled procession. As Fishel neared the bench where Adela and her mother sat, she ran toward him, seized his hand, and led him back to the bench. But Fishel was unable to wake from his trance and acknowledge the world around him. He couldn't focus his attention, and he stared ahead, apathy glazing his eyes.

It may be difficult to imagine that neither the Jewish police nor the SS bothered Adela and her parents as they sat watching the scene, but this was the case. The police had their hands full. This reality suggests how small numbers of Jews could evade their captors if they showed enough determination and had the right circumstances. Remaining on the bench until the captives had all been loaded into the train cars, Adela had little idea how to move on. It was almost noon. Her parents were in no condition to make a hasty retreat back to the ghetto, nor could they remain where they were. Adela couldn't even be sure the ghetto would be in the same condition as it had been before the raid. Then, in the distance, she noticed a young man waving at her. He gestured animatedly toward an opening in the fence, urging the three of them to follow. In their approach they realized the young man was Chaim.

After learning of the Modrzejów *Aktion*, Chaim had rushed over from Sosnowiec, hoping to save his family. As the mass of prisoners moved toward the transport site, the Gutermans' eldest child roved the *shtibel* area, at first having no luck in the search for his family. Despairing, he glanced at the empty area in front of the building and saw the three of them sitting on that bench. Once his parents and sister had passed through the fence, Chaim helped them all back to their room in the Modrzejów ghetto. The next morning, Rózia had returned to her senses, and the Gutermans resumed their life as it had been before the roundup. They discovered that a few other families still lived in the ghetto, and over the next days fresh transports from other towns arrived to replace those who had been deported. Chaim returned to Sosnowiec.

At the time of the Modrzejów ghetto *Aktion*, Adela was nineteen and, like most of her peers, she desired whatever freedoms she could salvage. Mainly in order to work, she moved from the Gutermans' room in Modrzejów to Środula, just under two miles away, where she lived with her aunt Lejcia, her mother's youngest sister, and uncle Isaac Apfelbaum in the newly formed ghetto. The couple had three children: Moshe, who was Adela's age, and twins Nathan and Edith. Uncle Isaac had once been the head of the *Judenrat* (Jewish council) for the Miechów area.

Though Adela had no nursing experience, she found work as a nurse at the Jewish hospital in nearby Old Town Sosnowiec. During the war anything was possible. A renowned medical facility, it was the first of its kind, in that Jewish communities around Poland collectively provided the funding. Adela's supervisor was a Czech named Dr. Dreifus. A second nurse taught Adela the basics: how to inject medications, insert catheters, and treat wounds of various types, and what to say when the Gestapo showed up. Because of a required work permit issued by the German department of labor, her employment in the hospital allowed for mobility outside the ghetto proper. By the time Adela started to work there, the hospital had been displaced from its original home and moved to a building that formerly housed an elementary school. The original facility had been shut down by the Nazis, who had sent all the patients to Auschwitz.

One night in May of 1942, a young man ran through the streets of Sosnowiec, not daring to turn his head to see if the Gestapo still trailed him. Yet he knew he could not run much longer: he needed a place to hide and time to catch his breath. Out of the corner of his eye, he spotted the entrance to a medical facility, which he recognized as the latest site of the Sosnowiec Jewish hospital. He knew exactly where he was, this having been his childhood territory. He rang the bell and the door opened immediately, as if someone were expecting him. The young nurse who let him in wore a welcoming expression.

The man's name was Shmuel Ron, and after he explained his predicament, Adela quickly checked him in as a patient and assigned him to a bed in the hallway. Because the hospital was already overcrowded, there was no possibility that he could stay in a room. The next morning, she explained the situation to Dr. Dreifus, who agreed to let him stay longer. Shmuel confided in the young nurse that he was an operative of HaShomer HaTzair, an organization involved in mounting resistance against Germans, and that this wasn't the first time he had run from the Gestapo. Shmuel remained in the hospital for a week. More than a year later, in the autumn of 1943, he and Adela would meet again in Katowice, but this is another story.

In January, some months after Shmuel Ron showed up, the Gestapo made an all too familiar appearance at the hospital. Natan E. Szternfinkel, in his book *Żydzi w Zagłębiu* (*The Jews of Zagłębie*), describes the SS *Aktion* that followed:

> When the hospital was surrounded, frightening things were happening. The ill were escaping in their hospital gowns. Many were jumping out the windows, and the ones who were unable to move were carried out on stretchers. The ill were placed on platforms one on top of the other. Next to one's head were the legs of another. They were driven to a train and loaded into individual wagons. The *Aktion* was run by the Gestapo officer Freytag. In addition, eighty children ages two weeks to five years old from the [nearby Jewish] orphanage were included in the hospital transport. The entire transport, consisting of approximately two thousand people, was sent to Auschwitz to be annihilated.

In this raid, the Gestapo spared the hospital staff, and the ward eventually filled with new patients. But the threat of a repeat visit from the Gestapo haunted Adela through every hour of every shift from that day on.

Being able to repress an apocalyptic reality was a prerequisite for survival... Like everyone else, I had to struggle to forget all that had happened to me from the beginning of the war. Every painful experience that might have sapped my will to live became a blank spot in my memory... It was suicidal not to detach yourself from the human suffering around you. The path to freedom from self-destructive qualms ran over the corpses of those nobler than you.

—*Roman Frister,* The Cap

Four

Final Solutions

IN SEPTEMBER OF 1942, the Germans began organizing a new ghetto in Sosnowiec-Środula. Unlike the setup in Modrzejów, this ghetto was to be fully isolated, surrounded by a wall of brick alternating with barbed wire and wooden fencing. It would be the destination of Jews from a few small towns in the area as well as some neighborhoods of Sosnowiec and Będzin. On March 10, 1943, when construction had been completed, the Germans closed the ghetto's gates. For the short term, they intended to let certain groups of Jews continue living on the exterior. Among them were Adela's parents, who remained in their room in Modrzejów.

After the ghetto had been sealed, the Germans moved to fill it as swiftly as possible. Street roundups and transports from neighborhoods and other towns throughout southern Poland occurred daily. As Jews were being targeted by the SS, and marched through the streets of Niwka, Modrzejów, Sosnowiec, and Katowice, most gentile Poles looked the other

53

way, going about daily matters just as they always had. The tram driver arrived at each stop on time; the butcher exchanged pleasantries with Mrs. Konieczny, one of his best customers, before handing her a pound of tightly wrapped pork; Dr. Mazurek finished his afternoon rounds at the clinic and headed home; and the miners of the Maurycy coal mine gathered in front of the entrance gate, waiting to start their shift. As they stood around, they chatted about the usual topics—children, wives, work, wages. They did not discuss the ghettos or the evacuations because the Jews' plight, they felt, was none of their business. And why should they worry about the Jews? Life might be okay without them, maybe even better. Neighbors tried to ignore events that were seemingly unignorable.

From the very beginning, living conditions in the ghetto were inhumane. An area less than one square mile was at times home to twelve thousand people. The population changed constantly, as the Germans organized transports to nearby concentration camps and then replenished the ghetto by dipping into other towns and villages. All along, maintenance of clean water and waste disposal presented major logistical challenges. It was difficult to uphold even basic hygiene, a problem that resulted in the spread of typhus, diphtheria, measles, and skin diseases such as impetigo and scabies. Lice and roach infestations were impossible to combat. Nothing, however, oppressed the residents as constantly as hunger and cold. After the ghetto was sealed, its residents—often children—would cross over to the Aryan side in search of food and coal for heating even though the act was punishable by death. Many were caught and executed on the spot. The SS officers and Wehrmacht soldiers often entered the ghetto and forcibly extracted from inhabitants whatever possessions they had held on to, always leaving a trail of corpses in their wake. Almost every day, a horse-drawn cart rolled through the streets of the ghetto to collect the dead bodies. An excerpt from Samuel Brechner's deposition for *Holocaust Testimonies* gives some idea of the scene:

> In March 1943, the Gestapo issued new orders on the basis of which all Jews displaced to Old Sosnowiec now had to move to Środula. Several days were designated for this purpose. The situation of the Jewish population was by now catastrophic. There began a hard fight for any place where it was possible to stay with one's family. In Środula, Jews lived with 15 persons in one small room. Many thousands of Jews wandered on the streets unable to find a roof over their heads. All this happened in March during very cold weather. Life in the ghetto became more difficult with each day. The concentration of all [these] Jews into one place made it easier for the Nazi criminals to prepare regular roundups and find more victims to send to labor camps for hard work.

While living in Środula with her aunt Lejcia's family, Adela could use her work pass to enter and leave the ghetto as she pleased. The only legal use for the pass was work, but such a restriction begged to be violated. Once a week, she would walk to Modrzejów to see her parents, a few kilometers away. But her hospital work ended abruptly one night, when the Gestapo emptied the entire building and barred the staff from ever entering it again. They declared the building *Judenrein*.[11] As for the patients, whoever wasn't gunned down on the spot was deported to a death camp.

The day after the closure of the hospital, still using her old work permit, Adela found a nursing job at the Skopek factory in Środula, a manufacturer of ice-making machinery, manual diaper dryers, and other household appliances that was also located beyond the ghetto proper. At the Skopek factory, gentiles and Jews worked side by side, and years later Adela recalled its German civilian owners to be decent people. In

---

[11] The term *Judenrein* is commonly translated as "Jew free" but means, literally, "clean of Jews" or "purified of Jews."

her new role, she alternated twelve-hour shifts with another girl, since the factory operated twenty-four hours a day. A dentist and a physician were also on duty for a few hours daily.

On January 20, 1942, at a lakeside villa on the outskirts of Berlin, Hitler met with his inner circle, including Reinhard Heydrich, Heinrich Himmler, and Adolf Eichmann, to discuss the final stage in the crafting of the Master Race. Though the meeting—later to be known as the Wannsee Conference—lasted no more than two hours, the participants agreed unanimously to the terms of the Final Solution, as well as to fulfilling their duty to the Führer and their Aryan nation. On Hitler's mind since at least 1933, the destruction of Europe's Jews had now become a priority order.

In 1961, during Eichmann's famed deposition in Jerusalem, the defendant admitted that "there was no difference of opinion. The opposite: all the representatives expressed their satisfaction with the role they were entrusted with—actually there was enthusiasm."[12] The Nazis subsequently ordered a rapid expansion of the Auschwitz death camp, setting their sights on additional barracks, gas chambers, and crematoria. With the help of German scientists, the SS set about to find more efficient ways to accomplish mass killings.

In their quest toward the Final Solution, the Germans first targeted the *Generalgouvernement,* organizing massive deportations of Jews to labor, concentration, and death camps. As in the early phases of German occupation, some people made last-ditch attempts to save themselves, attempts that failed almost without exception. Small groups tried to hide in the forests; hiked west toward Soviet Russia; or fled to the Reich, which paradoxically offered improved options for

---

[12] See Henryk Grynberg's *Polish-Jewish Monologue.*

hiding. (In Zagłębie, Środula was among the towns to fall within the *Reich.*) According to Yad Vashem documents, between May 10 and August 18 of 1942, almost twelve thousand Jews were sent to various extermination camps. During this period, my mother's sister, Hala, moved with Henia to Modrzejów to stay with her parents, while her husband, Israel, remained in the *Generalgouvernement,* relocating from Miechów to Kraków. Not much time passed before he and my uncle Max Czapelski (who happened to be walking near each other on the street) were caught during one of the Gestapo street roundups, ordered to drop their trousers, and sent to the Montelupich prison, notorious for abusive treatment of prisoners. Later they were transferred to Auschwitz, where both were murdered, likely in the gas chamber.

In early 1943, the Germans arrived to liquidate the Miechów ghetto, where Moniek Guterman was confined with his wife, Gitla, and their eleven-month-old daughter, Estera. Along with their neighbors, Moniek and his family were crammed into a cattle car, headed for Bełżec. But because their uncle Isaac Apfelbaum, the former head of the *Judenrat,* knew about the ghetto liquidation ahead of time, he persuaded the SS guards on the platform to let Moniek off the train. Unfortunately he could not negotiate the same for Gitla and Estera. So Moniek climbed back into the cattle car and reunited with his family.

That same evening, Adela was given a letter written by her brother. She could not be sure how the letter had got to her but later speculated that Moniek may have slipped it through the cracks of the wagon floor, or handed it to his uncle Isaac before the train left. The letter confirmed what she had already suspected: Moniek and Gitla would not allow the Germans to take them to the gas chamber. The family of three had taken cyanide pills and died on the way to Bełżec, a death camp where transports delivered straight to the gas chambers and their bodies incinerated in one of the camp's six crematoria. There were no living quarters in Bełżec. The Germans forced Jewish special commandos to administer this task. When the commandos had finished the work, they too were sent to be gassed. Each arriving transport thus initiated its own death cycle. Fishel and Rózia Guterman were never shown Moniek's letter, nor did they ever learn the circumstances of his death.

By this point in the war, ten major cities in Poland had large ghettos, and numerous smaller ones were scattered all over the country. Indeed, Jews were no less safe in the ghettos than they would be anywhere else—on the run, for instance.

By the time Moniek's family took their lives in the cattle car, Hala, Henia, Chaim, and Regia, along with her parents, had joined Adela and the Apfelbaums in the Środula ghetto. One of the main debates among the family was whether or not it was safe for Fishel and Rózia to continue living in Modrzejów. A different town—maybe a smaller one—would allow for better protection. Once again Uncle Isaac stepped in, visiting Moshe Merin, head of the *Judenrat* in Sosnowiec and Będzin, to ask for his opinion. Merin, who had firsthand knowledge of the Germans' plans for Jews in the area, advised that staying in Modrzejów offered a comparatively better chance for survival. Today it is impossible to judge if alternative advice would have yielded a happier outcome.

On an early morning in the spring of 1943, Adela left the ghetto with an SS commando (an escort, according to protocol) for her shift at Skopek. When later she ran into Moshe Merin on the street, he pulled her aside. "Where are your parents?" he asked. When she said they had remained in Modrzejów on his counsel, he apparently answered, "Then your parents are gone."

Adela ran back to the ghetto. As she passed through the gate, she sensed that everyone there already knew what had happened: There had been a total liquidation of the Modrzejów ghetto the previous night. One lucky exception was Hala Mandelbaum, Adela's aunt, who had escaped with the help of a friendly Jewish policeman.

The story cobbled together from a few eyewitnesses went like this: On the night of May 19, 1943, the SS encircled the Modrzejów ghetto in a huge envoy of trucks. They then ordered the Jewish policemen who joined them to comb through each house and chase the residents out. Once the people were in the streets, they faced the full force of the SS: the shouting, cursing, attacking dogs, beatings, shootings. Adela's parents and aunt Hala ran to the basement to hide, but the Jewish police discovered them and ordered everyone outside. Tens of trucks were loaded with human cargo and driven to Będzin, where the SS packed everybody into an old Jewish orphans' home, just as they had done in the Modrzejów *shtibel* seven months earlier.

Once again, Adela was assailed by questions: How can I get my parents out of this situation? Can anyone else help? Might I have been more useful staying with them in Modrzejów? Eventually she called on two of her cousins—Rózia's brother's sons—who lived on the Aryan side. They told her they knew of an SS officer who might be bribed to help. So Adela and Hala collected jewelry—wedding rings, anything of value—and the cousins promised to contribute jewelry of their own. The plan was then for Adela to call them from Skopek to arrange for a time and place to meet.

In times of peril, however, events seldom happen as planned, and here too a complication developed. That morning, a rumor circulated that the Środula ghetto would be liquidated that night. The rumor, like many others during the war, turned out to be just that, but Adela could not have known this beforehand. She thought only that if it were true, she would return from Modrzejów to an empty ghetto. Hala, Henia, and many others would have disappeared into some cattle train transport, like the family members before them. Losing Hala and Henia was not a chance she was prepared to take. After a long talk with the Apfelbaums, she decided that Hala and Henia should leave Środula and stay with her for one night at Skopek. This would not guarantee their survival, but at least it would spare them the liquidation.

Because of the curfew still in effect, only a work ID card was required for the nightshift, so Adela did not need an escort to the factory. This made it possible to smuggle Hala and her daughter out of the ghetto. Hala wore a black dress, black hat, and a veil, as though in mourning, and held her daughter's hand as they walked. By covering her face, she concealed both her fear and her Semitic features. As soon as the three of them passed through the gate, they removed the Shields of David from their sleeves. They proceeded without incident to the plant. Since children weren't allowed into the building, Adela had arranged for a female janitor to watch Henia through the night. Hala would stay with Adela at the factory, where they intended to place a call to their cousins.

According to the plan—yet another "plan" in a chaotic time—Adela left Henia with the janitor and instructed Hala to wait at the brick wall outside the factory grounds. She wanted to ensure that no SS officers were present, as they often inspected the place for irregularities. As she rang the bell to enter the factory, she heard voices from behind the door— shrill, unfamiliar voices. It was too late to turn back and she felt her heart rise to her throat. The door opened to reveal two SS officers and a woman in civilian clothing. They asked Adela for an ID and, after inspecting it, let her through without trouble. The agents then walked outside, where they immediately found Hala. She had no identification papers, and the veil aroused their suspicions. Neither Hala nor Adela had known that a veil, when used by Christian mourners, should not cover the face after sunset. Adela had instinctively followed the SS officers outdoors. She later explained:

> I was certain they would let Hala go, if only I could talk to them. I told them I was Hala's sister, but they wouldn't listen. They seized her and ordered me back to the factory, but I followed them to the tramway platform to bribe them with the jewelry. I removed the small pouch from my neck—the one I had hidden under my dress; it contained

the jewelry collected for my parents' ransom—and gave it to the SS officers. I said I would like to donate it to the Red Cross. My bribe had no effect on them. They threw the pouch back in my face. The woman dressed in civilian clothing collected everything that had fallen onto the pavement, and pocketed it.

When the tram arrived, the SS officers once more ordered Adela to return to the factory. But once more she defied them, waiting only a moment before jumping into the car right behind Hala and the officers. When one of the SS officers noticed her, he struck her in the face, and she fell to the floor, bruised and bleeding. The passengers—all gentiles because of the ban on Jews using public transportation—stared down silently. Nobody dared risking eye contact with an SS officer or otherwise bearing witness to the incident.

The SS and Gestapo offices were located in the basement of a building in Sosnowiec. There, the officers positioned Adela and Hala at opposite walls and forbade them to talk to each other. As an officer inspected Hala's purse, an alarm flashed in Adela's mind. Once the time came to search her bag, he would surely find her small box, known as a *paratus*. In the box, she carried needles and syringes, which she used to administer shots in the ghetto for extra money. But the *paratus* also had a false bottom meant to separate disinfectant from the other instruments. Adela used this compartment to hide a *palcówka,* a gentile identity card, which she had stolen from a factory worker who had needed treatment for an injury sustained on the job. From the moment she acquired the card, Adela had used the name Irena Siekańska[13] whenever she ventured beyond the ghetto walls. Here in the office of the Gestapo, she realized the danger she would face should the interrogators find it. Worst of all, only she and Hala knew where Henia was. So before the Gestapo officer could confiscate the purse, Adela spoke up: "I must leave for work

---

[13] Adela went by the name Irena after World War II as well, and both friends and family used it to address her.

now. Somebody might get injured in the factory and need my help." By some miracle he agreed and even gave her an escort out of the building. Adela walked back to the factory as fast as she could.

But the phone conversation with her cousins turned out disappointing when she learned that they would not be able to help after all. Adela also learned that the rumor about the Środula ghetto liquidation had been false. As soon as her shift ended, she rushed to the janitor's home to pick up Henia and returned with her to the ghetto. As she approached its gates, she saw the Apfelbaums waiting and knew from their expression that Hala had not returned. She and the Apfelbaums wept through the night.

I know that my mother would not have admitted this, but what truly spared her from sharing Hala's fate was that the Gestapo refused to believe that the two young women were sisters. They had hardly any physical traits in common.

What happened to Adela's uncle Isaac Apfelbaum and his family warrants a digression, because their lives were intricately entwined with hers. They had moved into Środula after having already escaped to Kraków following the Miechów ghetto liquidation. Isaac's days as an official in the *Judenrat* had long since come to an end, and he was facing the same fate as everyone else. Nevertheless, he maintained contact with the Jewish groups, the SS, and commissions that helped coordinate ghetto liquidations. Just a few days after Adela arrived to live with his family, he received a note from the SS that his oldest son, Moshe, should come to the *Umschlagplatz* to help liquidate one of the local ghettos. Moshe obeyed—and never returned. Eyewitnesses reported that the SS executed him in front of a crowd of thousands at Miechów's *Umschlagplatz*—without firing a single shot. To amuse themselves, they had loosed their dogs on Moshe; the animals ripped into his flesh, killing him swiftly.

Uncle Isaac hid this truth from his wife, Lejcia, until their deaths in Auschwitz in 1943. To make his deception more believable, he forged imaginary letters from Moshe to his mother. He had someone outside the ghetto place them in the mailbox. According to Adela, her aunt knew very well that the letters were fakes and that her son was dead. But she half-convinced herself of their authenticity as a way to soften the grief. Still, after her son's death, Aunt Lejcia stopped sleeping, lost weight, and could not stop sobbing. She also withdrew emotionally from her marriage, seldom speaking to her husband.

For Adela, it was bad enough to know that Hala was gone. Now, as she spent the night at the Apfelbaums' room in Środula, she had to confront her powerlessness to save her parents, who at that hour were locked up in the old orphanage along with the other prisoners. Closely guarded by German soldiers, they would spend another twelve hours inside. The conditions in the building were similar to, if not worse than, those that prevailed at the *shtibel* during the first roundup. A Jewish policeman and a former neighbor in Niwka later recounted seeing the Gutermans as they were forced into a cattle train, supposedly holding hands as they boarded. Among the other passengers were hundreds of young women with infants and small children, including several members of the Czapelski and Guterman families. When this transport arrived at Auschwitz, the prisoners did not benefit from the usual selection process. They were led straight to the *Rampe*—a train platform—to face the *Sonderkommando,* a squad of prisoners responsible for gassing arrivals, cremating them, and disposing of corpses from the gas chambers. No one survived. And Rózia's wish had not been fulfilled. Chaim had not been able to say Kaddish at his parents' grave.

Moments before the transport left the ghetto, Fishel Guterman gave the same Jewish policeman a map of his family's house in Niwka, showing where he had hidden a jar filled with gold coins—savings that might be useful to his daughter. He had tried sometime before to show Adela the jar but, unwilling to accept such a fate for her parents, she had refused to see it. When later she returned to the house with the map, she found only a freshly dug hole where the jar was to have been hidden.

At the time Rózia and Fishel were confined inside the cattle car bound for Auschwitz, murder and grief had become part of the daily order for Adela. First Moniek and his family, then her parents—and now Hala. Adela absorbed one blow after another, but there was no time for mourning. She must think of Henia first. Only the present mattered, and the burden of survival would require every bit of energy, every movement, every thought. Years later Adela explained that during the war, events happened so fast that "the situation simply did not allow for feelings to take precedence over the instinctive drive for survival. With so much tragedy and death around us, even the significance of the death of your kin took second stage."

The Polish journalist Hanna Krall, a Holocaust survivor who has written several award-winning books, concludes as follows in *Subtenant*: "Survived those who agreed not to allow entry of feelings of sympathy and suffering."

Five

Escape from Środula

ON THE NIGHT OF July 31, the Germans began liquidating the Środula ghetto, where Adela still lived with her aunt's family. In her words:

> It was a very humid and steamy night. The air and people's disposition on the street signaled an oncoming storm... At daybreak we heard shots and the howling of dogs. Squads of Gestapo and gendarmerie encircled the ghetto area. The sixth and final liquidation of Jews from Środula began.

The Środula *Aktion* was completed in three days, with the already familiar routine of previous ghetto liquidations replaying itself. A large SS regiment, assisted by Jewish police, coerced families out of their makeshift homes. Then came the dogs, gunshots, blows with rifle butts, gaunt faces lining up to obey marching orders, and the hellish *Umschlagplatz*. Anyone who failed to comply or tried to resist was killed instantly, and the dead bodies piled up on the streets. Children separated from their parents during the commotion retreated to their cramped ghetto rooms but found no one to comfort them. When discovered by the SS, these children too were murdered on the spot. Adela elaborated:

> The SS men amused themselves with a "game" of shooting children who from time to time would appear in windows or between the already emptied buildings searching for their parents.

In *The Jews of Zagłębie,* Natan Szternfinkel draws a broader picture:

> The ghetto was turned into a battlefield. Children running around in despair and without care [supervision] were being shot like rabbits. Every few steps [on the street] there were corpses. One hundred fifty corpses were thrown into one ditch [and were] later transported to a crematorium in Auschwitz. Groaning and the cries of the wounded that could not be helped [because of the overall mayhem] were echoing not just in the hospital but all over the ghetto. Each morning there were new transports sent to Auschwitz... Hundreds of people died on the spot from the bullets of the Gestapo and 10,000 were sent to Auschwitz to be annihilated.

Starting on August 1, the entire ghetto population was taken to Auschwitz-Birkenau. A survivor (No. 47746) of the *Sonderkommando* at Birkenau's *Krematorium V* describes the arrival of the Środula ghetto's last transport as follows:

> Their sweaty bodies were clad in rags on which the yellow Star of David was sewn. The excited dogs tore not only the people's clothes but snapped at their limbs... Anyone who fell and lay facedown in the dust never got up alive... As ordered by the SS...they began to undress, undressing also their children, and it was as though with every garment they were discarding a little of their

lives… Quite soon, they were all undressed. Husbands and wives embraced, caressing their children and trying to comfort each other… Zyklon B crystals extinguished their lives while life in the camp and in the *Sonderkommando* went on as usual.

Adela and Henia were not among those rounded up. In the heat of the Środula *Aktion*, Adela recalled an old bunker she knew of—an air-raid shelter—and wondered if she could hide there with Henia. Aided by the turmoil on the streets, and careful to avoid SS personnel and Jewish policemen, Adela hurried with Henia to the shelter. Climbing down the ladder, she turned around to get her bearings. There she encountered a shock: thirty pairs of eyes staring back at her. Among those hiding were friends and family members, including the Apfelbaums and their twins, and Iciek Ryński, an acquaintance from Modrzejów. The room was furnished with several cots, mattresses, a limited supply of food, and a few buckets. Though the people clung to hope, it didn't last long. Only an hour after Adela's arrival, a group of Jewish policemen burst in. The fugitives begged for a reprieve, but the policemen would not negotiate. They shoved everybody toward the *Umschlagplatz* to join the thousands already assembled. Somewhere along the way on the street, in the tumult, Adela found a small pouch of jewelry and hung it from her neck.

By late morning she and Henia had been waiting at the *Umschlagplatz* for hours. The air had turned increasingly hot and humid. In the crowds she spotted her brother, Chaim, and fought her way over to join him. Chaim and Regia stood in a long line guarded by uniformed SS soldiers pointing rifles and bayonets, and accompanied by their German shepherds. "Adela, you go!" her brother insisted as she approached. His eyes flamed with urgency, an expression at odds with his passive nature. "You go!" he repeated, nudging her so that she would step out from the line and make a run for it—which she did.

Sometime before, while Adela stood on the fringes of the *Umschlagplatz,* she had noticed a building less than two hundred feet away. Now an opportunity offered itself, and she ran toward it with Henia in her arms. They entered a small storage room filled with coal. Iciek Ryński had seen them running and followed them into the building. It was pitch dark inside, and the three of them sat on the coal piles, with no one uttering a sound. They knew the Gestapo would send Jewish policemen from the liquidation commando to seek out anyone hiding, and that the faintest noise would give away their presence. An hour or two had passed when they heard footsteps on the stairway. Any moment the door would swing open and a policeman or SS officer would order them to leave the room or else kill them outright. But after a few minutes, the footsteps faded. Still Adela and Iciek did not shift from their position. After what seemed like hours, Iciek opened the door to inspect the stairway. There he found a piece of bread, a bottle of water, and a message written by a cousin of Adela's, Samek Diamant: "I am now with the liquidation commando. I saw you run into the storage room. Stay put!"

Adela and Iciek remained in the room through the night. The note from Samek had given them the impression that he would return and perhaps lead them to a safer place. The next day, they heard steps again. Hoping it was Samek with more bread, Iciek emerged from their hiding place, but this time he did not return. As soon as the door closed behind him, Adela heard men shouting followed by two gunshots. She was certain Iciek had been killed right there in the hallway. Yet once again, out of caution she did not venture to open the door.

A few hours passed when the storage room door swung open again, this time forcefully. Two workers in blue uniforms stopped short when they saw Adela and a child huddled on a pile of coal. They stared at each other at first, then the workers began speaking to Adela in broken Polish with a Ukrainian accent. They would help her escape, they said, and would return later with food. But Adela knew better, and she hastily removed two rings from her fingers, handing one to each worker. The men were not satisfied with the bribe. Having noticed the pouch around her neck, they wrestled her to the ground, ripped it off, and hurried out of the cellar.

Adela waited for nightfall before opening the door a crack to see whether it was safe to attempt an escape. Expecting to see Iciek in a pool of blood, she instead saw nothing or no one at all. Exhausted, hungry, frightened, and broken down by the sheer intensity of the past several hours, she returned to her spot and fell asleep with Henia beside her. In the middle of the night, she was awakened by Iciek's stealthy reappearance. He explained that the Gestapo had been making one of its numerous *łapanka*s, Polish for "roundups," when the agents saw him on the stairway. The officers had arrested him immediately but hadn't bothered to search the building. Ultimately they proved no match for Iciek. Shortly after his arrest, he had sprinted off and eluded their pursuit by jumping from rooftop to rooftop.

Iciek had brought bread and water as well as a plan that entailed returning to the bunker where they had first hidden. Because the liquidation commando had already inspected the house above it, chances were good they wouldn't return for a while. A second point was that the house had a large coal stove in the kitchen, in front of which a steel plate was set to collect hot coal debris before it could ignite. This cover plate marked a secret entrance to the bunker, which would give them breathing room if an inspector were to show up. Finally, the move was advantageous because some food that had been stored in the bunker remained on the shelves.

Every minute counted as Adela, Henia, and Iciek sneaked out of the cellar and raced back to the bunker. To give the liquidation commando the false impression that the hideout had already been inspected, they positioned the cover plate so that it exposed the entrance. The few times officials did show up, this bluff repelled them. The bunker had no windows and the spray of light coming through the kitchen floor opening was all that the three saw. Switching on a bulb would be far too dangerous, as would lighting one of the candles they had found lying around. About a week passed before the food ran out and they needed another solution.

One night a powerful storm struck, with heavy rain pounding the earth and providing ideal cover for an escape. Though a party of guards marched back and forth, they would not be able to hear the three escapees. The storm was too raucous. Iciek crawled by himself along the roadside, and Adela followed with Henia at a safe distance. Every once in a while Henia would pinch her on the arm but Adela, knowing she could not waste a second, decided to ignore her. When they crossed the ghetto border into safety and Adela asked what she had wanted, Henia said, "Aunt Adela, you were breathing so heavily, I was afraid a German would hear us."

Adela and Henia were now beyond the ghetto, on the Aryan side. It was the first time they would be faced with the dilemma of living in exclusively gentile territory. From then on, different rules would govern their day-to-day life. A Jew caught on the Aryan side would be arrested, if not shot, at once.

Iciek led them to Ms. Horońka, a confidante and ex-girlfriend of his. Though panicked at the sight of three fugitives at her door—she feared a neighbor might inform the Gestapo—she agreed to hide them. It turned out that Iciek had used his ex-girlfriend's apartment as a shelter once before. Stashed away there, he had food, some clothing, and food coupons, enough for three to live on for a few days. But Ms. Horońka was in a constant fright. One day when Iciek was away, she burst in from the street with news of a Gestapo raid targeting Jews hiding in gentile homes—a risk neither Adela nor her hostess could afford. Though Ms. Horońka may have fabricated the rumor to protect herself,

Adela and Henia fled. They walked for a long while over roads and through fields until nighttime, when Adela detected the hum of an airplane motor in the distance. The plane neared swiftly, and for split seconds, Adela could see its metallic silhouette against the moon- and starlight. A searchlight shone over the landscape, and Adela was certain the plane had been sent to locate them. Hiding themselves in a haystack, they slept until morning. Adela recalled their next move:

> I remembered that there lived a friendly shoemaker in Niwka, a gentile. He would make shoes for the entire family. I tried my luck and I asked him to shelter us for a few days. He hid us in his attic, where we could only be in a horizontal position. There was no headroom.

Within a day or two, a few more people found refuge there. The crowd grew to a point that the host became frightened and all the refugees had to leave.

Six

Zawiercie Ghetto

ON AUGUST 14, 1943, when Adela came to the Zawiercie ghetto from the Aryan side, the carrying out of Hitler's Final Solution was entering its end stages. Within months the entire Zagłębie region would be declared free of Jews. As a refugee beyond the ghetto walls, Adela had exhausted all possibilities for sustaining herself and Henia, and she couldn't find Iciek Ryński, who up to this point had offered her best chance for survival. She and Henia were homeless, and they had to contend daily with hunger, lack of shelter, and basic hygiene issues. With no prospects for safe hiding, walking the streets presented untold dangers.

Though a ghetto was designed as an intermediate, strategic step in the dehumanization of the Jews on their journey to annihilation, it offered certain protections to its inhabitants, Adela included. For one thing, she was among her own in the ghetto and could let her guard down. She could cry and commiserate with those around her. And, odd though it may sound, she did not feel hunted while in the ghetto, not withstanding the SS or Gestapo raids. Here, she could be something like an ordinary person, a "gentile" with no particular reason to feel immediate fear. On the Aryan side, by contrast, the stress associated with always having to dissemble and hide could be unbearable. Adela had to watch herself continuously. Though statistics are not readily available on this question, survivors' testimonies and interviews that I have personally conducted bear out the notion that many Jews, like Adela, returned to the ghettos to seek relief from the strain of living on the Aryan side.

This brings us to Pola Buchner, the daughter of Rózia's older brother, Yankel Czapelski. A few months before, she and her husband, Stasiek, had been funneled into the Zawiercie ghetto. Although Adela and Henia couldn't remain in the ghetto legally, they took their chances and stayed with Pola and Stasiek. It sounds ironic to imagine a Jew being in a ghetto illegally, but according to the German rules, that was their standing. Adela was from Środula and, because that ghetto had been liquidated, she belonged "officially" at a concentration camp at best, not another ghetto.

Twelve days after Adela's arrival, on August 26, the Zawiercie ghetto was subjected to a total liquidation. During the liquidation, Stasiek recommended a hideout—an attic, shared with twenty other people, among them an older woman who had arranged to be rescued by her son, a Jewish policeman. When the son eventually did come for her, accompanied by the Gestapo, his mother was spared deportation, but the remaining attic occupants, including Adela and Henia, were hustled back onto the streets.

Years after the war, Adela learned that Iciek Ryński had come to the Zawiercie ghetto as soon as he'd heard about the liquidation. Though he couldn't have been sure Adela and Henia had relocated there, it was the most logical place given their options. Since his escape from Środula and perhaps even before, Iciek had worked as a railroad engineer, and his uniform allowed him to walk the streets freely. In this guise he roamed the ghetto the day of the liquidation. People with garment bags, rucksacks, and suitcases streamed from every direction as the Gestapo, the SS, and Jewish police surveyed the crowd for irregularities. Iciek stopped as many people as he could, asking if they had seen a young woman named Adela with a child. He even went to the *Umschlagplatz*, but the crowds and general chaos prevented him from finding her.

After the attic had been emptied, Adela joined the enormous crowd as it inched toward the *Umschlagplatz*. She had no immediate backup plan in mind, and the commotion forced her apart from those people she did know. Once she and Henia had reached the *Umschlagplatz*, they stood there for hours, awaiting orders to board the cattle trains. As it turned out, all options had not been exhausted, and Adela's mind was not the type to quit in a crisis. Adjacent to the *Umschlagplatz* was a large factory that manufactured parts for the Luftwaffe, and most of its workforce came from the ghetto. At one point during the liquidation, the factory attempted to retain its former employees. Anyone with connections to the staff or who offered a large enough bribe could work even if they had no experience. Among those recruiting for factory work was Shmuel Ron, whom Adela spotted in the crowd. She jostled her way over, and her hopes rose. Shmuel recognized her at once. An operative of HaShomer HaTzair with ties to the factory, Shmuel was to recruit as many workers as possible to spare them from the transport. "I can get you claimed into the factory. But the child must stay behind," he said. He motioned with his eyes to a group of children who stood frightened next to the factory building.

Addressing their departing children, women already reinstated at their Luftwaffe workstations would shout from the building's windows: "Yosele! Don't be afraid! Mommy is going to write you many letters." Or, "Shmulik! Be brave! You are going to a vacation camp with other boys! Mommy will visit you soon." Of those children younger than fourteen who were sent to Auschwitz from the Zawiercie ghetto, all were gassed on arrival.

Though Adela and Henia continued to stand with the crowd for some more hours, she instinctively sought a way out. The

Umschlagplatz was within the ghetto's borders, and opposite the guard post was a one-story corner house, in front of which stood a small barnlike structure with a few entrances. Old furniture cluttered the path to the street, suggesting a hasty attempt to move out by the former proprietors. People from the *Umschlagplatz* had been running into the barn in the hundreds to relieve themselves. Adela and Henia entered too, only they did not return.

Adela took advantage of what appeared to be the only promise for life: shit. She and Henia positioned themselves in a waist-high cesspool, hiding behind a large stove among the piles of furniture. Halfway submerged, they stood there many long hours, until all the former Zawiercie ghetto inhabitants had been evacuated. Sometime later, the SS sent a Jewish policeman to probe the area for hiding fugitives. He spotted Adela and Henia and ordered them to leave. But Adela wasn't about to give up. She pleaded for his mercy—it was their only chance—and he left without a word. A few minutes later, he returned to the barn entrance with a German officer. Adela listened as they stood in the doorway, her heart pounding, and the Jewish policeman informed the officer that he had checked the area and found nobody. An SS officer would never cross a waist-high pool of shit—even to hunt Jews. For the time being, they were safe.

Darkness had set in and the *Umschlagplatz* had fallen silent when Adela and Henia emerged from the barn and headed straight for the corner house, up to the attic. It was a large space used for furniture storage. Having been submerged for hours in a cesspool, Adela found herself overwhelmed by thirst. Never before or after would she experience a craving so intense. She elaborated years later: "I was so thirsty, I wanted to die. I will never forget the thirst that came over me. We were suffocating alive. Today, any time I am thirsty, I see myself sitting in the pool of shit in the Zawiercie ghetto."

Henia must have been going through a similar torture, but the child never uttered a sound. When she finally fell asleep, Adela cautiously descended the stairway to look for something to drink. In the pitch darkness, she found a jar with water. She took it upstairs, drank some, and gave the rest to Henia. The next morning, she saw that the jar was full of leeches and that the remaining liquid was brick red.

The ghetto was quiet for the duration of the night. It felt empty. Adela's sensation that she and Henia were the only two people left alive came over her like a fog, and stayed with her through the hours. She tried to sleep, but all sorts of noises kept her awake. It might have been rats, she thought, but she stayed in place out of caution. Because the noises kept on through the night, when morning broke she searched the area. She saw no rats, but she did find, huddled on the floor behind a commode, a young woman named Eva whom she had known from Modrzejów. The discovery was a great relief for both women. For Adela, a companion was especially helpful because it would allow her to forage food without having to leave Henia alone at night in the dark attic. It also meant grown-up company. For several days, the three of them stayed in the hiding place, subsisting on the raw oatmeal and water that Eva had found on the ground level. They watched the street vigilantly, though their peephole provided a view only of a lantern on the sidewalk and a small section of the ghetto fence.

Believing that the ghetto had been completely emptied, the two women decided to risk an escape. Their plan was to exit the building, crawl down a small hill in the direction opposite the guard station, and then climb the fence. Eva would climb first and then give a signal to Adela to hand over the child, after which Adela would climb over. If for some reason Eva were not able to wait for her companions, Adela and Henia would return to the attic. Should Eva succeed in reaching safety alone, she would send Kazik Budniak—her boyfriend from Niwka—to come for them. Because he was a gentile, he was far less likely to be harassed by the Germans. Adela was to watch the street for his arrival.

During their days of observation from the attic, Adela and Eva failed to consider a critical possibility: that the street in front of the house had been barricaded off, explaining its emptiness. In such a case, the street's perimeter would be guarded heavily. But given their desperate mindset, and the severely limited view of the street afforded by their peephole, Adela and Eva had little choice but to trust their instincts. On the night of the planned escape, they waited for what they thought was the right moment—the cusp of darkness when the lantern was not yet lit, a window of only a few minutes. The time came, and all three crawled up to the ghetto fence. Eva jumped it first, as planned, and Adela and Henia waited. Almost immediately Adela detected that her companion had disappeared into the darkness for good. In the night's silence they could hear themselves breathing, but no sign from Eva. Seconds turned into minutes, minutes into what felt like hours, until they abandoned hope and returned to the attic. The entire next day, Adela scanned the street through the peephole, but nobody showed up. She knew she and Henia could not stay in their hideout much longer. The day before, they had run out of food and water, and their hunger was quickly worsening. Adding to Adela's discomfort was loneliness. She missed Eva's company.

The very next night, after a long day of considering her options, Adela tied Henia to her chest with a rope and climbed the fence. On reaching the other side, they had taken no more than thirty steps when two flashlight beams blinded them. German guards stared forward in amazement:

"Wo kommst du her!"

Adela pretended she didn't understand German, so one of the guards spoke Polish to her. He had a Silesian accent. She replied, "I am coming from Siwierż, where I visited a doctor to take care of my sister's sick child." She drew Henia closer to her. "My sister and her husband were sent to work in Germany. I live in Sosnowiec and I work at the Skopek factory. Here's my ID." She produced the stolen card from the factory as the Silesian guard translated her message into German for the other guards.

Adela's act of incomprehension gave her a first reprieve. The Germans knew very well that Jews typically understood their language, so by pretending not to speak German, she might yet pass as a gentile. Yet the guards were suspicious. They wondered aloud how a woman and child could possibly traverse a street that had been barricaded for days. A plausible explanation was that she was a Jewess who had run away during the liquidation and had been still hiding somewhere in the ghetto.

The darkness gave Adela a second reprieve. In daylight, considering her filthy condition, the guards would have known she was lying.

"How did you get here?" one asked.

"I saw the barricades, but I only know this way home. I had no choice. The guards were talking to each other and I guess they didn't see us, so nobody stopped us. I need to get back to Sosnowiec, where I came from in the first place."

After a while, the guards appeared to be getting nowhere in their discussion. Adela felt the seriousness of her situation and knew she had to act decisively. She later recalled: "I felt that the ground beneath my feet was going to cave in at any moment. I understood that it was I who had to make things happen. It was a deadly situation, and having nothing to lose, I placed everything on one card."

That card was audacity. She declared her annoyance at the guards for stopping her. "I have to get home immediately. This child is ill and it is too cold for her out here." She pinched Henia's behind and the child joined in the protest by wailing, a prearranged signal between them for just such an emergency. "You can hold me over, but you must call the factory early in the morning to explain why I didn't show up for work. I promised to be back by then."

Adela's show of agitation succeeded in throwing off the guards. It also convinced the Silesian policeman to sell her story as authentic, and the Germans agreed to let her go. After taking a couple of steps, still in earshot of their conversation, Adela realized that the guards might yet rescind their decision. She turned around to face them: "I am concerned that somebody will stop me again. Could one of you accompany me and the child to the railroad station?" This marked yet another turning point for the better, as the German guards ordered the Silesian to escort

Adela and Henia to the station. The three of them walked in silence until, just before parting, the Silesian said, "You are too young to die, Jewess. This time you got lucky."

Exposure to other travelers at the railroad station presented new worries. After ten days in the attic, Adela and Henia were unclean and ragged and in no shape to face the world. Fortunately, the station's poor lighting obscured their condition to the other travelers, who were few in number anyway at such a late hour. Adela bought tickets for Henia and herself, and they boarded the train for Sosnowiec. They arrived just before dawn, and walked to Niwka in search of Eva's boyfriend, Kazik Budniak, their sole lead. Once they had located Kazik, he informed them he'd had no knowledge that Adela and Henia had been awaiting him from the ghetto attic. He did, however, confirm that Eva had arrived safely. Adela made no attempt to solve the mystery. Kazik was the only chance for help.

Kazik arranged for Adela and Henia to hide at the house of Heniek Ostalowski, a widower whom Adela had known from the times when he patronized her parents' fabric store. This arrangement continued until one late afternoon when Adela and Henia were alone, and their attention was drawn to unfamiliar, determined faces nearing the gate, then heading straight for the door. She overheard a few German words and suspected them to be undercover Gestapo agents. Such an encounter she was unwilling to risk. As the men stood at the front door, Adela grabbed Henia and fled down a ladder on the backside of the house. They ran through the woods to Bór, a small nearby village, to the home of a woman named Mrs. Tatarczucha. Ostalowski had made the plan with her only a night before in case of such an emergency. The Gestapo gave no pursuit and later that night, to Adela's surprise, Heniek Ostalowski showed up at Mrs. Tatarczucha's house "just to make sure that they were safe."

Adela never learned the identity of those agents at the door, but the story as a whole didn't make sense. First of all, no other house in Niwka had been searched for Jews, which would have been the usual Gestapo protocol. Where one home was suspected, an entire neighborhood went under the magnifying glass. Second, Ostalowski's visit to Mrs. Tatarczucha was tough to reconcile with his explanation. The Gestapo would pursue and interrogate a suspected collaborator for days before letting the issue drop. Ostalowski, however, had apparently been left to go about his business. According to my mother's testimony, Ostalowski may have staged the raid to protect himself, and the men at his door may only have been posing as undercover agents. After all, many Silesians spoke perfect German.

In the years after the war, my mother could never explain why Eva did not wait for her at the fence in the Zawiercie ghetto. Nor could she explain why, after Eva showed up in Niwka, Kazik did not retrieve Henia and her from the attic. A few decades later, after learning that Eva had survived the war, the two exchanged letters, yet my mother still stopped short of asking her what had happened. She later suggested as follows:

> Fear and terror often prompt even the bravest and ordinarily decent people to act in ways that can only be understood as motivated by the urge for self-preservation. Is this natural and justifiable conduct between humans? I don't know. What happened cannot be reversed, and putting Eva in a compromising position now will not lead anywhere.

Later, invoking a Jewish adage, Adela added: "Besides, even though it does not feel just, I wasn't there on the other side of the fence.... I have no right to judge."

Seven

Bór

ADELA AND HENIA HAD been hiding at Mrs. Tatarczucha's house for two nights when, after making sure Henia was asleep, the hostess took Adela's hand and led her to an adjacent barn. "I must show you something," she said placing her index finger across her lips as she opened the large creaking doors. Mrs. Tatarczucha called into the barn, "It's all right. It's me with a friend." A few seconds passed before the flame of her lantern revealed at least ten faces, which hesitantly emerged from the hay and behind the rafters. As Adela stared in disbelief, Mrs. Tatarczucha smiled. "You are not alone," she whispered. "I have been hiding several people for many weeks. You and the child are my newest guests."

While the others stayed in the barn, Adela, Henia, and a former Jewish policeman remained sheltered in the house. Adela never understood what criteria led Mrs. Tatarczucha to choose who stayed in the house and who went to the barn. It simply could have been the sequence in which the newcomers arrived. But that didn't really matter. What mattered was that she and Henia felt safe again. At least in the short run. Living with the Jewish policeman brought to light a further truth: that a Jewish policeman may have harbored the illusion of authority, but it was only that, an illusion. His power was meaningless and temporary, and ultimately he would be hunted like every other Jew in Hitler's reach.

When at first Adela and the policeman heard the metallic clanking and strident voices coming from outside, they suspected it might be from the Sunday market. But this was Bór, a kilometer or so away from Niwka, where the market was held. And it wasn't Sunday. The voices continued, accompanied by heavy static, as if from a radio broadcast. As the volume increased, Adela and the policeman listened closer:

> *"Żydy!"* (Jews!)
> *"Wygonić?"* (Chase away!)
> *"Zabić!"* (Kill!)

The voices grew louder by the second, and Adela pulled back the corner of a curtain just far enough to peek out. Despite all she'd been through, nothing yet had touched a nerve as raw as the scene out the window. Only a hundred feet away marched what seemed like the entire population of Bór. They waved rakes, spades, axes, clubs. Their faces were wild and feverish—and all their rage swelled toward Mrs. Tatarczucha's little house.

There was no time to ask questions or to prepare a reasoned escape. There was no time to take a warm coat for Henia, or to do anything one normally does when leaving a house, even in flight. Adela threw open the back window, and set Henia outside. Then she climbed out herself, scooping the child into her arms and dashing toward the woods. She thought only of getting as far away as possible from those savage faces. The Jewish policeman had put on

84

his police hat and run to the front of the house to face the villagers. He hoped to negotiate, to fight, to slow down the mob in any way he could.

Adela lost her breath as she ran, but she refused to stop. Trees blocked her pathway and she brushed against them with her shoulders. Branches and leaves whipped against her hair, her face, her arms. A few times she stumbled and fell, with Henia clinging to her all the while. The clamor of the villagers eventually quieted down, but Adela kept running, propelled by the images of peasants waving tools and shouting, their faces hard and murderous. In not much time, the Jewish policeman appeared at her side. Together they ran through a meadow and then a dense birch forest, until finally they reached the bank of the Biała Przemsza River. Without deliberation both understood they would have to ford it. It was either the river or the mob. Several minutes later, drenched and shuddering from cold, they climbed up the other bank. This had been Adela's closest call. It was also the first time she had felt truly like a hunted animal.

Resuming their escape, the three once again reached open fields. Darkness had now come and only the moonlight let on to their disheveled condition. In the fields they stopped briefly so that Adela could check on Henia. The child seemed all right. Then she examined her own condition. In addition to the bruises and lacerations covering her face and arms, she had lost a shoe while crossing the river. The policeman had broken his hand, though it's not clear whether he did so in his brief scuffle with the peasants or during the river crossing. Whatever the cause, his pain was acute.

Now that they were out of the range of their pursuers, they had some luxury to plan. Adela remembered that years ago a cousin, Iciek Rosenfeld,[14] had urged her to go to Dąbrowa Górnicza, eight kilometers north of Niwka, if ever she needed help. There, a woman named Mrs. Feboch would

---

[14] Son of Fishel's brother and a survivor of World War II.

take her in. So that's where Adela and the policeman walked after resting in the field. Of course she could no longer remember the house number, so they walked from building to building and examined the posted names.

When at last they found the right house, Mrs. Feboch arranged for a doctor to set the policeman's hand. She then agreed to let them stay for two nights, despite her terror of a Gestapo reprisal. This fear was very much the norm among gentile Poles who agreed to shelter Jews. On the third night, after dark, the policeman, Adela, and Henia set out on foot for Katowice. There they split up. With all the ghettos in the area already liquidated, the Aryan side was the only remaining option for fugitives such as themselves. But survival on the Aryan side was not possible without the help of gentiles. In addition to shelter, clothing, and food, one needed valid documents.

I was unable to locate either documentation or eye-witness testimony about what happened to the people who were hiding in Mrs. Tatarczucha's barn after the peasant mob encircled her property. I can only surmise that they were all killed by the villagers or captured and turned over to the Gestapo.

During one of my visits to Niwka, I mapped out my mother's approximate escape route from Bór. I tried to retrace her and Henia's footsteps through the field and the birch forest, until I reached the embankment of Biała Przemsza. The thought of fording it didn't cross my mind because such an attempt would have been suicidal. The river is thirty feet wide and over five feet deep, and the potent current is obvious just from looking.

Biała Przemsza River

One is unable to grasp the Holocaust without having been there. We are talking about unbelievable times, a nightmare that invades its victims every night, and makes them break into a cold sweat as they open their eyes and scream in horror, only to realize that it wasn't a dream. Extraordinary times lived by ordinary people. Even Jews who survived outside of concentration camps or ghettos did so with the stigma of a hunted animal, or with the consciousness of being not a human but some kind of an insect that others not only want to kill but must kill.

—Michael Moshe Chęciński, author of My Father's Watch *(Gefen Books)*

Eight

The Aryan Side

ZAWIERCIE WAS THE FINAL ghetto to be liquidated in Zagłębie-Silesia. Except for the scattered Jews still hiding in basements or nearby forests, and a few Jewish policemen assisting the Germans in a ghetto's "cleanup," the entire Jewish population in the region had been delivered on cattle trains to Auschwitz-Birkenau or other camps in southern Poland. Now a kind of an open hunting season on Jews began. Almost overnight, the streets of Zagłębie filled with *szmalcownicy*—repulsive characters of many nationalities, including a handful of Jews, who would sacrifice others' lives for profit or, in the case of Jews, to preserve their own. These were not just a few opportunistic criminals. In Małopolska alone, the southern province of which Kraków is capital, about sixty thousand *szmalcownicy* roamed the streets. By turning Jews over to the SS, they might earn an extra food coupon, a kilogram of sugar, a hundred grams of meat, or a bottle of vodka or whatever else the Germans decided to offer on a given day. Only those who carried with them money or objects of value were able to buy time until their next encounter with a *szmalcownik*.

So how would a young Jewish woman, a "hunted animal" with a four-year-old child, a "hunted small animal," walk the streets of Katowice in broad daylight? How would she avoid being recognized by those who once knew her? How would she conduct herself to prevent the suspicions of passersby? How would she steer clear of the *szmalcownicy*, whose senses were sharp as radar and who devoted their time exclusively to hunting Jews? She would have to be constantly aware, with the glances of pedestrians inciting paranoia in the worst way. It wouldn't have taken much for Adela to imagine their thoughts: "What are you Jews still doing here?" "Don't you belong in the ghetto?" And the rest. For their first two nights in Katowice, Adela and Henia slept on the urine-soaked staircase of an old building. There they would have aroused curiosity for a number of reasons: their frightened eyes, their unwashed faces and unkempt hair, the odor of their bodies, the stench of their unlaundered clothing.

In the days that followed, as they wandered the streets, their difficulties did not let up. Once when someone approached them, Adela and Henia turned toward the window display of a furniture shop and feigned interest in a sofa and chair. Pointing out the set to the child, Adela gazed at the merchandise as if she intended to purchase it right then. When the same day another person came perilously near, they strode into a building's entrance, hoping to convey the impression they lived there. Once sheltered in the dark stairwell, having slammed the gate behind them, Adela wondered if their pursuer had been a *Blockmeister*, a Gestapo affiliate who carried out janitorial duties for the whole block. This made him a greater threat than a *szmalcownik*, who worked essentially on his own. In this particular close call, the stranger walked by, perhaps never even noticing the unusual pair. But Adela and Henia would have to repeat such maneuvers over and over again. They couldn't ever let their guard down.

Hunger challenged Adela and her niece every waking minute—exhausting, debilitating, painful hunger that consumed their minds as well as their bodies. Not only did every movement of Adela's limbs require great effort, but she also couldn't think straight. Such hunger is a portrait of extremes. Along with slow speech and laborious movement of the limbs come sparkling, seemingly vibrant eyes and a swollen face. Aching from malnutrition, Adela feared fainting and worried about what would then happen to Henia. Anything that might be chewed began to approximate food. Leaves, grass, rinds, even pets entered her imagination. For a moment she thought that maybe if they stayed hungry long enough, they'd get used to it, and the pain would eventually ease. But hunger does not work that way. Whenever they passed a restaurant window, Adela wondered what the patrons would do if she were to dash in and snatch the food from their plates. Sometimes she saw people leave potatoes or a piece of bread untouched, but she wouldn't dare act on the obvious impulse.

Katowice was familiar territory to Adela. So often, before the war, had she walked its streets, admired the window displays, visited with family and friends. So many times had she enjoyed a pastry in a café while her mother ordered coffee. One evening—without her parents' know-ledge, of course—she had even gone out dancing with David Glejcer at the Café Bagatela. But now the town was entirely hostile. As a refugee, along with her niece, Adela had run out of options. No money, no food, no place to go. Mrs. Feboch, who had sheltered Adela briefly in Dąbrowa Górnicza, had been her only known hope. Survival on the Aryan side was possible only with the help of gentiles.

One evening, after she and Henia had been wandering for long hours with no prospects for a reprieve, they retreated to a bench in Kościuszko Park. It was there they tasted what might be called redemption. A tall, firmly built man who gave off a faint odor of alcohol approached them on the bench. "Who are you?" he asked in Polish. Perhaps the man inspired confidence, or otherwise Adela's hunger and the exhaustion may simply have taken over body and mind, causing her to momentarily let down her guard. "I am Adela and this is my niece Henia," she replied. "We are Jewish and we have no place to go. We are very hungry." Once she'd made this admission, Adela somehow wasn't frightened anymore and felt a little bit of relief. She didn't care if she and Henia fell asleep on the bench never to wake up again, or if this man delivered them into the hands of the Gestapo. At least there wouldn't be any more uncertainty, wandering, desperation, hunger. Their fate would be decided. And even if they were arrested by the Gestapo, at least they might get something to eat. The man stood motionless for a few seconds, looking at them with steady yet unfocused eyes. He seemed to be pondering an idea temporarily lost, perhaps a memory of a distant relative. "Please wait for me here," he said reassuringly, then smiled and walked away. Although Adela did not take the tipsy fellow entirely seriously, she felt they should remain on the bench. Perhaps he would return—at the least with something to eat. Besides, there was no place to go.

The man's name was Paweł Jaworski, and he did come back later that night. "Follow me, if you please," he said, and they did: instinctively, mechanically, unquestioningly, and hungrily.

The interaction on the park bench began a thaw in Adela and Henia's troubles, with Paweł becoming the force behind every step they took. He made sure they had food, and he made arrangements for people to house them. Their first host was Paweł's ex-wife, Bronka, with whom he had an amicable and cooperative relationship. When a dutiful *Blockmeister* inquired about the new tenants, Paweł sent

92

them to work as domestic help in the house of Frau Bülger on Kościuszko Street, in Katowice's fanciest district.

During the war, the term "Volksdeutsche" referred to people of German origin living in territory occupied by the Germans, mainly Eastern Europe. If you could prove German ancestry, you could claim certain advantages over ethnic Poles, though the advantages varied depending on the jurisdiction. Under the Volksdeutsche umbrella, there were three loose categories, based on the geography and bloodlines of one's ancestors. The Germans used and bent these categories to their liking.

Frau Bülger was a Volksdeutsche in what was known as category III, the least privileged level. According to this designation, she was not entitled to a housekeeper, which the state employment office sometimes assigned to first- and second-category Volksdeutsche. She employed Adela on her own, providing food and a place to sleep in exchange for housework. There was no pay. In addition to Adela's housework, Paweł supplied Frau Bülger with food, including meat, poultry, and dairy items—anything to keep her interested in sheltering the tenants for as long as possible. The Bülgers presumably had no idea who the young woman and child were. In their minds, they might really be a poor young mother and child passing through town, in need of work and a place to stay.

Frau Bülger had a large, richly decorated flat, and she gave Adela and Henia a room to share. Her husband was a medical doctor who worked far from Katowice and came home only for holidays. Adela cleaned, helped with the cooking, and did laundry. Twice a day, she carried sacks of coal briquettes from the storage room a few blocks away to the apartment. Most homeowners would use a horse-drawn delivery service for the coal, but Frau Bülger was not known to spend more money than was necessary. She was parsimonious not only where Adela and Henia were concerned but also with her daughter, little Iva, and herself.

Even though Pawel brought abundant food, Adela and Henia were incessantly hungry. Most of the food stayed with Frau Bülger under lock and key.

The one task Adela had trouble with was the laundry. She knew how to wash small articles of clothing, but the bed sheets confounded her. They were enormous and unwieldy and she would never know whether she had already laundered a particular section. Over and over she would scrub the various sections. One day Frau Bülger noticed her struggling and enlisted the building janitor's wife to do the laundry from then on.

Except for her extreme thriftiness with food, Frau Bülger treated Adela and Henia well. Sometimes, when she prepared a coffee cake for her friends, she would ask Adela and Henia to join the group at the table. Although they were all Silesian Volksdeutsche, they surely felt Polish inside because only when they feared being overheard by the authorities did they speak German. Usually at tea times they whispered to each other in Polish.

Adela kept Henia with her at all times. The child had been through one trial after another and she was perpetually frightened, especially of strangers. She also had needs common to any little girl, such as new clothing and shoes. She was growing. "I learned that if one is in need, one can accomplish almost anything," Adela once said. "I remember when Frau Bülger gave me a cut of fleece. Using this fabric, I made a coat with a hood and a pair of mittens for Henia. Do not ask me how I did it. I never knew how to sew and I don't have a clue to this day, but it was an excellent coat; it had buttons and everything."

Sometimes Adela and Henia would fall asleep hungry and go through the whole day with their stomachs growling. Frau Bülger would bolt up everything, even sugar and spices. One day she prepared ground meat into cutlets. Leaving the house with her daughter, she instructed Adela to fry them before she returned. Henia stood on a small stool, watching her aunt work. She asked for one cutlet. Adela answered, "I cannot possibly give you a cutlet, Henia, because they are counted. I must serve as many as Frau Bülger prepared."

"Auntie, please take away a small piece from each cutlet and put it together to make a new one. Then let's hide it under our bed and at night, when everybody is asleep, we shall eat it!" That was one of the few nights when Adela and Henia went to sleep sated.

A number of weeks passed when another prying *Blockmeister* inquired about Adela and Henia, and Paweł arranged for them to stay with the Halicks, Volksdeutsche who had two grown children in the German forces. They served away from home and, like Dr. Bülger, returned home only for breaks. Since Paweł paid regular rent to the Halicks, Adela did not have to work for her keep. She and Henia lived in the rented room under the pretext that Henia's mother was in the hospital awaiting a serious operation. The cover story went that since the family lived out of town, they were staying in Katowice in order to visit Hala more often. Twice a week they would make pretend visits to the hospital. Frau Halick would bake cookies meant for Hala, and Adela and Henia would wander about town and eat them while Adela coached Henia on the "facts," in case they were questioned en route back to their room: They had visited Mama at the hospital, and she was feeling better. She was responding to treatment and her fever was gone, and so forth. Indeed one day, when they had returned from a mock hospital visit, Frau Halick turned directly to Henia to inquire about her mother's condition. The child answered politely, "Mama feels good now. She has no fever and she has red cheeks."

"Was your mama still in bed or is she already getting up?"

"She can sit now," Henia said. Upon which Adela quickly changed the subject. Henia's awareness of their reality, her instinct for spotting danger, and her ability to adjust to various situations were astonishing for a young child. At only four years of age, she appeared to be fully cognizant of Adela's and her mission. Shmuel Ron wrote the following in his book *The Memories Never Let Go of Me*:

> My attention was drawn to the little girl, who answered such questions as "Who are you?" and "What's your name?" with great composure. She had a set line meant to persuade the listener that she was going with Adela to visit her mother in the hospital. (In fact, her mother was already in a concentration camp.)

During one of their leave periods, Frau Halick's children came home for a visit. After dinner, Frau Halick went to sleep but her son stayed up talking to Adela. He remarked, "I once attended class with a Jewish girl and she looked a lot like you." Adela shuddered then excused herself to her room, even though the son wanted her to stay up for another glass of wine. The next day at dawn, while everyone slept, Adela and Henia stole out of Frau Halick's house. They returned to Paweł's ex-wife, as they always did when Adela needed to reach her benefactor. Paweł arranged for a room at yet another family's home—the Halińskis—but after a few days, Adela and Henia had to vacate that apartment too.

By this point, Adela knew that Paweł Jaworski was connected to the Polish underground. He had a network of contacts, and access to money, food, and firearms. Paweł had elevated the lives of Adela and Henia immeasurably. But his relationship with her was hardly uncomplicated. In not much time it had become intimate, which on its own increased the risk for both of them. And now Adela wanted to be active in the resistance herself, with Paweł alone able to open this door. She needed a sponsor to vouch for her before other members of the organization. Because the last thing Paweł wanted was to endanger Adela further, it was with great reluctance that he agreed to use his influence on her behalf.

Though it's clear that Paweł introduced Adela into the resistance, I have neither documents nor direct testimony from Adela or any other witness establishing the circumstances that confirm her underground work. In fact, my interviews with her and my discussions with others who knew of her involvement suggest she was not a formal member of any organization at all. She participated on her own, without any ideological affiliation and without being recruited. Shmuel Ron explained the situation in his book:

> It is a rather prevalent assumption that activists in the underground were affiliated, in one way or another, with an ideological body, a youth movement, or a party. Adela is perhaps the best refutation of this assumption. She had not been educated in a youth movement and was not identified with any party. She joined of her own free will and at first had no help from others… Although not officially, perhaps, Adela fulfilled important roles in the Polish underground and took me along on several missions.

Once Adela had been accepted into the underground, daily life for her and Henia gathered new complications as well as perks. Until now, her focus had been merely on survival on the Aryan side. Joining the underground resistance meant allying oneself with the Nazis' chief opponent in Poland. Because the collapse of the Polish army gave rise immediately to organized opposition, the Nazis zeroed in on two immediate goals: the elimination of Polish Jewry, as planned, and the uprooting of the resistance.

As a participant in the organized resistance against the Germans, Adela worked mainly as a foot soldier, delivering food, falsified documents, money, arms, ammunition, and messages to other cells. She also escorted people sought by the Gestapo to hideouts in the area, and was called upon to spy on various maneuvers of the SS. Now she was more than simply another Jew on the run. If captured, members of such groups were interrogated and tortured. In addition, the Germans would often retaliate against resistance actions—or any anti-German act—by annihilating the entire village where the offending organizations or members resided or where the action had taken place. This was a legacy no resistance member would want to contend with. Perhaps the most frightening large-scale example of a Nazi reprisal took place in June 1942 in Lidice, a village in Czechoslovakia. An event that haunted members of the resistance, the Lidice massacre was sparked by the assassination of SS officer Reinhard Heydrich, the architect of the Final Solution. Though Hitler's order that ten thousand Czechs be murdered as punishment was never carried out, the Nazis killed all 192 men who lived in the village and 71 women. The remaining women and children were deported to a concentration camp. Afterward, the entire village was burned to the ground.

Adela knew that her participation in the underground would put her at greater risk, but at the same time, it provided security for Henia and for herself in other ways. Henia's presence had restricted Adela's mobility, limited her options for hiding, and hampered escapes. At only four years old, no matter how disciplined she was, a child might slip when confronted by yet another *Blockmeister*. The underground network had more possibilities for hiding a small child than did a single young fugitive exposed to all the risks posed by the Aryan side. In addition, the constant fear, hunger, lack of shelter, and loneliness had worn Adela down. She needed companionship. It was bad enough to be in a constant state of fear, but to be frightened alone was unbearable. Anyone who knew my mother would agree that she was the antithesis of a loner.

Falling in love during the war had a lot more to do with "falling" than with "love." It happened in snatched moments and with little sentimentality. Emotions were intense but brief, prompted more by circumstance than high-flown notions of romance. The line between emotional closeness and physical desire faded away sometime between the day of the German invasion and the image of cattle trains bound for the death camps. To lie in a bed next to a lover meant first of all that you were still alive and you were breathing. Physical pleasure gave comfort to a young person knowing that, against all odds, one had snatched an ounce of life for oneself. Adela had no visions of a future with Paweł after the war. Nor did anyone else plan for the future, a concept that was too abstract to comprehend. The future practically didn't exist. Yet in her interviews with me, Adela made clear that she was deeply in love with Paweł, and there is good reason to believe that the feeling was mutual. Paweł also cared for Henia as if she were his own daughter. And it would not be a stretch to say he was prepared to give his life for both of them.

After her stint with Henia and the Halińskis, Adela moved into Paweł's apartment and immediately involved herself with resistance missions. For Henia, Paweł arranged for a more permanent sanctuary at the home of Ewald Pradela—Paweł's friend, a Volksdeutsche, and an active resistance fighter. In an act of great caution, Ewald chose not to tell his wife, Janka, that Henia was Jewish, and even though Janka had been told about Adela, they did not meet for some time.

In the fall of 1943, only Hala, Adela, and Henia remained of the immediate Guterman family. That made Adela's relationship with Hala all the more indispensable, and over the course of the war, they never lost contact thanks to smuggling networks that enabled the exchange of letters and even packages. Their correspondence was especially remarkable considering Hala was frequently transferred from one camp to another. Adela received her first letter from Hala while still in the Środula ghetto. In the following months their corres-pondence involved more than mere updates on family news. Hala requested packages with dyes to treat fabrics, which she could trade for bread, the most precious commodity in the camps. In return, she would send packages consisting of simple clothing that she had sewn for Henia: pants, blouses, dresses, and gloves. Bound together tightly and ingeniously, to an untrained eye these packages appeared to be collected scraps of fabric. But once the thread was removed, voilà, Adela would discover fully sewn ready-to-wear outfits.

After Hala's arrest at the Skopek factory in spring of 1943, Adela instinctively attempted to rescue her. Her first attempt had come when Hala was being held at the Gestapo station in Sosnowiec. Later, she tried again to exert her influence when Hala was transferred to the building's cellar, used as a *Durchgangslager,* a transit camp for detainees destined for death camps. Those held on the ground floor were to be sent to forced-labor camps. With the help of Uncle Apfelbaum and Yolek Feiner, an operative of the Jewish community, Adela succeeded in relocating Hala from the cellar to the ground floor. Had her sister remained in the cellar, she would have met the fate of her parents. The next day, Hala was sent to an *Arbeitslager*, or labor camp, many of which were turned eventually into death camps.

Many months had now passed since Hala was captured by the Gestapo. Along with Paweł and his underground contacts, Adela formulated another plan to free her sister, who was then imprisoned in the Graben *Arbeitslager*, where she worked in a textile plant. Through a fellow prisoner, Hala made contact with Georg Wittich, a German foreman in his seventies who helped detainees smuggle letters in exchange for payment. Wittich was a civilian who lived outside the camp in the town of Graben, and he allowed Adela and Hala to use his address as a post-office box.

In an intrepid gesture, Paweł arranged for himself and Adela to board a German military supply train bound for Graben. From the station, they walked straight to Georg Wittich's house, where they would stay for two nights. As a gesture of goodwill, they gave their host a suitcase full of food. (In the Reich, where the Graben camp was located, food was so scarce that even the Germans had to use food stamps.) A second suitcase was for Hala, to be delivered one half at a time.

Shortly after Adela and Paweł's arrival, Mr. Wittich smuggled a letter to Hala containing Henia's photograph and an outline of the escape plan. That entire week Hala was assigned the night shift. The plan was to wait for her at a predetermined time outside the wall that enclosed the factory. Its upper tier was lined with glass shards as a deterrent to potential escapees. For the probable cuts and minor injuries she would sustain in clearing the fence, Adela had brought along first-aid supplies.

Around midnight on the day of their arrival, they slipped out of Wittich's home and walked to the factory perimeter. Hopeful at first, they waited at the wall for the next two nights, but Hala never showed up. After those two nights, communication had broken off, and staying too long in Wittich's house might stir unwanted attention from the neighbors, so Adela and Paweł boarded a train back to Katowice. Adela later recounted:

> I was heartbroken. We took the train back. We had a stopover in Wrocław, for a long period of time. For the first time in my life, I saw Jewish camp prisoners. A large group of men, under guard, crossed the tracks. Their heads were completely shaven. They wore some kind of bluish uniforms. They were very skinny and looked hungry. It was a depressing sight. I asked Paweł to give them some money. He jumped off the train, managed to approach the group, and quietly slipped some money into a prisoner's hand.

After the war, when Adela finally reunited with her sister, the details from the other side of the factory wall came to life. Hala confirmed receipt of Adela's letter and the picture of Henia. She also said that once the contents of the suitcase had reached her, only half a loaf of bread remained. As for the attempt to climb the wall, she simply had felt it was too risky. But by the time she'd decided to back out, she had no way of notifying Adela.

It was while living at Mrs. Halick's house that Adela bumped into Shmuel Ron on the street in Katowice. He wrote of their encounter in his book:

> Toward the end of 1943, while I was working on the Aryan side of Katowice, Adela passed under the bridge near the former "Rialto" cinema. She was dressed modestly but tidily, and was followed by a four-year-old girl. We were both surprised, but we knew to restrain our joy so as not to arouse suspicions among passersby. We did not talk much on that occasion, so as not to arouse attention. We arranged a meeting at a safer place…

As a member of HaShomer HaTzair, Shmuel helped smuggle small numbers of Jews who had evaded the SS to Hungary, one of the few European countries still not fully occupied by the Germans. Because Shmuel lacked adequate resources for his smuggling operation, Adela turned to Paweł for help. He wasn't easily persuaded to meet with somebody like Shmuel, as it added to the risk for both of them. But in the end he did so anyway, though very cautiously, and their collaboration eventually developed into a friendship—a luxury during the war. Against strong opposition from Paweł, Adela decided to take part in Shmuel's actions as well as in her already initiated underground activities. Aiding two different resistance organizations increased the level of peril exponentially for her and for Paweł. It is almost inconceivable to me that he would have permitted himself to be drawn into such a situation. But he had.

"Wo meine Faust hinlangt, da wird kein Gras mehr wachsen!"
(Where my fist reaches, no grass will ever grow!)

—Gestapo officer interrogating prisoners in the Bielsko prison

Nine

Eighteen Days

THE SECOND HALF OF 1943 and the first half of 1944 constituted one of the darkest periods in the German occupation of Poland. The process of ghetto expulsions had reached its end phase, and many labor and concentration camps were being converted to death camps. On the Nazi agenda, the pressure to declare villages and towns *Judenrein* gained ever higher priority. Daily transports arrived at the Auschwitz platform from all over Europe, including Amsterdam, Brussels, Lyon, Paris, Prague, Vienna, Munich, Rome, Athens, Rhodes, Belgrade, Bucharest, Minsk, Riga, Tallinn, and Bergen, just to name the major cities. These transports increased the demand on the Nazis to improve their killing efficiency, a challenge they embraced in every area of the war. The obvious answer in the camps was more crematoria. So in section BII of Auschwitz-Birkenau, three gas chambers and accompanying crematoria were added, along with the rapid construction of new holding barracks. In a short time, an entire new camp section, BIII, had been built to hold over fifty[15] barracks, with more in the works.

Instead of reassuring gentile Poles that a better life without the Jews was on the horizon, these developments redoubled their angst. The message originally inscribed on the trains carrying Wehrmacht soldiers into Poland—*"Wir fahren nach Polen, um die Juden zu versohlen"* (We are off to Poland to thrash the Jews)—offered no solace to Poles. They had experienced deep losses too, and their suffering, though not always as direct, or of a magnitude comparable to that of the Jews, was profound. They wondered what the Germans would do once all the Jews had been liquidated. Would they be next? Long before the years of the Weimar Republic and the Third Reich that followed, certain Germans had always looked down on Slavs, particularly Poles, whom they disdainfully called pagans despite their strong Catholicism. The most recent enmity dated to the 1921 League of Nations plebiscite, at which Poland was awarded the coal-rich areas of Silesia when the region was divided with Germany (and the Germans were not permitted even to participate in the plebiscite). Now, after four years of brutal occupation, hopes had long since faded that the war might end quickly. The Polish nation was demoralized and apathetic. News of German failures on the Soviet front arrived late, and few knew what to believe and what to doubt. In 1943, even the weather—an exceptionally cold winter—seemed to be on the Germans' side.

For the Jews who remained alive, whether in the camps, on the run, or in hiding, the sense of resignation was reinforced by news of mass killings of Jews on the Eastern Front. Reports from Soviet Russia, Latvia, Lithuania, and Estonia chronicled the execution of entire shtetl populations. News also came of the SS mobile killing squads known as *Einsatz-gruppen,* which followed the advancing soldier battalions into Soviet territory. Their assignment was to purge

---

[15] Fifty barracks translated to room for forty-nine thousand new prisoners.

entire Jewish communities by rounding up Jews, including women and children, marching them into secluded locations in the forest, and shooting them at the edge of a ditch so that the bodies would fall to the bottom. Later that year, the killing squads employed mobile gas chambers, vanlike vehicles in which Zyklon B was administered to victims as they were driven to dumping sites.

On December 31, 1943, Adela was assigned to help transport a small group of Jewish refugees to Lokca, Slovakia, a town on the southern edge of the Beskid Mountains. This particular group consisted of stray family members, homeless youths hiding in nearby forests, and fugitives who had otherwise managed to elude the *szmalcownicy*. In locating such refugees, members of HaShomer HaTzair such as Shmuel Ron would go on search missions throughout the Aryan side. Once a sizable enough group had been assembled, a new transport would be organized.

Adela was to accompany her group by train from Katowice to the village of Jeleśnia, a few kilometers beyond the Polish border. But at the last minute the destination was changed to Bielsko, Poland, about fifty-five kilometers south of Katowice. From there, professional smugglers were to lead the group on mountain trails to Lokca, the last stopover before Bratislava. Once in Bratislava, the head organization, HaShomer HaTzair, would take over the transport to Hungary. The same routine had been used in past operations. At that time, the organization leaders could not have known that in first half of 1944, the Germans would start sending massive transports of Jews from Hungary and Slovakia to Auschwitz. Many people successfully smuggled into Hungary by HaShomer HaTzair would end up back in Poland in Auschwitz.

For this transport, the original destination had been modified, suggesting complications that made Adela uneasy. At the time of the operation, a typical Silesian winter evening was under way: snow, biting cold, gusting winds, and air so dry that one's lips cracked and bled. Adela waited by the track for the group of refugees, her eyes continuously scanning the platform from far end to near, looking for Gestapo agents, German soldiers, rail engineers, or other possible abnormalities. For the duration of this trip, these lives would be in her hands. She could not ignore the minutest inconsistency.

As planned, a group of eight people discreetly arranged themselves on the platform. They knew exactly what Adela would look like, what she would hold in her hand, along with other details that confirmed she was the agent. They were instructed to always follow her at a distance and to do exactly as she did. For this stage of the operation, everything went smoothly. The transport consisted of two women, four men, and two boys—a four-year-old and a thirteen-year-old.

All boarded the train, which had been waiting at the platform for some time. The teenager was pale and tense, and his hands trembled. Adela could see panic in his eyes. She was concerned that the fear would get the best of him, and that in an unchecked moment he might act foolishly, endangering the rest of the party. She decided to keep him next to her at all times. The rest of the group maintained its distance, watching Adela's every move. Later, when they had already boarded the train and taken their places in the same compartment, the teen appeared calmer, and after a while, she felt convinced he would not cause a problem.

Because the transport originated in Katowice, familiar territory for Adela, it was no surprise when she spotted Fredzia Feder[16] with her husband, Jerzyk, and her mother among the group. On other such transports, she would also recognize people from her hometown. But when she learned that the four-year-old was Fredzia's nephew, Adela realized she was connected to half the group, an unusual number even for a transport from Katowice. This discovery made her

---

[16] A distant cousin of Adela's.

especially tense, because outsiders can often sense when people know one another, even if they pretend to be strangers. Adela sat silently, trying not to gaze at the others in her compartment. Another agent was on board the train—Shmuel Ron. Since Adela had to stick with the group at all times, Shmuel was to tend to all higher-level details, such as communication with agents at the various transfer points. The refugees had no idea about their clandestine companionship.

The train arrived in Bielsko late in the evening. An agent was already waiting at the platform, and he directed Adela to lead the group to a restaurant near the station. Shmuel Ron remained on the platform in order to meet up with Roman Brzuchański, one of the professional smugglers who would pick up the transport beyond the Slovakian border. Once the coast was clear, Shmuel would join her and the group at the restaurant. After receiving a direct order from Shmuel, she was to hand over the group to Roman Brzuchański and board the next train back to Katowice.

Adela sat at a table with the teenage boy, while the rest of the group arranged itself at another table not too far away. To her surprise, instead of Shmuel, Roman Brzuchański approached her table. Adela knew Roman, a trusted veteran, from previous transports.

"Where is Edward?" she asked, using Shmuel's alias.

"He still needs to take care of a few things."

Almost fifty years later, Adela recounted this change of events:

I hoped that the sudden chill that traveled through my entire body passed unnoticed by Roman. I became very suspicious. This was another unexpected twist, which we had never discussed in our meetings. Shmuel would not have had anything else to do except to take care of the transport, making sure that everything would go according to plan. I would have known about it. I tried not to let my suspicion become visible to Roman. To make things worse, Roman was a little bit drunk. It made me even more nervous because he never drank, and this was not a time to allow oneself to be intoxicated.

We ate soup or drank something, whatever did not require food stamps, but I could not help feeling that everything was over. Roman talked with me about many things, most of them totally irrelevant, and he wasn't focused. At one moment, though, he asked me about Henia. He knew that I was hiding a child and he wanted to find out where she was. I had spoken with Roman about Henia a few times before. He would come to the *melina* (Polish slang for hideout) for the meetings. Once I told him that a time would come when I would have to cross the mountains with a small child. Except for me, only Shmuel and Paweł Jaworski knew of Henia's whereabouts. Roman insisted that I tell him where Henia was. Of course, I would never do that, but his insistence reinforced my suspicion that my transport wasn't going anywhere.

Time was against Adela and her group; each moment was an eternity. The greasy clock on the wall became their worst enemy, and with each tick and tock her fear would jump another notch. Adela was surely still hoping that, the next minute, Shmuel would enter the restaurant and defuse the entire situation. But every time the door opened, there was another stranger. At one point she asked Roman for a cigarette. He did not have any, but since he lived next to the station, he promised to go home and get some. In that instant, Adela realized that he wanted to leave. She tried to stop him, but he left anyway. Now she knew for certain that everything was over.

A few moments later, four undercover German officers entered the room. They locked the doors from the inside, announced themselves, and proceeded to pace between the tables. Adela's back was to the officers, but she felt them coming directly toward her. The teenage boy moved closer to her, pale as a wall. She paled too. One of the Gestapo officers asked her for an ID. When she produced the *palcówka* from Skopek, they examined it and continued from table to table, collecting everyone else's IDs.

108

At the table next to hers, Fredzia sat with her husband. The waitress came to collect their money and gave Jerzyk some change. As he attempted to place the change in his pocket, one of the Gestapo men came up to him and grabbed his hand: *"Du bist ein Jude!"* (You are a Jew!) They took Jerzyk into custody right away, and later detained the entire group, including a few other restaurant customers not involved in the operation, at least to Adela's knowledge. All the detainees were taken to the Gestapo station in Bielsko and later to the jail, located in the basement of the same building. From the Gestapo agents' assured manner, it appeared they already knew quite a bit about the operation. At the jail, women and children were placed in separate cells from the men. This meant Adela was confined in the same cell as Fredzia, Fredzia's mother, the young child, and other female prisoners whom she didn't know. As often as twice a day, the officers would take the prisoners out of their cells for interrogations. Shmuel Ron's version of events goes as follows:

> One day I was due to meet one of the border smugglers who worked for us. Adela insisted I should not go—she had a premonition something might happen. I did not completely trust her feelings, as I had met this man before and this time, so I hoped, he might be able to help me with the plan to save my father. Against my wishes, Adela decided to come with me. All through the trip I kept insisting that she should leave the train, but she refused. Adela's suspicions turned out to be justified. Our man was caught by the Gestapo and informed on us in exchange for his release. Adela and I were arrested, and after an inquiry during which we were cruelly beaten, we were thrown into the Balice [Bielsko] jail awaiting transfer to Auschwitz.

Adela's prison cell consisted of an iron-barred door, a small basement window with a steel grating, and a light bulb suspended from the center of the ceiling. It had no heating, no running water, no bunk or cot, and only a bucket for a toilet.

109

Alongside eleven fellow women prisoners, she slept on a long wooden platform placed diagonally across the room. The women took turns sleeping because the platform wasn't large enough to accommodate them all, and the cement floor was too damp and too cold to sleep on with any comfort. Storage shelves outside the cell did hold blankets for use during the night.

Even though Adela was not the lead agent, the Gestapo beat her several times. Sadistic, bloody, merciless beatings. Using whatever objects or means within their reach—clubs, whips, boots, fists—the Gestapo tried to extract information. Adela would respond only to the obvious questions—name, age, address, and so forth—though she even lied about her name, claiming to be Irena Siekańska.

Not long into the interrogations her body was covered with bloody bruises and purple blood clots. Each day thereafter brought a fresh beating. And with each beating, the bruises and clots multiplied. During one assault, blood from a head wound poured into her eyes, nearly blinding her. Her breasts turned black. The Gestapo agents would come up with new tricks daily, their favorite being to place Adela with Shmuel Ron on opposite ends of the same room. They would tell him she had confessed to knowing him and, likewise, they would tell her he had admitted the same about her. Back and forth a Gestapo officer paced between them. He would stop in front of one, ask a question, and apply a savage blow to the face without waiting for the answer. Then he would spin around, stalk to the other end of the room, and repeat his performance, until neither Shmuel nor Adela could stand up. Once the two captives struggled back to their feet, the guards would prod them back to their cells.

Underground collaborators knew about German interrogation methods, so no Gestapo measure surprised them. Once caught, they harbored no hopes for survival. The only question was how much each of them was willing to suffer. Shmuel Ron wrote in his letter to me, dated September 1991, "I witnessed how [the Germans] interrogated Adela. I was interrogated in her presence as well. I remember how one of the Gestapo officers commended himself: 'Where my fist reaches, no grass will ever grow!' And his fist kept reaching, and reaching."

Although her underground training had prepared her for the likelihood of torture by the Gestapo, Adela recalled that "the mere thought of torture made me want to die." Another thought troubled her. Even if she were to survive torture and imprisonment, she was sure to be sent to Auschwitz, a fate she refused to entertain. The specter of the gas chamber, which she had heard about secondhand, was far worse than death. Moniek's pledge not to allow his family to be killed in this manner also played out repeatedly in her mind. Maybe it was the fear of torture combined with the idea of a future at Auschwitz that prompted my mother to make an attempt on her own life. Adela knew that Henia was waiting for her, but now even that responsibility could not steady her mind. Not Henia, not the underground, not life itself. Cornered as she was, taking control of her own death appeared to be her only option.

Every time during our interviews when Adela related to me details about standing next to death, she would pause, lighting a cigarette and taking a sip of cognac. She would drift into a trance that lasted long enough to make me uncomfortable, and then suddenly start talking, though hardly audibly. My mother loved life, and to imagine her at the depth of human misery is not something I can process easily.

Adela's sketchy recollections along with testimony I once read about a prisoner in similar circumstances prompt me to imagine her world turning to a white, radiating, abysmal space with the only sound being a continuous murmur. We can understand this phenomenon as white noise, used in courtrooms to cancel out other sounds. Or else we can imagine the sensation of bumping our head against a blunt

111

object and, for a moment, experiencing a suspension of reality. Here in the cell, Adela's stupor lasted much longer than a moment. She had fallen to the core of this white depth, yet she felt dark and heavy. Just holding up her head, moving her hands and fingers, breathing, and sitting on the crate tested her will. Even the eventual effort of reaching for the knife required superhuman strength. She felt no pain as the blade slit her wrist open, and the sight of blood streaming down her hand seemed to her as detached from her body as water running from a faucet.

Fredzia's mother was alone with Adela in the cell at the time, with the other cellmates either under interrogation or out on work crews. Though at first her back was turned to Adela, when she saw the blood pouring from Adela's hand, she screamed until she attracted the Gestapo's attention. A few minutes later, the prison guards had thwarted Adela's suicide attempt. Years later, she recalled, "Apart from the time when I escaped Tatarczucha's house, when all the village Volk surrounded us and the peasants waved clubs, rakes, and iron rods, and the time I stood in the line to the gas chamber at Auschwitz, this was the darkest moment in my life.... Until my last hour in the Bielsko prison, I was not tortured. I was beaten, but not tortured."

I will never find out what details Adela knew about Paweł Jaworski's resistance cells (about these later) or Shmuel Ron's HaShomer HaTzair, and possibly others: scheduled actions, munitions depositories, names of agents and smugglers, the *melinas*. But what she knew troubled her, for her fear of torture was not only fueled by the anticipation of unbearable physical pain but also by the concern that in a moment of weakness she would release information that would have fatal consequences for her comrades. Had the Gestapo taken the time to find out the reasons for her suicide attempt, their decision to forgo torture might have been different.

It was while she was incarcerated at Bielsko prison that Adela learned of Roman Brzuchański's role in her arrest. Periodically during the evening hours, prisoners were ordered to leave their cells to allow the cleaning crew to do its work. This was the only opportunity for male and female prisoners to exchange words. On one such break, Mietek Kobylec, an agent from a previous transport who was imprisoned in the same basement, confirmed that indeed Brzuchański had given away their identities.

But whether Roman Brzuchański had betrayed her, and why, was not her main concern anymore. Adela's thoughts had returned to Henia and what would happen to the child should she die in the prison or at Auschwitz. Believing that Shmuel had a much better chance for survival than she did, she felt an urgent need to communicate with him. Underground agents trumpeted his legendary escapes and evasions of the Gestapo, and Adela herself had witnessed his skill when he hid at the Sosnowiec Jewish hospital. At the least, she felt, he could ensure that Henia would get reconnected with Hala or some other family member, if ever the killing stopped. Shmuel must have sensed Adela's impulse because it was he who bribed a prison guard in order to talk to her. He writes:

> The Kapo in my cell fancied my shoes and, in exchange for them, he agreed to lead me to the door of Adela's cell. I remember her burning eyes, which seemed to cast a spell on me, telling me: "Run away! Run away! For the child's sake, escape!"

The spell alone wouldn't be enough to help Henia. Adela whispered to Shmuel all the details of her niece's latest whereabouts. She also pressed a small soft object into his hand. Back in his cell, he removed a *palcówka* folded in quarters once belonging to Irena Siekańska, a worker at the Skopek factory. "There was nothing I could do with an ID of a female, but it was all she could give me," he told me once when I visited him at his home in Jerusalem.

113

At the time of her arrest in Bielsko, Adela wore overalls and a long overcoat. Fredzia's mother had on a Chinese bathrobe, which she had wanted to take with her to Slovakia. "God only knows why in this situation a Chinese bathrobe was so important to her," Adela later wondered. Once the women had been jailed, the Gestapo took away her overalls and gave them to Shmuel Ron. Somebody else wore his suit, and Adela, the bathrobe. These actions typified the Gestapo strategy of forcing prisoners to wear clothing in the most ridiculous combinations. The more comical a detainee looked, the less likely he or she would be able to make a successful escape.

After a week of interrogations had failed to yield answers from Adela and Shmuel, they were assigned to regular work commandos. One day a large group of prisoners was taken to work at the railroad yard—a chain gang of sorts but without the chains, because even the thought of anyone escaping in such outfits was laughable. Adela, Jerzyk, and Shmuel were among the workers. On this work outing, Adela decided to run away when her first opportunity arose. A moment came when she was able to hide from the guards, who were preoccupied by their conversation. But she could not stay hidden. The cold, the pain from all her beatings, and the absurdity of the Chinese bathrobe all prompted her to reconsider. She emerged from her hiding place and quietly rejoined the group, giving the excuse that she had needed to urinate. The guards may not have believed her, but they let the matter go. A few minutes later, Adela saw Jerzyk and Shmuel dart under a waiting train and into a wooded area. The guards positioned their rifles and fired several rounds, but the two prisoners were gone. Adela had witnessed one of Shmuel's legendary escapes.

On January 18, 1944, the Gestapo concluded its investigation of the conspirators and emptied the entire Bielsko prison. All the inmates were packed into military trucks and driven to Auschwitz. The group included Jews and gentiles, children and adults. In the eyes of the Germans, Adela was not to be trusted in the least; she was placed in the jeep of the chief Gestapo officer, who wanted to deliver her to Auschwitz personally. A driver with a guard sat in the front seat; the officer and Adela, wearing the Chinese bathrobe, sat in the back. A few military trucks filled with prisoners followed behind them. This is how Adela arrived at Auschwitz. Except for Jerzyk and Shmuel, everybody from the original transport reached the gates at the same time: Fredzia Feder, her mother and four-year-old nephew, the teenage boy, and the two men whom Adela did not know. (Years later, my mother learned that the teenage boy had belonged to the family of Hala's first husband, Israel Wajcman.)

In two hours' time, they were marched into the Auschwitz registration building. Terrified, the thirteen-year-old from the original transport to Bratislava again stood at Adela's side.

I do not know if the action of December 31, 1943, was Adela's only failure, or if there were others. Nor do I know how many lives she saved in her successes. Or, in comparison, how many were lost. It also goes unrecorded how many friendly lives were compromised so that the resistance could go on. Evidence suggests, for example, that Paweł himself ordered the murder of the Jewish policeman with whom Adela escaped from Mrs. Tatarczucha. Though I never discovered the specific connection between the two men, I did learn that the policeman was killed because of his blatant Semitic features, a liability for the resistance—and yet a bitter irony considering what the organization stood for. Finally we can only speculate as to how many Jews actually made it to Palestine thanks to these smuggling operations. On the other hand, we do not know how many were smuggled to Hungary only to be recaptured and delivered to Auschwitz after the Nazis invaded in March 1944. Even the testimonies in Shmuel Ron's book, *The Memories Never Let Go of Me,* offer no concrete information. One unnamed person who knew secondhand of my mother's underground activities said that the Bielsko arrest terminated her very first action, although Shmuel Ron's book suggests otherwise, and his letters to me indicate that Adela participated in numerous resistance operations. By the time I decided at last to write this book, Adela was no longer alive. But even had I asked her directly about her underground activity, I am sure she wouldn't have produced numbers to validate her accomplishments. Numbers in themselves connote a grand deed, in her case maybe a claim to heroism, and this was a position she would never adopt as her own. Shmuel Ron wrote in his letter of September 1991: "Lately, historians are looking into these events. I doubt if Adela's name will be mentioned, because it is a typical trait of her character—she was often on the front line of action but would step aside when credit was being distributed. This made her different."

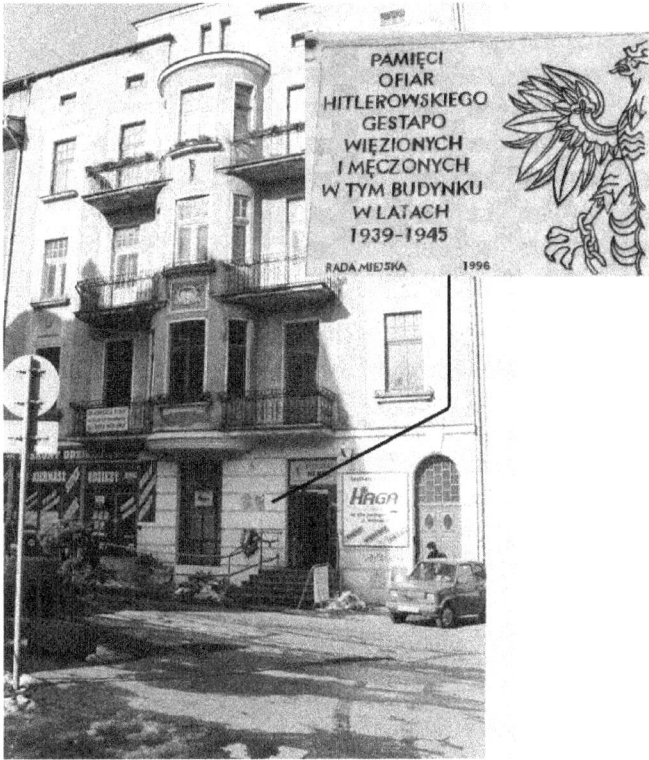

*Plaque posted at the former Bielsko
Gestapo station. It reads:
"In the memory of the victims of Hitler's
Gestapo imprisoned and tortured in this
building in the years of 1939 to 1945."
City Council 1996.*

O you who know
did you know that hunger makes the eyes sparkle
that thirst dims them
O you who know
did you know that you can see your mother dead
and not shed a tear
O you who know
did you know that in the morning you wish for death
and in the evening you fear it
O you who know
did you know that a day is longer than a year
a minute longer than a lifetime
O you who know
did you know that legs are more vulnerable than eyes
nerves harder than bones
the heart firmer than steel
Did you know that stones of the road do not weep
that there is one word only for dread
one for anguish
Did you know that suffering is limitless
that horror cannot be circumscribed
Did you know this
You who know

—*Charlotte Delbo*[17]

---

[17] Auschwitz survivor (No. 31661), journalist, writer, and poet, Charlotte Delbo was brought to the camp on January 27, 1943, just less than a year before Adela. She arrived with a cattle train transport of 230 female political prisoners from France, having been accused of resistance against the Germans.

Ten

Auschwitz

ON JANUARY 18, 1944, Adela entered the Auschwitz compound after traveling with her personal guards from the Bielsko prison. She and the other prisoners were marched into the administration office. There they merged with a train transport, and were ordered to face the SS officers of the *Aufnahmegebäude* (receiving building). Soon the SS separated the Jews from the rest of the new prisoners. As he came out of the *Aufnahmegebäude*, the officer who had personally escorted Adela to Auschwitz looked her directly in the eyes and, addressing her for the first time since they had left Bielsko, said, *"Mach's gut"* (roughly, good luck). He said this, according to Adela, as one would bid farewell to a friend leaving home for a trip. "His words actually comforted me a bit," Adela recalled.

An hour passed as she and the rest of the Bielsko transport remained standing. Then a group of women marching in rows of five passed by their area, and somebody shouted, "Adela! Adela!" A young woman stepped out of the formation in order to be seen. It was Cesia Monshain, an acquaintance from Modrzejów. "Don't be afraid!" she shouted several times. Later Adela learned that Cesia and the others in the group had been designated to carry clean laundry. They still had hair and were dressed well. Yet Cesia lived in Block No. 11, known by prisoners as the "death block."[18]

Armed guards with dogs and rifles showed up and ordered the entire group to march to Birkenau, a satellite camp four kilometers away from the main site. It was at this time that Adela noticed certain prisoners with favored status—those who worked for the SS in various capacities. As Adela moved about the camp she wondered why, given the horrific stories she had heard, Cesia and her group and many of the male prisoners she now saw looked relatively fit. In fact, the Kapos (orderlies designated to control a prisoners' block) and other functionaries did not look like prisoners, even though many wore striped suits. They appeared clean and well nourished. After one of these observations, she remarked to the teenage boy still by her side, "See, it isn't as bad as we thought. People live here. They seem clean and they look healthy."

During their walk to Birkenau, however, they witnessed increasingly grim scenes. As they passed various groups of prisoners, Adela could hardly distinguish between men and women. She saw gaunt caricatures of human beings whose heads were completely shaven, causing them to resemble comic-strip aliens. These prisoners moved their limbs slowly,

---

[18] Here the SS placed resistance suspects, both men and women. Other inmates included those sentenced to death by starvation. The SS conducted a trial use of Zyklon B gas for mass killing in Block No. 11's basement in September 1941, murdering six hundred Soviet war prisoners and 250 Polish patients. Between 1941 and 1943, the SS shot several thousand prisoners at the Death Wall located in the courtyard between Blocks 10 and 11. In this same location, the SS administered floggings and a punishment known as "the post," whereby prisoners would be hung by their wrists, which had been twisted behind their backs (State Museum of Auschwitz-Birkenau).

I could not determine why Cesia lived in Block 11, but Mr. Kozielczyk, a Jew from Białystok and the block Kapo, saved her life a few times. He later arranged for Cesia's transfer to a regular block, where she was given a job in the camp dental laboratory. Cesia survived the war.

mechanically like windup dolls, and their eyes were dull and lifeless. Adela saw two prisoners carrying one brick and supporting each other as they walked, because neither could manage on his own. The boy turned to Adela: "Next to the SS office was no Auschwitz. *This* is Auschwitz."

Adela had heard many things about the Auschwitz death camp. People in every town in Zagłębie had stories to tell, some of which strained the credulity of even the most hardened listeners, many of whom had themselves witnessed monstrous acts by the SS in their own villages. In spite of Cesia's urging to not be afraid, Adela now wondered how long it would take before she resembled the two *Muselmann*[19] who had just passed by. Yet she still asked herself why some prisoners seemed so strong and healthy, and how they had been chosen.

The group stopped before an elongated building, where a roll call was taking place. At the head of the group a young Jewish girl acting as a *Läuferin*, or gofer, stood beside the *Aufseherin* (a female supervisor of prisoners), a uniformed German SS woman named Frau Hasse.[20] Turning to the guard, Frau Hasse demanded: *"Was hast du hergebracht? Eine Zigeunerbande?"* (What did you bring here, a gang of Gypsies?) *"Nein, eine Judenbande!"* he replied (No, a gang of Jews).

Frau Hasse disappeared inside the building for a short while and when she reemerged, she barked, *"In die Saune Nummer Drei!"* (Into sauna number three.) Adela had never heard the word "sauna" before, and she had no idea what it meant. She entered an enormous shell where a series of showerheads hung from the ceiling and groups of prisoners stood about haphazardly. These groups included prisoners of

---

[19] Literally "Muslim," the term was used among concentration-camp inmates to describe prisoners who appeared near death due to starvation, exhaustion, or hopelessness; in other words, walking skeletons. Symptoms included lethargy, indifference to one's surroundings, and an inability to stand upright for more than a few minutes. Prisoners often avoided *Muselmann* for fear of contracting the condition themselves (*Encyclopedia of the Holocaust*, Yad Vashem).

[20] Elisabeth Hasse became an *Aufseherin* in October 1942 (*Auschwitz Chronicle 1939–1945*, by Danuta Czech).

different ages and nationalities as well as both sexes. All of them seemed to be Jews. Those arrested at the Bielsko railroad station remained together in one group. An escape from the bathhouse was impossible; guards observed prisoners at all times and even escorted them to the toilets. Attempts by Adela and her compatriots to communicate with other groups failed at first, even when permitted by the guards. Presumably out of fear, the prisoners refused to talk, even in a whisper.

Eventually Adela and Fredzia approached a group of prisoners who stood alongside some children, all nude. This time they had more success. "Who are you? Where are you from?" they asked in Yiddish, keeping their voices low. "We have been standing here since yesterday," came the reply. "We arrived together with the group standing there, behind the glass wall. Then somebody came and ordered us to take our clothes off. They separated the young group from us and placed them there, behind the glass wall. We think we are next to die; them—perhaps not."

Presently a group of about forty naked prisoners of both sexes shuffled past. They were silent and despondent, and their skin was jaundiced and stretched over their protruding bones— they were *Muselmann*. The life had been sucked from their eyes, and many needed the support of the people next to them. They were led down a stairway and soon the entire group vanished.

The Bielsko prisoners remained standing as the hours passed. Adela understood that the stairway down which the *Muselmann* descended led to the point of no return, the gas chambers. But questions remained for those still alive: Were the old to be separated from the young? And what would be in store for people who appeared capable of work? Adela knew about the selection process and the two lines that usually formed at the *Rampe* of new transports arriving at the camp. But she had not been a part of such a process, because the Bielsko Gestapo had escorted her directly to the camp office.

A man in apparent health passed by. He had a yellow strap on his arm, with the Star of David and a number beside it on the left side of his chest. The word "Kapo" was sewn onto his uniform in black letters. Because the Bielsko group lacked the Star of David on their clothes, they attracted the Kapo's attention. "Who are you?" he asked in Polish.

"We are Jews from the Bielsko prison," Adela said. "Sir, where are we? What is this place?"

"You are in a place where nobody ever leaves alive," he replied with indifference, in the way one might say, "I'll have tea" or "It might rain today." Like a steel beam to the head, these words struck Adela. The world around her blurred; the Kapo morphed into the raconteur of a tasteless Nazi joke tacked onto a ghetto wall. But she toughened herself and immediately begged the Kapo, with Fredzia's help, to get them out of the building. "I can't get you out of here," he said leaving. "The time will come when I won't be able to get out of this place myself."

A while later when he returned, they begged him again. Adela had taken note of the Kapo's privileges, his freedom to come and go at will. "Do you have any jewelry?" he asked. Adela had nothing left after the Gestapo confiscations at the Bielsko prison, but Fredzia miraculously produced a wedding ring. When she offered it to the Kapo, he departed without an acknowledgment one way or the other.

The two women were left to wonder. Had the Kapo gone for help? Why hadn't he bothered to collect the ring? Time crept so slowly it was sickening, yet now the discomfort of standing, the silence, and even curiosity about the people around her no longer troubled Adela. Only one thought occupied her mind: whether the Kapo would return.

When he did, a meticulously groomed man in a white apron accompanied him. Under the apron Adela could detect a military uniform. This suggestion of a doctor had a peculiarly distant and sterile bearing, as if he weren't a member of the human race but instead a kind of automaton. Pocketing the ring, he ordered both Adela and Fredzia to strip. Then he performed an examination in the careful yet detached way a mechanic might appraise a broken machine part. This was the first time Adela would have to remove her clothes in front of a strange man and, determined to influence him with her youthful body, she did so as seductively as she could manage. Though she didn't yet know the doctor's name or reputation, she did know that he could save her life if he chose to. It was only after a few weeks at Birkenau that she would identify him as the notorious Dr. Josef Mengele.[21]

When he pointed to the wounds covering her body and to her breasts, still black from the beatings in Bielsko, she did not answer. Then both she and Fredzia were told to dress, and the two men exited the room. They returned only a few minutes later, shoving both women toward the door. *"Geht! Raus! Raus mit euch!"* (Go! Out! Out with you!) "For today, you have been saved," whispered the Kapo into Adela's ear as the two women were swept out of the building.

That was how Adela and Fredzia escaped sauna number three and were transferred into the camp's quarantine building. The rest of their group stayed behind. Only now the actual registration process began. Both Adela and Fredzia were taken to the bathhouse again, but this time they stood in a different section. In the presence of Gestapo officers, they were ordered to undress and to place their clothing in a large paper bag. After showering, they were sent to yet another room, where other prisoners shaved off their hair. Next came the *Effektenlager*— nicknamed "Canada" by inmates—where camp clothing was distributed. All these actions played out against a continuous barrage of racial slurs, shouting, and physical abuse from the SS guards. Each prisoner would have to catch his or her clothing while running. Adela received underwear, a long narrow skirt, a pink knitted sweater, a man's house jacket, and a pair of wooden shoes. Among those who cleared the selection process, only gentiles and functionaries wore striped suits; Jews and Gypsies received the various garments of those already gassed to death in the crematoria. All new inmates

---

[21] Nicknamed the Angel of Death, he served as the chief physician at Auschwitz and was responsible for the selections. He also conducted sadistic pseudoscientific medical experiments on prisoners.

filled out a form known as a *Häftlingspersonalbogen*, on which they put down information such as their address and next of kin. Once the form was completed, each inmate was assigned a number. From that moment on, like all the other prisoners before her, Adela would identify herself and be addressed by this number alone. Her new name was 74721.[22] The last step of the process involved the tattooing of this number onto her left forearm. The crude and painful method required the repeated insertion of an ink-dipped needle into the skin until thickly crowded dots had formed each numeral. This function too was performed by prisoners.

Later that evening, Adela and Fredzia were escorted to BIIa—a section of the women's camp—into one of the quarantine buildings. Designed originally as a stable for fifty-two horses, the building now housed eight hundred, sometimes one thousand prisoners. Only now at night, as Adela's first day at Auschwitz neared its end, and as she and all the other prisoners lay in their bunks, was she able to run her hand along her shaved scalp. She tried to examine the tattoo but the room was too dark. And when she rested her head against the bunk post, tears welled in her eyes. She then wept for her parents, for Chaim, for Moniek, for little Estera, and for the Bielsko transport. She envisioned Fishel's and Rózia's faces as they waited their turn in the bathhouse. She saw them clinging to each other, trying to conceal their nudity. She wondered what they had been thinking, whether they knew their fate. And how frightened they must have felt, how lonely and abandoned by humanity. She replayed the image of the *Muselmann* who had soundlessly shuffled down the stairway to the gas chambers, but this time their faces were familiar. They were the faces of her parents, her brother, her aunts and uncles.

---

[22] *Auschwitz Chronicle* shows an entry of numbers 74703–74737 for thirty-five Jewish women who came on a transport from Wrocław. Evidently, because of Adela's unusual arrival at the camp, the recording clerk fused her with this transport. The records mistakenly show her arriving on January 20, when in fact she'd arrived two days earlier.

Adela had once again evaded death, but she felt little relief. She had eaten nothing since leaving Bielsko that morning, and shivering from the cold, she finally fell asleep. On her way to Auschwitz, Adela had imagined the worst, but what she found was simply beyond the threshold of human imagination. Four weeks earlier, she had turned twenty-one.

According to *Auschwitz Chronicle*, on the day Adela was admitted to Auschwitz-Birkenau, the camp housed relatively few female prisoners: 27,053 out of a total prisoner count of 87,410. On that day, four baby girls were born in the women's camp and assigned numbers 74739 to 74742. These infants were then starved to death within a few days, having been separated from their mothers and given nothing to eat. In Auschwitz, newborns were not allowed to be nourished, either through breast-feeding or otherwise.

> Dying was simple. You just had to make do with what you were given to eat, and obey every order. Living was more complicated. You had to disobey, stand clear, and not hit back. The common moral law no longer applied. It was an abysmal world. On our side the victims, on their side the butchers, who often belonged to our own group, and who felt all the more separate from us because the privilege earned was great.
>
> —*Primo Levi* (No. 174517)

It took another two days before Adela received her first meal, a quarter pound of bread, no soup, no water. According to camp regulations, each prisoner was to be given daily 300 grams of bread (more than a half pound), a cube of margarine, and a small portion of jam. But the regulations meant nothing to the Kapos and the block guards. They stole as much as they could, apportioning whatever was left among the prisoners.

The quarantine period was designed to isolate the newcomer *Häftlinge* (prisoners) from the existing camp population—to prevent the spread of diseases they may have brought in from outside and to introduce them to camp rules. Orders were enforced more rigorously during quarantine than at the Auschwitz main camp, with the prisoners subjected to crippling physical exercises, nightly roll calls, German lessons, and the incessant singing of German songs. All on a piece of bread and a bowl of soup—a smaller food ration than for ordinary Auschwitz prisoners.

The quarantined population was a mix of nationalities, separated by gender. In those first days, Adela witnessed scenes she could never have conceived of: "There were many insane people in our block. Some became insane during the quarantine. I remember seeing one young woman who constantly recited *Pan Tadeusz*.[23] Another woman pretended to hold an infant in her arms while singing lullabies. There were many scenes of that nature."

During her second evening, Adela received an object lesson in the rule among prisoners that nothing was free and the usual currency was bread. The pink sweater she was given in the *Effektenlager* had a series of holes at the breast level. No matter how she wore it, her naked breasts would pop through. She remembered, "I was unable to fix the holes. Each time I had to show up for the roll call, I would wear the man's jacket—back to front. My breasts were freezing." Having decided to shorten her skirt and use the excess material to cover the holes, she asked a fellow woman prisoner from Greece if she could borrow her scissors, sewing needle, and thread. But Adela had not offered anything in return. The woman answered by thrusting the scissors at Adela's head, cutting the side of her scalp just above the ear.

Adela also quickly learned the slang prevalent among prisoners. To "organize" meant to steal, "Canada" stood for the *Effektenlager*, and "Mexico" for a new camp section at Birkenau. Of course, she had also learned of the *Muselmann*.

---

[23] A famous epic poem written by the revered Polish poet Adam Mickiewicz (1798–1855).

After a short time, Adela must have experienced something of what Krystyna Żywulska, a political prisoner at Auschwitz, expressed in her book *I Came Back*:

> After three weeks or a month, camp life becomes all absorbing. All thoughts and attention are focused on the immediate problems. How to get a spoon so as not to wait until someone had finished. How to "organize" a sweater, or warmer underpants.... Each one would remember herself as she had once been. Her thoughts, gestures, actions, and manner of living. But that was extremely difficult. We had lost ourselves and forgotten. Some fragments of remembrance would reach our consciousness—some misty, unreal pictures of the previous life.

A month into Adela's quarantine, Frau Hasse entered the building looking for ten girls to work at Weichsall-Metall Union Werke, a munitions factory located a few kilometers away from the women's camp. Known commonly as the Union factory, it specialized in the production of V2 missiles. Adela volunteered, and she was reassigned to a block at the Birkenau women's camp that housed Union workers only (section BIa). A wood warehouse-type structure, her new barrack had just two windows on each wall and extremely narrow, three-level wooden bunk beds (no mattresses) that slept 720 prisoners. Though the number of inmates in the camp fluctuated daily, the barracks were always overcrowded. There was no plumbing or heat but some lighting, which seldom worked. A typical block also contained two additional small rooms—one for the *Blockälteste* (block eldest, referring to a prisoner functionary) and the other for storage. Adela slept on the upper bunk, where only a few centimeters separated her head from the roof. The icy water that leaked through and dripped onto her neck during rainstorms and snow melts would be responsible for the motion restriction and muscle spasms that tormented her for the rest of her life.

It was not unusual to wake up in the morning and learn that your bunk neighbor had died during the night. Sometimes inmates would be tipped off to a death by the lice that had migrated to the "healthy" neighbor, since lice don't feed on a lifeless host. In fact, lice were one of the chief menaces in the block. The camp administration fought the pests by conducting frequent inspections and disinfections, and by threatening the prisoners with reprisals and punishments, including the gas chamber. But no matter how often the so-called lice commando disinfected, the creatures kept up their raids. One can hardly be expected to believe that the camp authorities didn't understand that living conditions prompted the infestations and not prisoner behavior. More likely, they used the issue as just another tool to dismantle prisoner morale. Morning roll calls focused mainly on counting the prisoners who had died the previous night against those who had survived. Only after the numbers were correctly tabulated and the corpses removed could the block go about its daily business.

The *Häftlinge* made every attempt to learn about newcomers to the camp and vice versa. People wanted to locate family members or friends or anybody who might know something about their former lives. Though communication between barracks was off limits, inmates found ways around the restriction. And despite men and women living in separate camps, their paths still crossed on occasion, such as at the Buna, Union, and I. G. Farben plants, where both sexes were used as slave labor, and when men were assigned to make repairs at the women's barracks. This was why maintenance men and factory workers made for the best messengers.

Another place where male and female prisoners could exchange a few words was at the common dumping ground for human excrement. The *Häftlinge* would relieve themselves, fifty women at a time, on long wood platforms covered with a top board containing fifty circular openings. In *I Came Back*, Krystyna Żywulska describes the women's latrine:

> There was a passage through the middle of the holes. That
> was where the latrine Kapo ran back and forth beating us

over our heads with a stick. "Enough! Get off! No resting! This is not a cafe...." More or less in the center of the latrine stood a stove, and on it a pot of soup. Two of the women who worked in the latrine were eating out of the pot with their spoons. They were not disturbed by the stench, the sounds, or by what they saw. They ate with gusto. Nowhere had I felt so humiliated.

In her biography of Primo Levi, Myriam Anissimov depicts a scene at the men's block:

At 5:30 each morning came the ominous summons, spoken in Polish. "Wstawać!"—"Get up!".... The light goes on, the bunks are made, the prisoners put their clothes on, their vertical stripes. Moments later they emerge into a biting cold and rush to the collective, open-plan latrines, an effort at modesty, where two hundred inmates [fifty at women's blocks] must defecate together, harassed by those who wait to take their place so tortured by dysentery that often they cannot contain themselves. Those who retain some strength of will hurry to the unheated washroom block, where they are entitled to "wash" to the waist in ice-cold water, with neither soap nor towels. The washroom floor is thick with mud....

It was at the excrement dumping site where Adela sought to meet Shmuel Ron after learning that he had been captured and brought to Auschwitz. Knowing the waste-collection crates had to be emptied frequently and the contents driven to the site on wheelbarrow-like carts, and that Shmuel Ron had been assigned this job on the men's side, Adela arranged to perform this same task. Mornings and evenings, she pushed the shit cart while leaning her battered body against the two long wooden planks, balancing the cart against her own weight. Like Sisyphus, she struggled to move it across every stone in the pathway, through every mire and puddle. The cold oppressed and disabled her. And it took three days of shit hauling before she and Shmuel spotted each other at close range, later arriving simultaneously at the dumping site:

One day, I saw Shmuel. He saw me too. We were no farther than five meters away from each other. He was madly in love with me, and there must have been a little bit of woman still left in me. We had a lot of important information to exchange, but the first thing I said was, "Look what they did to me!" Pointing at my bald scalp, I repeated, "See how I look!"

Adela then leaned her head toward him as if he needed a closer look. Shmuel turned around charmingly, and without blinking an eye, replied, "Your hairdo is beautiful! Once we are liberated, you should never change it!"

During this meeting Shmuel confirmed a second time for Adela that Roman Brzuchański had betrayed their plan to the Gestapo. They talked briefly about a few other subjects but had to part quickly. It was too dangerous to remain standing in one spot for too long.

A few days later, when the SS brought an all-men's orchestra to the women's camp for a concert, Adela met with Mietek Kobylec, the former underground operative, who now played in the camp orchestra. In their brief conversation, Mietek told her what had happened to Paweł Jaworski. An agent in his resistance group in Katowice had been caught by the SS, which had threatened to torture and execute him. So Paweł, through his contacts, arranged to meet with a corrupt SS officer in Kościuszko Park to negotiate his comrade's release. On a bench close to where he had first met Adela and Henia, he removed the bribe money from his pocket. The SS officer took it and shot him dead.

Mietek Kobylec was murdered in Auschwitz a few weeks after his conversation with Adela.

Adela worked the night shift at the Union munitions factory, drilling holes into the metal housing of hand grenade heads. Every evening, led by an armed escort, she and the other women would walk the four kilometers to the factory. Though she had no knowledge of the individual parts of a hand grenade, or of any other explosive material or its means of delivery, she drilled each tenth hole skewed, her personal attempt at sabotage.

Birkenau's Block 25 for women was what might be called the inner circle of hell at Auschwitz. Though I don't know the exact block where Adela lived, I do know that through the cracks in the wallboards of her barrack, and while enduring the never-ending roll calls, she could see women's Block 25. She also passed near this block while entering and exiting her own. She refused to give me details, but I watched her hands tremble each time she said "Block 25." And each time she said these words, she would pause for a long while in her characteristically unsettling way. Because my mother would always associate Block 25 with a hospital stay, it never left her memory, even on the last day of her life.

Starting in September 1942, Block 25 in BIa (women's section) of Auschwitz-Birkenau was known as the "Death Block."[24] The SS would send to Block 25 female prisoners who were dying, or too weak, too sick, or otherwise seen as unfit to continue living. Once a sufficient number had been collected, the guards would deliver them by trucks to the gas chambers. Block 25 also stored corpses of inmates who had died within the past day, having either collapsed while working or perished during the night in the barracks. The dead and the barely living shared the same quarters for days before being ushered together to the gas chambers. Often, especially in winter, the corpses were placed in front of the building's entrance. Because I cannot possibly describe one scene in the life of Block 25, I will borrow the words of former prisoner Charlotte Delbo, who, like Adela, faced the prisoners of the Death Block at each roll call:

---

[24] Not to be confused with Block 11 in the main Auschwitz camp.

Look. Look.

At first, we doubt that we've seen what we've seen. It's hard to tell them from the snow. The yard is full of them. Naked. Stacked side by side. White, a bluish whiteness against the snow. Heads shaved, pubic hair straight and stiff. The corpses are frozen. White with brown toenails. There is something ridiculous about these cocked-up toes. Horrifyingly laughable.

…The women lying there in the snow are yesterday's companions. Yesterday they were lined up for a roll call. They stood in ranks of five, on each side of the Lagerstrasse. They were setting out to work, dragging themselves towards the marshes. Yesterday they were hungry. They were lice-infested and scratched themselves. Yesterday they gulped the murky gruel. They had diarrhea and were beaten. Yesterday they suffered. Yesterday they wished to die.

Now, they are there, nude corpses in the snow. They died in Block 25. Death in Block 25 has none of the serenity one associated with it, even here.

One morning, because they fainted at roll call, because they were more ashen than others, an SS beckoned them. He formed them into a column which magnified the sum total of all the degradations, all the infirmities which until then, lost in the human mass, had escaped notice. And the column, commanded by the SS, was driven towards Block 25.

Some went alone, willingly. As if to commit suicide. They awaited the inspection of an SS for the door to open—and stepped in.

There were also those who failed to run fast enough on a day on which they should have.

There were also those whose companions had to abandon them at the door, and who shouted: "Do not leave me! Do not leave me!"

133

[L]ocked with a suffering and solitude unlike any other, the prisoners generally could only adapt to their condition—and either be submerged by it or carried along by time. The apparatus of murder was too perfect not to crush people weakened by hunger, forced labor and punishment. But…the executioner did not always triumph. Among his victims were some who placed freedom above what constituted their lives.

—*Elie Wiesel*

Eleven

A Boit'l of Freedom

FROM THE VERY FIRST week of her imprisonment in the camp, word spread that Adela had been a leader of a major underground organization. Though this wasn't exactly true, it earned her respect among the prisoners, and those few groups involved in resistance at Auschwitz-Birkenau considered her as a potential collaborator. Some of these groups had connections to outside resistance movements, while others operated entirely within the camp and were organized by prisoners with a pointed goal in mind, such as blowing up a crematorium, facilitating an escape, obtaining food, or smuggling photographs of German atrocities to the outside world.

Adela participated in one of these groups and, as with her resistance activity before her Bielsko arrest, she didn't always know how her isolated tasks contributed to an overall mission, a practice enforced for security reasons. As long as the goal was to sabotage her oppressors, she would participate. Within the Auschwitz resistance, a number of agents knew Adela by name, and they would contact her from time to time, but she knew only of a French woman named Susan, a single link in the chain of command.

In her main role, Adela was assigned to organize a group of five women factory workers to perform subversive tasks, such as smuggling tools and transporting small amounts of gunpowder from the Union plant to Birkenau. In *Women of Valor: Partisans and Resistance Fighters,* Anna Heilman writes of her own involvement in this activity:

> We smuggled the gunpowder from the factory into the camp. It was smuggled in tiny little pieces of cloth, tied up with string. Inside our dresses we had what we called a little boit'l, a pocket, and the boit'l was where everybody hid their little treasures, wrapped in pieces of cloth. Often there were searches. When [the SS guards] conducted searches we used to untie the string and spill the gunpowder behind us on the ground so it wouldn't be found.

Specific tasks associated with the mission would be made clear a night in advance. On one occasion, Susan asked Adela to smuggle from the factory an insulated wire cutter needed to rend the electrified barbed wire that surrounded the camp. The next evening, as Adela operated her drilling press, a young boy wordlessly dropped the cutter beside her. In turn, she gave it to a woman named Cyla, who had been assigned to deliver it from the plant to the barracks. As the factory workers returned en masse to Birkenau, each woman on the team concealed a bag cobbled together from scraps of material. Inside they might have kept bread, soap, a pair of slippers, a pocketknife, a mirror, a comb, a small rag—any of an assortment of carefully hoarded, forbidden items. In this case, they planned to use the bags should Cyla need to hand over the wire cutter.

Those on the nightshift worked until dawn, and the entire group marched out of the factory in rows of five, always in the same order. By the time they reached Birkenau, daylight would have come. Cyla and Adela marched next to each other. The women had successfully smuggled items out of Union in the past, despite frequent checkpoints on the way back to camp. Though they were usually waved through the checkpoints, on this particular night the guards ordered that they kneel and undergo a search. Cyla surreptitiously tossed the bag containing the wire cutter into a ditch that ran along the path, and the other five women followed her lead with their bags.

Although the SS found nothing during this spot check, the next day during evening roll call, just before the workers headed for Union, Frau Hasse announced that a bag with a wire cutter had been found in a ditch. Placing it on the ground as evidence, she ceded the floor to an SS official, who threatened various penalties, including the gas chamber, for the entire work commando. But no culprit had been identified. And the inmates offered only silence in response. When they had reached the factory that night, Susan instructed Adela to keep quiet under all circumstances.

Two nights passed without any reprisal, and it seemed as if the SS had given up on its investigation, when a woman who marched in the row behind Adela, having recognized Cyla's bag, informed on her to the SS. The next evening, Cyla was interrogated in the factory's office and was beaten repeatedly before the SS finally released her—unconscious. Adela had to drag her out of the office. Recalled Adela: "She didn't crack. Cyla didn't tell them anything."

By October of 1944 Adela had been imprisoned for almost ten months, and her responsibilities in the resistance had increased steadily. In addition to smuggling gunpowder, she now helped coordinate explosives storage and had succeeded in completing tasks such as forging a sustainable connection between the *Sonderkommando* in the men's and women's camps. More generally, she herself had become a principal liaison between the two camps.

One of the agents with whom Adela worked closely was Estera Wajsblum, alias Mala. Each time Adela would smuggle gunpowder from the Union factory, she would later transfer the contents to Estera. Though the smuggling of gunpowder suggested a major operation, Adela did not know its ultimate goal. Perhaps because of these clandestine missions, rumors began to spread among the prisoners of "something big," perhaps a revolt meant to inflict major casualties on the SS.

It was one of the few times in the camp that the rumors were founded on truth. Estera Wajsblum turned out to be one of the head conspirators in a *Häftlinge* plot to blow up Birkenau's Crematorium IV and spark a prisoners' revolt. Aside from destroying the crematorium, the conspirators aimed to kill Germans and enable the escape of as many inmates as possible. On the day the operation was carried out, smoke and flames rose from the crematorium building, and as many as five SS men were killed. During the commotion of the revolt, one of the SS guards was even shoved alive into a crematorium oven. Along with the destruction of the crematorium, several hundred inmates escaped, including the special commando. But aided by vigilant locals, the SS caught every last escapee within just twenty-four hours. Back in the camp that evening, the entire *Sonderkommando* was ordered to lie facedown on the ground. They were killed execution-style the following morning, with shots at close range to the back of the head.

Four female inmates were also to be executed for their roles in the conspiracy, including mastermind Rosa Robota, Estera, and two young women identified as explosives smugglers. On their walk to the gallows, which took place in front of the entire women's camp, these women needed help with every move; their bodies were mangled and their faces bruised from the torture inflicted by the SS. Adela stood near the women as they walked. Despite her condition,

Estera Wajsblum still had the presence of mind to wink and tighten her lips at Adela, indicating that the interrogators had failed to extract any other names. Had one of these young women, Estera in particular, buckled during the SS interrogations, Adela would have joined them on the gallows.

In an account published by the Rosa Robota Foundation, the event is described as follows:

> The explosives were hidden in the carts and lorries used by this "special commando" to haul the corpses. Unfortunately, before the revolt could occur as a concerted effort, the *Sonderkommando* staged their own uprising with the explosives they had—for they had found out they were about to be gassed in their own turn (members of this work group were normally selected out and gassed about every 3 months). Subsequently, on October 7, 1944, Crematorium IV was suddenly blown up and an unplanned haphazard revolt began. Four SS men (some records say 5) were killed and several wounded. In the panic and pandemonium, around 600 of the *Sonderkommando* were able to break through the wires and escape. Unfortunately, all who escaped were caught and shot—with the usual German efficiency and the ever-present cooperation of the people living in the surrounding area. A special Gestapo team was called in to investigate the revolt. The explosives were traced back to the Union plant and several suspects were rounded up. Using typical techniques of torture and "persuasion" under the auspices of the "Political Dept" (operated by the Gestapo), the names of Rosa and 3 other women were extracted.

For the first time since she started taking part in sabotage at the camp, Adela now saw the faces of her fellow conspirators—young women like herself. To see them killed crushed her, and their abused state made her sick, but this sort of sadism was a daily fact of life at the camp. To stay alive and functioning, a prisoner, to a large extent, had to block out such realities. And on the whole, the revolt had been more a cause for hope than for despair. At least a couple of examples demonstrate why. First, there was the SS's inability to break the perpetrators' will. Second was a scene that occurred before their execution, as an SS officer pontificated to the *Häftlinge*. In the aftermath of the revolt, the inmates didn't seem to be listening to the rant. In those moments, Adela realized that whatever acts of cruelty the Nazis inflicted, however dehumanizing their practices, they could never destroy her freedom of spirit or that of her coconspirators. This prompted a deep sense of liberation despite the barbed wire and crematoria smokestacks. As for the women on the verge of being executed, they had triumphed. They, the parasites, would not be defeated—not by beatings, not by torture. Their program of resistance would go on. *Auschwitz Chronicle* has the following entry about this particular day:

> In the evening four female Jewish prisoners, Ella Gartner, Roza Robota, Regina Safir, and Estera Wajsblum, are hanged in the women's camp in Auschwitz. They were condemned to death because they assisted in the uprising that broke on October 7, 1944, among the members of the Special Squad [*Sonderkommando*] in the crematoriums in Birkenau. They provided the Special Squad with explosives and munitions from the depots of the Weichsel-Union-Metallwerke, where three of the women worked. The execution takes place in two stages. Two female prisoners are hanged during the evening roll call in the presence of the male and female prisoners who work the night shift at Weichsel-Union. The other two female prisoners are hanged after the return of the squad that works the day shift. The reason for the sentence is read by First Protective Custody Commander Hössler in Auschwitz; he screams that all traitors will be destroyed in this manner.

When I think about Adela's resistance activities in Auschwitz and elsewhere, I can't help associating them with a feeling of glamour, or bravura. But that is a false association, one that can only be made from a comparative distance, both in time and space. People involved in the camp resistance would never have been in touch with a sense of anything beyond the needs of the moment. They would have been dragged down in the monotony of camp life, with each passing day no different from the last. After only a few weeks at the camp, prisoners would typically lose track of time entirely. They wouldn't even have a sense of how many weeks or months had passed since they'd entered the camp. Not only that, but all prisoners of both genders—with their shaved heads, skeletal frames, and sagging skin—would look virtually alike. If Adela and her bunkmate were to be separated for a few days, it is almost certain they wouldn't recognize each other on the next encounter. Overshadowing these realities was an all-consuming hunger—a craving that manipulated every thought and every movement. Only *Muselmann,* on the border with death, were perhaps too far gone to experience hunger. (I want to emphasize the word "perhaps"; how could I possibly know what they felt?) As for time, it did not pass in the usual way for Auschwitz prisoners—it crept, it edged toward each meal, a bowl of watery soup, a piece of stale bread. Adela never asked herself, "How long has it been since I was brought here?" Or, "Will the war ever end?" The only question relating to time was, "How long till the next meal?"

The prisoners could hardly remember, much less imagine, the world outside the fence. For Adela, to resist under these circumstances was certainly an expression of will, perseverance, and character, but at the same time it was an assertion of freedom. Until this time and in the years to come, her ability and readiness to redefine and reinvent freedom, regardless of where she happened to be, struck me as one of her most consistent personal traits. Adela entered Auschwitz in a state of crushing fear—much as she felt while detained with her parents in the *shtibel*, while escaping from the mob in Bór, and during the nearly lethal interrogations at the Bielsko jail—and she declared war from the first day. Adela fought for her life and against her captors, earning the respect and recognition of fellow inmates in the process. This gave her an identity and it distinguished her in a world where distinctions had become all but impossible to make. For me, this episode in Adela's story has provided an enduring lesson: that hope and optimism can, and even must, be drawn upon in the darkest and most sinister places. Otherwise, those qualities carry no real purpose at all.

In the relationship between the SS and the prisoners, little subtlety existed, even when the latter were given preferential treatment, particularly in the form of assignments as Kapos or orderlies. The *Häftlinge* might be given the opportunity to live another day or a week or a month, but the price was unconditional submissiveness and obedience. Such traits came in handy as camp commanders sought to administer the work of slave laborers in the nearby factories and agricultural fields. Often, prisoners did the SS's dirty work by assisting during selections at the *Rampe*, working at the crematoria, and performing countless other tasks necessary to run the camp and its satellite sites. Maintaining order in the barracks also fell largely to prisoner orderlies or Kapos. Such titles came with privileges such as control of bread distribution within the barracks, but in return the Kapos were expected to display toughness and exercise discipline.

Even as death loomed in every square inch of the camp—the stench of burning flesh mingling with physical exhaustion, disease, and the inmates' ever-present hunger—life in the barracks had its own dynamic, much of which owed itself to the personality of the Kapo. In Adela's barrack, this position belonged to "K," a woman in her thirties who came from the town of Chrzanów, about twenty kilometers away from Auschwitz. K contributed to the amusement of the SS with regular displays of cruelty toward her fellow prisoners. When supervising work crews, she would administer punishments to the weak and those unable to perform to her liking. Women who dared commit the smallest infraction could expect harsh retribution from K's own hand and boot. But the Kapo's favorite penalty was to reduce a wayward fellow prisoner's bread rations. K also had an excellent command of German, a skill that enabled her to mimic the SS men as she barked out orders, including her own pet slurs directed at individual *Häftlinge* who shared her own barrack. On her own initiative, K would submit the names of near-death prisoners to Frau Hasse for relocation to Block 25. Yet K did not understand that her appeal to the SS was entirely temporary, and that it couldn't possibly be a down payment on a better chance at survival. To the Nazis, each Jew amounted to no more than the dark blue, sloppily tattooed number on his or her forearm. Whether a barrack was well run, or its inmates worked efficiently, had only passing value. All Jews' fates were sealed from the day they entered the camp, regardless of their function, rank, or place of origin. And for every Kapo, whether brutish or laissez-faire, thousands of others waited eagerly in the wings to take over the job.

It may be difficult to imagine that on that "other planet," as Ka-Tzetnik called it, where all rules of humanity had been suspended, a raw—if only instinctive—code of ethics, solidarity, and communication still existed. During one morning roll call in autumn of 1944, K was found dead on the floor of the barrack. The night before, she had been beaten to death with the only weapon available to her barrack-mates—their shoes. Her corpse was promptly delivered to the crematorium. During the same roll call, Frau Hasse appointed a new Kapo to head Adela's barrack.

Neither the SS nor the prisoners from other barracks ever inquired about what had become of K.[25]

Regina Guterman was Adela's first cousin, the daughter of Isaac Guterman, Fishel's brother. Though she grew up with her family in Dąbrowa Górnicza, she often visited Adela's home in Niwka. Regina and Adela were the same age, and their friendship and a sort of common destiny caused their paths to cross many times during the Second World War. Like Adela, Regina and her family were forced to live in the Środula ghetto. And Regina's parents were taken to the Jewish orphanage building and later to the gas chambers on the transport with Fishel and Rózia. Both Adela and Regina managed to stay alive on the Aryan side, aided by the same organization and frequently by the same people. And they met again in Auschwitz-Birkenau following Regina's arrest by the Gestapo in Katowice.

After the liquidation of the Środula and Zawiercie ghettos, Regina escaped and tried to get by on the Aryan side. Owing to an accident of fate, Ewald Pradela—the same man then caring for Henia—found Regina in Katowice and offered to hide her. At the time, Mr. Pradela's offer had been a last chance for Regina, and his timing could not have been better. A collaborator with Paweł Jaworski, Ewald worried so intensely about his wife's jealousy that he threatened to shoot her if she said anything to the Gestapo. For Regina, he arranged for a forged ID card and a cleaning job in one of the town's hotels. The underground resistance branch for which he and Jaworski worked belonged to the Polish Socialist Party, known as the PPS, which helped facilitate the printing of forged food coupons, personal ID cards, employment certificates, and other relevant documents in addition to carrying out its main function: organizing civil resistance against the Germans. In

---

[25] Over the years, Adela told the story of K a few times, never deviating from the main details, but I have been unable to verify it. K's origins, as described, have been fictionalized and her first initial changed.

the beginning of 1944, a man named Bolek (last name unknown), a Jewish refugee and a member of Ewald's underground cell, betrayed the operation to the Gestapo. The entire group, including Regina, was arrested and locked up in the Katowice jail. A few months later, in July of 1944, the Gestapo concluded its investigation and Regina was brought to Auschwitz. By this time Adela had already been at the camp for six months. Because she had established a network of contacts, she learned of Regina's presence on the day of her arrival. After Regina's new name (No. 82323) had been tattooed onto her left forearm, and she'd been assigned a bunk, Adela came to greet her with a piece of bread. Years later, Regina said, half jokingly, "There were eight of us assigned to one bunk. The space was so tight that if one of us wanted to turn, all eight had to do the same."

For the half year of Regina's incarceration at Auschwitz-Birkenau, Adela supplied her with extra food, clothing, and other favors vital to survival in a concentration camp. For example, the wooden shoes given to Regina in the *Effektenlager* were awkwardly shaped and didn't allow sufficient space for her toes. In a short time, her skin became so infected that a recovery seemed hopeless. When later she developed gangrene, a sure death sentence for Auschwitz inmates, Adela arranged for Regina's transfer to the camp hospital.

In the closing months of 1944, the rumor began to circulate among the *Häftlinge* that a long forced march to another camp could take place any day. Adela organized for herself and Regina clean civilian clothes and warm boots should such a march occur. Both women were planning to escape, and for that, unmarked ordinary clothing was of the highest importance. If strangers recognized someone as an escapee, that meant a far diminished chance of surviving. When the Great March, later called the Death March, did take place in January 1945, Regina escaped on her own because she did not march in the same column as Adela. Exposed to freezing temperatures that disabled her legs so that she had to crawl on all fours, she almost died twice before receiving help from a Polish farmwoman. None of this was unusual in the experience of an Auschwitz prisoner.

Months earlier, however, long before the Death March, Regina had an experience to distinguish herself from the other prisoners: she testified at a trial outside the barbed wire fence. As far as I know, she is the only Auschwitz prisoner ever to have done this.

Ewald Pradela had been arrested by the Gestapo in Katowice during the same raid that landed Regina in jail. The charges were conspiracy against the Third Reich and *Rassenschande,* a dishonor to Hitler's race defined by a sexual relationship between a Jew and a German. Because he was a Volksdeutsche category I (the highest ranking), he received the benefit of a trial. For Ewald this was a welcome postponement of death; for the SS, an opportunity to run a show trial with the hope of deterring similar activities in the future. But the prosecutor needed witnesses, and the best one, Regina Guterman, was already in Auschwitz. After being reassured that the witness was still alive, the prosecutor ordered her presence at the trial. Per a directive from the *Aufseherin,* Regina ate well for a number of days before the trial and, on the day the Gestapo sent for her, she wore clean clothing and even makeup. It was during the actual court proceedings that Ewald communicated Henia's whereabouts to Regina. How he achieved this while at a distance from Regina is cloudy. One witness told me that they communicated via subtle facial expressions, as it is hard to believe they would have been permitted to speak to each other directly. Another witness said the message was conveyed through Janka, Ewald's wife, who waited outside the courtroom because the SS would not allow her to be present at the trial. She probably shouted the message in Polish as Regina passed her in the hallway, and out of incomprehension, the German guards ignored it.

When Regina brought Adela the news that Henia was still in Janka's protection, Adela's joy was immeasurable. The thought of having lost control of Henia's life had haunted her, not least because nobody knew exactly where the child was. And should Adela die in the camp, Henia would not be able to gain contact with her mother or any other family member. By then, Adela already knew that Paweł Jaworski, the only person with direct knowledge of Henia, had been murdered. Shmuel Ron, who knew about Henia too, was in the camp, and his chances for survival were as slim as hers. Given the conspiracy charge against Ewald, he too would almost certainly be killed. The knowledge that Henia was alive and well gave her a reason to go on. "It was one of the happiest days of my life," she later said.

Twelve

Death March

FACED WITH INEVITABLE DEFEAT in the war, the Germans started to consolidate their prisoner populations at the beginning of 1945. The word *Todesmarsch*—Death March—became synonymous with forced mass treks over great distances, from one camp to another. Although such marches had also taken place earlier during Hitler's occupation of Poland, they only became regular toward the end of the war. Prisoners en route would be exposed to disabling winter conditions, with the accompanying guards inflicting abuse at will.

The evacuation of Auschwitz and its satellite camps began on January 17, 1945, when tens of thousands of mostly Jewish prisoners were ordered to march west toward Włodzisław, over sixty kilometers from Auschwitz. Inmates from the men's and women's camps traveled separately. The SS planned, on reaching Włodzisław, to load the surviving prisoners onto an open coal train bound for Germany. There, "protected" from the ever-growing threat of the Allied forces, the prisoners would be used as slave labor until they could work no more, and then they would be killed. Meanwhile, the Red Army was nearing Kraków, less than fifty kilometers from Auschwitz.

On the day of the Auschwitz Death March, Adela's *Blockälteste* and the block leaders from adjacent barracks summoned the *Häftlinge* to a morning roll call. Block by block, the prisoners were arranged in long columns, where they received their final portions of soup and bread.

At that same roll call, the rumor spread that the Soviet army was approaching. But the prisoners knew better than to yearn for the unimaginable possibility of a rescue. Even the uncommon nervousness of the SS officers failed to spawn much hope. This was because Auschwitz, like every other concentration camp, was rife with rumors, some started by the camp administration and even more by the prisoners themselves—about escapes, food, resistance actions, newcomers, deaths. Rumors born in the morning often died by night of the same day. Even when the first blocks began marching out of the camp, the prevailing thought was, "If the Germans haven't killed me yet, what will a few more days change. I will mind my own business."

Adela's block left Auschwitz late in the evening and joined with others during the night. They walked in two long columns, one thousand women each, surrounded by SS guards. Only able bodies went on the march; the sick were left behind at the camp. The columns marched through the night in a freshly fallen snow, and the air was bitter. Many women struggled to continue, dogged by overexhaustion and frostbite, among other afflictions. If a prisoner fell, the SS guards would either shoot her or leave her to freeze to death. Stopping spontaneously to rest was not an option. Anyone who could not walk fast enough or who otherwise delayed progress was killed. Hundreds never made it even to the first stopover. Anna Heilman writes in *Women of Valor*:

We went on the famous death march in January. We walked on foot in snow piled up so deep we felt we were walking on our knees. We didn't see our legs anymore. Marta [her companion] took me bodily. She had to force me to join along; I wanted to stay in Auschwitz. It was worse than a nightmare.

In the early-morning hours of January 18, after a twenty-five-kilometer walk, the prisoners stopped near Pszczyna in a village called Łąka, a rural community with only a few farm buildings and scattered hay barns. The prisoners rested sitting up, side by side on a barn floor because there wasn't enough space to lie down. Hoping for a chance to bolt, Adela and two other women nearby tried to stay awake. After a fourth woman overheard their plotting, she joined along. She had known Adela in the camp, and she also remembered that Adela had worked in the resistance on the Aryan side before her arrest. The newcomer implored, "Let's run away together. You surely have contacts on the other side, and I have some jewelry that I organized in Canada [*Effektenlager*]."

Adela and her comrades watched the scene closely. At some distance from the barn the German guards rested in a one-story building, leaving the prisoners practically unguarded. From time to time, a tall man in civilian clothing crossed the yard, and the women decided to ask him for help, delegating Adela as their spokesperson. She was to ask him to hide the four of them, with the jewelry as his reward. When the right opportunity came, Adela set out. The man listened to her very carefully, but before she could finish, a disquieting noise emanated from the building where the SS guards were resting, and the tall man quickly forced her into a nearby shed, locked her inside, and left.

For the first time in more than a year, Adela found herself completely alone—an unimaginable situation only a day ago. Though the fear of being discovered by the SS infiltrated her thoughts, she savored every second of this long-forgotten sense of privacy. At Auschwitz, even the latrines were shared by fifty other women. Being locked in the room also gave her some freedom to look around. She found tools, small pieces of machinery, and some furniture. Adela also noticed a green uniform and a revolver on a table. Darkness fell and the guards commanded the prisoners to line up for the next leg of the march. In little time, the procession departed, leaving an eerie quiet. She heard the calls of the other three women but answering them, or even nearing the window, would put her at risk of being spotted.

With the Germans and the prisoners gone, Adela could not imagine what would happen next. After Auschwitz, she expected no kindness from another human, yet she knew very well that without the help of strangers she would never survive. Still, a sense of panic grew in her, and she grabbed the gun from the table, and positioned herself behind the door so as not to be seen when it opened. She cocked the gun, a trembling finger on the trigger. It was still dark when she heard a key turning the door lock. A light came on, and two men entered— the one who had locked her in the room and another, in uniform. Seeing that she held the gun, the men froze before one of them jumped at her and wrestled it from her hands. Now that they had the pistol out of the woman's hands, they stared at her for a few seconds—and began to laugh. Their laughter struck Adela as healthy and sincere, different from the laughter she'd grown accustomed to hearing from the Germans. As she watched the men talk with one another in Polish, her fear gradually dissipated. The uniformed man left the room, and the civilian asked her about the jewelry. When she explained that it had belonged to one of the girls who left with the column, the man no longer seemed interested. "I want to help you," he said, and these are words she would never forget. She was not sure how to react or what to say. Not for a very long time had anybody said anything like that, especially so directly, and free of restraint. At that very moment Adela knew that Auschwitz—and perhaps the war—was over.

He then instructed her to trail him at a distance, and they stepped outside. After about two hundred yards, they entered the large, well-heated kitchen of the man's home. They were greeted by a woman—probably his wife—a young girl, a cat, and most important, a loaf of bread. In the camp, Adela had seen many dogs but never a cat. The animal seemed to be from another planet. She was given a small bowl with warm water, a towel, soap, and a place behind a curtain to wash. When she proved unable to take her eyes off the bread, the woman apologized for not cutting into it: "It is still too fresh, you may get a stomachache." Next came a large bowl of steamy soup.

Mr. Kloc was the man's name, and he showed Adela to the attic. The next day he brought along another young woman, who had been hiding in the haystacks since before the Auschwitz group arrived, to keep her company. Because of his fears about the neighbors—fears that the women shared—Mr. Kloc only felt comfortable housing them for a few days. While her companion left the very next day, Adela decided to wait one more night. On the day of her departure, Mr. Kloc took her on his bicycle to the railroad station and bought her a train ticket to Sosnowiec. Once there, she headed straight to one of her former hideouts from her time as an underground agent with Paweł Jaworski—the *melina* at the home of the Sitko family in Sosnowiec.

On January 27, 1945, approximately two thousand female prisoners from Auschwitz-Birkenau arrived at the Nazi concentration camp Ravensbrück, near Fürstenberg, a town about seventy kilometers north of Berlin. This marked the end of the Death March, which had begun ten days before. Partly on foot, and partly by train in open cars filled with coal, according to *Auschwitz Chronicle,* the prisoners bridged a distance of three hundred kilometers. Adela was of course not among them. The Red Army liberated Auschwitz-Birkenau on January 27, and six days later marched into Sosnowiec and Katowice.

In all interviews with her about the German occupation, including those on the Death March, Adela refers to herself and her female camp companions as *dziewczyny*, "girls." Yet she had turned twenty-two only thirty days before she hid in Mr. Kloc's attic. In that era, as now, it was not common for a woman of Adela's age to call herself a girl. By contrast, when my mother talked about her life after 1945, she referred to herself as a woman. This distinction struck me as interesting, and I wondered if the war had robbed her not only of six years but also of her awareness of growing into adulthood. Or it may have been Adela's subconscious way of expressing the void that should have been filled by the everyday experiences of young womanhood.[26]

---

[26] Many survivors appear to have made this distinction, which recurs throughout Holocaust literature. For example, see Krystyna Żywulska's *I Came Back*.

Thirteen

Sixteen-Kilometer Walk

BY EARLY 1945 THE RED Army was making deep inroads into Poland, but for the residents of Sosnowiec the war remained a reality. They saw how the German soldiers lingered in the area, and how Allied air raids repeatedly drove them into their bomb shelters. One resident of Sosnowiec was Wanda Sitko,[27] who throughout the war had done her part to flout the Nazis's occupation. In her flat she had sheltered up to twelve people at a time—men, women, children, members of the resistance, stray refugees fleeing the Germans. Most were Jews. Those in the resistance movement usually needed a place to stay only for the night. Others would remain for weeks, even months. To protect their guests when the *Blockmeister* came prying, the Sitko family had constructed a phantom second wall in their home's front room. In the narrow space between the two walls,

---

[27] The testimony of Wanda Gelbhard (b. Sitko) was recorded on May 15, 1982, during her visit to Adela's home in Frankfurt am Main. In February of 2003, the details were confirmed in another interview.

the refugees would often stand for hours without uttering a sound until the threat had passed.

One day in January 1945, Wanda heard the secret cadence rapped against her window. Not expecting anyone—the air raids had kept all her guests cooped up indoors—she hesitated before opening the door. As the knocking increased in urgency, she peered outside and saw a scrawny young woman with a shaved head, whose pale complexion accentuated enormous sunken eyes. When she opened the door, she slowly understood that this woman, who had a blue number tattooed crudely onto her arm, was Adela.

The meeting with the other guests was emotional for everyone involved. Though none had met Adela in person, pretty much all of them knew something about her resistance activities. And though they had undoubtedly heard stories about Auschwitz secondhand, they were now shocked by the details Adela provided. Late into the night, they all stayed up listening and asking questions.

Even after Adela had entered Wanda's home, she appeared restless, with only one thought in her mind: Henia. It took some convincing from the host to persuade her to wait until the next morning before beginning her search. On her first night at the Sitkos', Adela slept fitfully, with Henia's likeness filling every crevice in her mind. Was she even still alive? How would she look? Would she recognize Adela?

More than a year had passed since Adela had parted with her niece, five months since Regina Guterman had returned to Auschwitz from Ewald's trial with news of Henia's whereabouts. Five months within the madness of any war is a very long time, but the same period spent in Auschwitz equaled an eternity, and any number of events might have imperiled Henia's situation. First, there was Ewald's conviction, which put Henia under the protection of his wife, Janka. This in itself was not so much a cause for worry, but Adela knew the Gestapo often went after the families of resistance fighters. And she could only hope that Ewald had not leaked

156

information about Henia during his interrogations by the Gestapo.

The next morning Wanda offered to accompany Adela on the sixteen-kilometer walk to Mrs. Pradela's home in Zatęż, near Katowice. She knew it was not yet safe for a Jewish woman to wander the streets of Zagłębie alone. It was a week before the war would end for Sosnowiec, and long-distance public transportation was nonfunctional. Most Germans had already vacated the area, but remnants of the Wehrmacht forces stayed around, retreating reluctantly. They knew that they had lost the war and this fact made the soldiers more furious than ever. They could be set off by the most unpredictable act—a wrong movement, a smile, the lack of a smile, a scowl. The point was you had to be extremely careful in their presence. Recalled Adela:

> We set forth on our walk toward Katowice at the break of daylight. The air was bitter and the road was covered with snow. Now and then, we would see dead bodies scattered along the side of the road, all German soldiers. It made a big impression on me, because I had never seen dead German soldiers before, but there was no time for reflection. The day was short and we had a long way ahead of us. After four hours, we arrived at Janka's place in Zatęż.

At Janka's residence, the tenants were just emerging from the bomb shelter, having taken cover during one of the frequent air raids. Adela immediately recognized Janka but saw no sign of Henia. A panic filled her as she approached to introduce herself. When Janka, an extremely cautious woman, feigned ignorance, Adela answered with a litany of personal information. Still Janka did not acquiesce. She knew an "Adela" would come looking for Henia one day but had seen her only once—at a resistance meeting—and wasn't at all sure this was the same person. (Besides, this woman looked nothing like the Adela she remembered meeting.) Adela's frustration mounted as she provided details about Ewald and Paweł Jaworski, and she unrolled her sleeve to expose her tattooed

Häftlingsnummer. Only then did Janka let down her wall, explaining that Henia was alive and staying with her relatives in Herby, near Częstochowa: "I visit her often and know she has been well cared for. When the Gestapo came to search my home [after Ewald's arrest] they found Henia and my son playing together. The Gestapo took an interest in her, but I told them that she was my sister's child and simply visiting at my home."

Wanda Sitko remembered:

> We did not get to see Henia that day, but Adela was overtaken with joy, which by the way was very contagious. Henia was alive and safe, and Adela knew that she would reunite with the child within days or weeks. We started to walk back to Sosnowiec. We wanted to arrive home before dark, but there were still sixteen kilometers to go. In Bogucice, approximately halfway there, I decided to stop for a rest at Mrs. Nowak, who once had almost become my mother-in-law. She was an elderly woman with a big heart. We were exhausted. The long walk and the bitter cold had taken a toll on us. Our feet were cold and our lips were bleeding, and we were hungry. Mrs. Nowak received us with open arms. She immediately sent her daughter to buy food: bread, sausages, and more. We were able to wash and rest. Two hours later, we started walking again. Mrs. Nowak gave us a loaf of bread for the way and she showed us some shortcuts.

Wanda and Adela were still a few kilometers from Sosnowiec when a German officer driving an open-top jeep pulled over next to them. At first, they were certain he would kill them right there. But he only wanted directions. Since Wanda did not speak a word of German, the entire conversation took place between Adela and the officer. Wanda knew the way, but Adela knew the language, so in concert they were able to get from his questions to the answers: *links*, *rechts*, *gerade aus*, they would point with hands in various directions. The officer noticed that the two young women were traveling in the same direction as he was, so he offered them a ride. "German or no German, we were so cold that we gladly accepted the offer," Wanda said. Six kilometers later, they got out and Adela gave the officer a few more pointers, all lies, and this time she needed no help from Wanda, who continued:

> We had another few hundred meters to go when Adela stopped and nudged me gently. "Look what I organized," she said. I was a little bit confused, because ordinarily I did not associate the word "organize" with what came after. Adela had stolen the entire food supply that the German officer had in the backseat: canned meat, sausages, a bottle of cognac, and some other goodies. "What is he going to eat?" I asked. She gave me a bewildered look that made me want to go ten meters underground and hide there forever. "Wanda, I was going hungry in the camp for a long time. It is time now for that son-of-a-bitch to know how it feels."

> The feast that we had that night was a splendid one. It was the best food I ever had. I remember the taste of the canned meat until today. Delicious.

Several weeks passed before Janka had an opportunity to visit her family in Herby. During this period, Sosnowiec had been liberated by the Red Army. Most Germans had escaped, but those who hadn't were now frozen corpses in the snow, scattered all over town in ditches, on sidewalks, even on staircases. Adela passed her days at a makeshift repatriation center, searching for family members, friends, acquaintances, just about anyone from her life before the war. Sometimes fellow Auschwitz inmates recognized her, and, on a memorable occasion, she was offered a job at the State Bureau of Security (*Urząd Bezpieczeństwa*) by a former prisoner who worked there. She accepted the offer, and within a short time had been given an office and an apartment in Katowice.

A source of comfort for Adela during the weeks after Auschwitz was the reunion with her cousin Regina Guterman. Having escaped from the Death March, Regina caught up with Adela in Wanda's apartment. She too had knocked at the

Sitkos' window, and now she joined Adela and Janka on their visit to retrieve Henia from Janka's relatives—the Marciniaks—at their small farm in Herby. God-fearing, deeply religious Catholics, the Marciniaks had five children, not including Henia, and lived in great poverty. On her arrival at the farm, Adela was overcome with relief when she saw Henia playing in the yard right before her. But she was reluctant to approach the child herself, preferring that the Marciniaks help ease the transition.

The process would not be so easy. Perhaps temporarily unaware of who Adela was, the Marciniaks allowed Henia to meet the three visitors. But when the couple learned the purpose of the visit, they flatly refused to let the child go. After all, they had acted as parents for Henia for the past year, and the bond that had developed was not negligible. They had loved her as one of their own. It is also possible that, as devout Catholics, the Marciniaks felt an obligation to continue caring for Henia. She had come to them as a homeless child, and they may well have seen her as a mission from God. To give up such a child now could mark not only a personal tragedy but also a betrayal of their faith. My conversations with Ana Sobel, a close relative of the now deceased Marciniaks, solidify this theory. Upon further research, I realized that withholding children who should have been returned to their birth parents or other family members after the war wasn't an uncommon occurrence.

This episode prompted questions about Henia's allegiance, in whatever way allegiance can exist for a young child. Had she remembered that somebody would come looking for her one day? Had she even known? And did she remember Adela? For a five-year-old child, a year would feel much longer. But a telling thing happened during the brief time Adela and Henia stood near one another: Henia grasped her aunt's sleeve and would not let go of it. For the Marciniaks, Henia's instinct was no more than a reflex from the past. They also cast doubt as to whether Henia's mother was alive, evidence Adela was unable to refute. At that time, nobody knew whether Hala had survived the war. The ensuing discussion between Janka and her relatives began civilly but soon turned rancorous. As Janka argued furiously, Adela stood by speechless.

From this point on, the details of Henia's return become sketchy. Two other witnesses claim to have traveled with Adela to bring the child back, which allows me to assume that my mother visited Herby a few more times. But on none of these visits could she get the Marciniaks to budge from their position.

This was why she called upon Leon Winiawski, the director of the repatriation camp where she worked. He had returned to Poland from exile in the Soviet Union together with Michał Jachimowicz, Adela's future husband. I am not sure if Adela had yet met Michał, but I *am* sure they were not yet in love. It must still have been winter of 1945—spring at the latest—when Adela, Janka, and Leon Winiawski paid a final visit to the Marciniaks. Leon wore his Polish army uniform for the occasion. Again, I was unable to reconstruct all the details of this trip, but Leon's wife told me that when he and Adela arrived, Henia was locked in a room, nowhere to be seen. Almost at once, a shouting match erupted between Leon and Mr. Marciniak. But shortly Leon's threats of legal action, his rank (first lieutenant), and a pistol that protruded from an open holster forced the Marciniaks to change their mind. They wept bitterly as they handed Henia over to Adela.

To most of us today, Henia's condition would suggest neglect—she was alarmingly skinny, unbathed, and full of lice. Her skin was infected in several places and spotted with vesicles that oozed puss. A fungus covered part of her scalp, and her hands trembled constantly, all results of the lack of hygiene and malnutrition that stemmed from the Marciniaks' poverty. According to Janka and Henia, she'd been treated the same as every other child in the family.

All four returned to Katowice to Adela's new apartment. Henia was five years old and had adopted the way of life on the farm, including the hosts' local accent. Not surprisingly, on her first evening away from the farm, she refused to sleep in a room without a cross or picture of Jesus on the wall, sobbing for hours in protest. The next morning, Adela bought a small cross and hung it on the wall above Henia's bed, which helped her sleep much better in the nights to come. In those first days, Adela made it her mission to improve her niece's health. A doctor's visit, followed by applications of ointments and strict hygiene, achieved this end quickly, but no treatment would ever stop the trembling of her hands.

Henia's mother, Hala, spent time in several concentration and labor camps during the German occupation of Poland. At the time of liberation, she was at Bergen-Belsen,[28] where she had been since the end of 1944. Though prisoners at Bergen-Belsen did not work, there was little food and extreme overcrowding. Large numbers of inmates died of starvation, disease, or exhaustion. Just before the British forces liberated Bergen-Belsen, a group of prisoners from Auschwitz arrived after having endured the Death March. One of them told Hala that Adela had been hanged at Auschwitz with the three other women charged with collaboration in the revolt.

Soon after Bergen-Belsen's liberation, Hala fell ill with typhoid fever and the British army transferred her to a facility in Sweden for medical care. It was there, in the convalescent unit, that a better-informed Auschwitz prisoner told Hala that her sister had survived. The source's name was Adam Kowalski, and he had known Adela from the Union factory, where they had worked together and collaborated on resistance activities. Unfortunately, he could not comfort Hala with any such news about Henia. Upon his return to Poland, Adam coincidentally began working at the same office with Adela. He was the first to share the news of Hala's survival.

---

[28] A concentration camp in Germany established in 1943 to hold prisoners to be used in political exchanges. Administered by the SS, it included five subcamps where some 50,000 Jews, political prisoners, and others died of starvation, disease, and sadistic medical practices. The camp was liberated by the British in 1945 (Museum of Tolerance, Wiesenthal Center).

Eventually, Hala recovered and was sent back to Poland, directly to the repatriation center in Dziedzice. Like the vast majority of newcomers, she kept herself busy posting search notes and asking whatever familiar people she could find about her sister. But Adela and Adam were no longer working in Dziedzice, having been reassigned to a different location. One day, Adam had to return to the repatriation center and Adela asked him to inquire about Hala. He did so, and as he affixed a message to the community board, he noticed Hala's note nearby. Not unusual considering the chaotic first half of 1945, the two sisters missed each other a few times before their reunion. Nonetheless, the sighting by Adam marked the start of the sisters' postwar relationship. "I remember this moment like it happened yesterday," recalled Adela:

We lived at 39 Plebiscytowa Street in Katowice. Hala came in a dress made out of a blanket, which she had sewn for herself. Henia had always known that I was her aunt, and that she had a mother who was about to come through the door any day. "Is this my mom?" she asked curiously when Hala walked into the apartment. Henia was almost six years old then.

It was summer of 1945.

163

Henia, 1946

I would like just to be silent
but being silent I lie

I would like just to walk
but walking I trample

—*Jerzy Ficowski*

Fourteen

Revenge

IN OCTOBER OF 2003, I met with Adela's first cousin David Mandelbaum in Amsterdam. My main interest was to learn about a few days the two of them spent together in Sosnowiec toward the close of the war. The Germans were already gone by this point, and former Jewish residents were trickling back to their hometowns in search of a familiar face.

As we sat in a cozy café in the city center, David began with his own story. In the years before the war, his family had moved out of Niwka, where they had shared the unit with the Gutermans, to Sosnowiec. There, near the end of 1941, he had his first head-on encounter with the Nazis, when the Gestapo abducted him from his family's home during one of their patented night raids. He was imprisoned at a transit camp, or *Durchgangslager*, before being transferred to the Johannesdorf forced-labor camp near Wrocław. Over the course of the German occupation of Poland he would be moved from one camp to another until, near the end of the war, he ended up at Gross Rosen, in Rogoźnica in Lower Silesia. It didn't take long for the SS to organize another Death March, which emptied the entire camp. David escaped with a small group of fellow prisoners during that march. On foot, under the cover of darkness, they made it as far as Gerlitz, where they hid in the crawl space of a utility shed at the railroad station, a place they never dared to leave during daylight. After a few days, they consumed their last drop of water from a bucket that they had "organized" earlier at the station. Sometime later, Soviet soldiers discovered them huddled together under a building. A few had already collapsed from fatigue. The soldiers took them to their quarters, and this was how the war ended for David and his comrades.

Returning to his hometown of Sosnowiec in March of 1945, David wore a striped prisoner's suit, his only possession. In his first days of freedom he wandered from house to house looking for an acquaintance. "I was in my home city, but I had no place to go. Sosnowiec felt like one big cemetery. It was depressing. There wasn't even one Jew left there. Later I did bump into my uncle, who told me that Adela was in the area, but he did not know exactly where."

Exhausted, hungry, with no place to sleep, David scoured Sosnowiec for three days in search of Adela before he ran into someone who helped unite them. Tears filled David's eyes as he recalled the scene of almost sixty years earlier. After pausing for a few moments and regaining his composure, he continued:

> I knew I had to leave Poland. My return to Sosnowiec felt like a cold shower. Nobody was left. The few who survived did not want to stay there. Nobody was waiting for me. Occasionally a passerby on the street noticed my striped suit, and I would hear him mumble to himself, "Look! The Jews are already back." I asked Adela to help me leave for Palestine. She was already working for the State Bureau of Security, and she had connections.

At this point I realized I knew the end of David's story: My mother had set him up with a job at the bureau, and in turn the bureau issued him a valid ID. Two days before he was to report to work, he boarded a train to Vienna and left the country using this very ID. "Indeed this is true," he confirmed. "I was very lucky, for without the ID I wouldn't have been able to leave Poland."

As David traveled south for Vienna, Adela remained firmly in Poland. I asked David for his opinion on why my mother chose to stay behind. Had something held her back? His response was emphatic: "Revenge!" "Revenge?" I repeated. "Yes…revenge!" David continued:

> The night before my departure, we talked until the morning hours. Adela was devastated by my decision. I was devastated too. The thought that I might never see my beloved cousin again made me shiver. We had survived the Nazi hell, and almost all of our loved ones had vanished. As if this wasn't enough, we were about to part from one another for God only knows how long, maybe forever.

I asked David to elaborate on the part about revenge.

> That night before my departure, I asked her the same question: "What is holding you here?" "Revenge," she had said. "Revenge. My revenge…. Our revenge…. Our revenge is to stay here and to nurture and to reeducate these people, to build a new nation on the principles of Marx and Lenin. To build a nation, a whole world like never before. My revenge will be to see a nation born out of unity and equality, a nation that one day will bear witness to a new humanity, and the self-destruction of capitalism." The whole night, she talked about communism, her new philosophy of life. A philosophy that, according to her, saw only humanity, not ethnic divisions. In a short time the boundaries of race and religion would be obsolete anyway. Adela was to show the Germans that her suffering and the suffering of her country had only strengthened their resolve; enough so that they could sit back and watch Germany's decline…. She was charged….

"How did you part?"

"Oh, it was very sad. As I said, we talked the whole night through. Next morning she accompanied me to the railroad station. We stood at the platform for a long time, locked in embrace. Neither of us wanted to let go. We wept and wept. I jumped into the train when it was already moving."

I am not wholly certain when my mother's rendezvous with communism began. Although her brother Moniek tended to be progressive, especially in comparison to his older brother, Chaim, he was as much a capitalist as anyone. Nor could her husband-to-be have introduced the ideology to Adela, because her conversation about revenge with David Mandelbaum took place before she and Michał had spent much time with each other.

I will therefore deduce that Paweł Jaworski brought the principles of equality, freedom, and independence (both on a political and a personal level) into my mother's worldview. And he did so not through formal discussion—certainly not indoctrination—but direct experience. First, in a broad sense, Adela saw how Paweł resisted the Nazis and fought for his principles while few other Poles stood up publicly for anything. Citizens kept quiet and guarded their opinions, principally out of fear. But not Paweł—and, by extension, not the socialists. As a member of the Polish Socialist Party (PPS),[29] which was banned first by the Polish government and later by the Nazis, he fought underground not only *against* the occupiers but also *for* his party's promotion of social democracy. Philosophically, Paweł likely harbored many of the views found at the nexus of Marxism and social democratic thought, which included PPS bona fides such as the elimination of racism and inequality and the elevation of the common worker. The latter of these causes was embodied in policies such as a forty-hour workweek and

---

[29] During the Nazi occupation, the party actually went by the name PPS-WRN, with the latter part of the acronym standing for *Wolność, Równość, Niepodległość* (Freedom, Equality, Independence).

free education. Adela also saw the character of Paweł's associates and friends, people like Shmuel Ron, Ewald Pradela, and Mietek Kobylec. These were not only kind, intelligent, loyal individuals, but they all showed a willingness to risk their lives for a cause. Where Adela's parents and most of the older crowd of Niwka had rejected both communism and socialism with words, she now had witnessed through courageous acts the thousandfold redemption of those philosophies. She would have been hard-pressed to reject it.

Yet despite the impression David's testimony may give, my mother never craved an unquestioned ideological path, and she valued the egalitarian intent of communism above its theoretical framework. Even after her formal political training in 1947, and throughout her life thereafter, she hardly spoke of Marxism or Leninism. She supported the ideology out of an instinct regarding the possibility to create good—from the same sensibility, I presume, that had always compelled her actions. She did see beauty in communism, and it seems to have intoxicated my mother by embodying her personal values. Had the Polish government not curtailed her stay in the country in 1968, she would have remained a communist in the best sense, however utopian this may have been—collectivist, humanist, and empathic.

My interview with Adela's cousin David may lead to a second misconception: that Adela's desire for revenge stemmed from communist zeal. I believe that though she did attempt to goad him into staying by peddling the ideology, she mainly wanted to get back at the Nazis for personal, even primal reasons, not to vindicate a political agenda. From my conversations with other survivors, including those who spent time with Adela immediately after the war, I came to understand without equivocation that she held a profound desire for retaliation. She wanted to avenge the death of her parents, her siblings, her aunts and uncles and cousins; the loss of David Glejcer, Iciek Ryński, Paweł Jaworski, along with the nameless millions murdered. She wanted her due for every day the Nazi agents hunted her as if she were an animal; for the cowardly acts of the SS and the *szmalcownicy*; for her humiliation, hunger, and deprivation, and for every time the Bielsko Gestapo dealt another blow to her face. At times she wanted to inflict pain with her own hands, along with other forms of suffering. This desire for revenge emerged, without a doubt, after the brutal actions of the Germans in Upper Silesia during the war's early years. Stays in the Środula and Zawiercie ghettos intensified such feelings, along with the knowledge of the murder of her family members. But not until her incarceration in the Bielsko prison did her longings take specific shape in her imagination. There, in her cell, she concocted elaborate tortures that she herself would inflict on her captors, who—she fantasized—would endure slow, agonizing deaths. I am not sure when these musings were transformed into determination or the seeds of a mission, but I am certain her time in Auschwitz-Birkenau had a lot to do with it.

Naturally, this desire for retaliation against the Germans was widespread in the aftermath of the war. Europe lay in ruins, with Jewish life on the continent decimated. Most Polish Jews, including Adela's surviving family members, carried their vengefulness with them in tattered valises and on fusty garments as they boarded ships for Palestine—the most popular destination—as well as for the United States, Canada, and South America. They felt especially inclined to leave Europe after learning that none of their loved ones had survived. Yet for those few who remained in Poland after the war, my parents included, I believe a central goal was to retaliate against the Nazis in the most direct, effectual way possible. Employment with the State Bureau of Security offered an easy and, to a large extent, sheltered venue in which to achieve this end.

In the interviews I conducted for this book, I got some sense of the revenge acts that took place, though interviewees usually would not volunteer details. One exception was Adela's cousin Manus Diamant, who told me how he and one of his colleagues had "finished" a former *szmalcownik* in his own apartment a few days after the war ended. At first when I heard insinuations about revenge, I figured the material wasn't relevant to this book, but later I reconsidered. Even for Adela, the subject came up on occasion in the years after the war.[30]

According to the Yalta and Potsdam treaties, which laid out postwar terms of settlement, Germany lost nearly half its land, which became a Soviet protectorate, and did not retain a single territorial victory. In addition, four million Germans died over the course of the war. Yet the Nazis had succeeded in implementing their mindless agenda until the last moments before surrender—by slaughtering and debasing Jews and Gypsies and anyone else they saw as defective or impure. They also silenced untold numbers of people who attempted to resist, either belowground or in plain view. These "victories" they kept.

Now, for the approximately fourteen million people who had been displaced and were trying to reunite with their families, the war's end produced unimaginable chaos. The dislocated traveled by train, boat, military convoy, horse-drawn cart, and bicycle and on foot. Thousands came and went in all directions at the same time. Despite refugee camps and repatriation offices set up all over Europe, few could see through the confusion. Into and out of Adela's office at the Security Bureau traipsed individuals of all description: returning prisoners from concentration and POW camps, soldiers and officers from the Polish unit known as the Anders Army, and inmates of forced-labor camps in Germany and elsewhere in Europe. The Allies set up displaced-persons

---

[30]See "New Journalist" John Sack's controversial book *An Eye for an Eye* for an extensive discussion of revenge acts committed immediately after the Second World War. Though I do not have much respect for Sack, who strikes me as viewing the Holocaust in relativistic terms, and who presents what I consider suspect statistics and statements in his book, he nevertheless managed to document numerous undeniable acts of revenge. Sack actually visited with my mother in conducting the research for his book but concluded that her "act of revenge"—discussed on the next pages—was too negligible to document. With this conclusion, I agree.

171

centers in Austria, Germany, and Italy to help refugees find a way home or at least a temporary solution. For anyone returning to Poland, Soviet and Polish units were on hand to repatriate nationals and offer a semblance of direction.

In late summer of 1945, while working for the Security Bureau, Adela cooperated closely with the Central Repatriation Bureau. During this brief period, she wore a Polish army uniform (her rank unknown to me), and carried a Walter pistol. One day, two colleagues entered her office and asked her to accompany them to the building's basement to a small, dark room where a heavyset man, around forty, sat undressed to the waist. Adela's colleagues lifted the man's arm to reveal a tattoo under his armpit. (Members of the SS had their blood type tattooed under the left armpit.) They explained that two Polish POWs who had arrived at the Repatriation Bureau had recognized the man, who spoke fluent Polish with a Silesian accent. They reported him to be an SS man disguising himself as a repatriate. When a colleague handed Adela a nightstick, rage swirled inside her, and she struck the man three, four, maybe five times. But suddenly she stopped—then left the room and vomited. Adela later explained:

> Certainly I did not feel compassion for the SS man. I wanted revenge badly, but not this type of revenge. It was too easy. Sure, I wasn't hitting an innocent person, but at the same time I was hitting a defenseless prisoner. I had more satisfaction looking into his face, for not so long ago he was a proud member of the SS, the *Herrenvolk*, who now was standing before me panic-stricken, with fear in his eyes. Today he was afraid of me, the humiliated, the undesired subhuman, the cause of evil and an impurity of his world, the parasite—a Jewess.

World War II devastated Poland. Of the major Polish cities, only Kraków had been spared. Warsaw, a cultured European center before the war, had been virtually leveled. Not only did the Poles now have to rebuild their cities and infrastructure, they also had to deal with the new government, largely under the control of the Soviet Union. Complicating matters, the Polish exile government based in London, which had been formed at the beginning of the German invasion, refused to give up its claim to power. This led to factional guerrilla clashes, which erupted around the country in the immediate aftermath of the war and contributed to the feeling of national disarray.

For Jews trying to emigrate in the year or so following the war, the confusion made crossing the Polish border a relatively easy task. But this situation didn't last for long. In mid-1946, the Polish government sealed the country's borders, making it impossible for anybody to travel abroad. Such a policy showed the new regime's paranoia, while previewing the corrupt policies that would shadow Poland for the next several decades.

Nor did Hitler's fall bring an end to the murder of Jews. In the Polish city of Kielce, a Nazi-style hunt for Jews took place in July 1946. Mobs attacked a group of Jewish residents of an apartment building, and forcibly removed Jews arriving by train at the Kielce station. At least forty-two people were murdered and eighty wounded. Order was restored, and the main rioters were executed, but the pogrom caused many remaining Holocaust survivors to attempt to flee Poland. To their misfortune, the government's hard-line immigration policy made such an exit impossible—at least within the law. In a country so recently and devastatingly touched by the Nazi slaughter, the Kielce pogrom exposed a thriving postwar anti-Semitism, a seemingly inconceivable thought. The reluctance of the Communist Party authorities to stop the mob, and the silent cooperation of the police, the army, the Bureau of Security, along with local and national politicians and the Catholic Church, stung every Polish Jew with the reality that they still could not be safe in their home country.

So, as she had so often before, Adela stepped into the underground in the interest of forwarding justice, an early confirmation that she was first a humanist, and a communist second. By calling on her knowledge of escape routes used during the war, she once again helped organize transports of Jews to Hungary via Slovakia. Though I have no information on her particular role in these operations, or their success, I do know the Polish security agents uncovered her involvement and imprisoned her. It took serious intervention from her future husband, Michał—then too a member of the Security Bureau—to gain her release. I extracted this information from family members and friends, for my parents kept it to themselves until their last days.[31]

When my brother, Felek, was born, Adela was studying Marxism in Poznań, where my parents had moved in late 1946, following my father's new assignment. Ursula, our housekeeper, would bring Felek between lectures to be breast-fed. Two and a half years later, in 1950, I was born during the family's brief stay in Łódź. The family ended up in Warsaw several months afterward, when my father was reassigned once again. In September 1952, Adela was hired by the Polish Academy of Sciences (PAN), where she would work in an administrative position for the next sixteen years. The memoirs of her boss, Professor M. Śmiałowski, shed some light on postwar sentiments among even highly educated Poles. In the book, he laments that during a brief sojourn of his from Warsaw, PAN had hired two women of Jewish background to work under his supervision, though he goes on to praise my mother and her colleague for their performance. The book also includes disdainful words about my father—surprising, given that the two men had never met. My mother wasn't aware of her boss's feelings until her time in Frankfurt in the 1970s.

The other woman hired by PAN was Janina Mordzińska, with whom my mother—and, by extension, the entire family—developed a fast friendship over their years working together. During my 2007 visit to Warsaw, I bumped into Mrs.

---

[31] Adela began her smuggling operation before the government yielded to pressure from Kielce victims, granting them permission to leave Poland. Some 80,000 Jews ultimately fled the country as an immediate response to the pogrom.

Mordzińska on the street, and she grabbed hold of my shirtsleeve with such urgent affection that only when we arrived back at her flat, and unlocking the door required two hands, did she let go. Over tea and cake while sitting on the sofa, she talked about my mother:

> Irenka [Adela] was my best friend. [After 1968] she practically clothed me from head to foot. She always managed to send us food, money, and clothing from Frankfurt. This leather jacket and the white shoes [pointing to the clothing she was then wearing] are from Irenka. When Andrzej [her only child] fell ill with cancer, she sent medications, even medical instruments from Frankfurt so that he could be treated. He only lived so long thanks to her. Irenka did not live to see the end of my son's life.

Since our encounter, I have continued corresponding with Mrs. Mordzińska, and in a letter dated February 17, 2008, she wrote:

> Sometimes after work, Irenka and I would come to my apartment to chat. I remember the three of us [the third being Mrs. Mordzińska's husband] sitting around the small table in the kitchen. We would have a piece of marinated herring and a shot of vodka. We used to talk for hours.

The passionate ideal-driven new world required passionate ideal-driven love, leaving no room for documents and clerical monotony or the traditions associated with marriage. That explains why, though my parents lived as husband and wife since almost the time they fell in love in 1945, they did not marry officially until years later. Only the demands of living in a bureaucracy ultimately compelled them to tie the knot. The actual piece of paper meant nothing to them. In fact, once my parents did wed, they held no ceremony. The story goes that the civil clerk had to wait four hours next to my father's office, until Michał finally emerged from his meetings and signed the papers. The clerk apologized sincerely for taking up my father's

175

valuable time. The marriage certificate states that my father's chauffeur was his witness.[32]

The call came in 1963. "Adela, is this you?" It had been a long time since anyone had called her "Adela." During the war, and for almost twenty years after, she had continued to use her assumed name, Irena—the name written on the *palcówka* she had stolen from the Skopek factory. None of her new friends knew anything about an "Adela."

"It's me, Jerzyk! Jerzyk Feder. Remember?"

Jerzyk was calling from Katowice. He had located Roman Brzuchański, who was then serving as district chairman of the Polish United Workers Party (PZPR), and wanted to confront and expose him as a wartime Gestapo informer. After learning of his plan, Adela caught the next train to Katowice, where Jerzyk awaited her at the platform. For a day or two, they tried to arrange a personal meeting with Brzuchański, but he was elusive, using his influential position to claim unavailability. After additional attempts failed, Adela and Jerzyk filed a suit in the district court of Sosnowiec. But the desired face-off never came to pass. Adela recollected:

> I returned to Warsaw and waited for the legal process to engage. But nothing happened. Two years later, Jerzyk left Poland and neither of us followed up on this. Until my last day in Poland, I wanted to confront Brzuchański face to

---

[32] More than a half century later, I learned that technically my parents had been married once before this. Shortly after they decided to move in together around the end of 1945, Hala hired a rabbi to perform a marriage ceremony for the young couple. When the idea was broached, Michał not surprisingly showed opposition to having a ceremony "tainted" by religion, God, and the symbolism of the very world he was determined to reject. All he wanted was to be together with Adela. But Hala had a deep regard for tradition, and she would not be at peace until her sister's marriage was sanctified according to Jewish custom. So, after a healthy dose of persuasion from Hala and Adela, who mainly saw the event as a way to please her sister, Michał agreed to a Jewish wedding. A brief and very modest ceremony was held in the couple's apartment at 39 Plebiscytowa Street in Katowice.

face, but I lost the urge for revenge. I wasn't at peace with myself. After all, Brzuchański had saved many lives. He brought many transports across the border safely to Slovakia. Sometimes, when the organization had no money, he would do it for free. Brzuchański was smuggling food and arms when the Gestapo caught him. In order to buy himself out, he betrayed us. So does he deserve to be punished for lives lost because of him, when on the other hand he rescued many others?

It took years for Adela to return to her native Niwka, and she only passed through town when she happened to be in the area and felt curious about the house at 7 Piłsudski Street. As she recalled, there was "no sense in returning to a place where nobody is waiting for you." And no one was. Indeed not a single former Jewish inhabitant of Niwka-Modrzejów had moved back to his or her former home. Jewish life there had simply ceased to exist. The overwhelming majority of the community's members had been murdered by the Nazis, and those who survived had no reason or desire to return.

By the time the killing had finally stopped, Adela had lost her parents, two brothers, two sisters-in-law, one brother-in-law, six aunts, seven uncles, twenty-one first cousins, one niece, and a husband-to-be. A family of fifty-three, comprising the Czapelski relatives, had been reduced to eleven.

Michał and Leon Winiawski, circa 1945

Adela types while Michał dictates, 1945

*From left: Fishek Viener, Gucia Viener (b. Mandelbaum),
unknown, Michał, Adela, unknown, Hala, fall of 1947*

Fifteen

March 1968

THOUGH JEWS WHO STAYED in Poland felt lingering bitterness toward certain of their gentile neighbors for their passivity during the war—and to others for their aid to the Nazis—most preferred to focus on the hopeful future they saw in communism. This future seemed ever more radiant considering the Soviets' role in liberating Poland and the camps. For these acts, the Soviets were cheered by remaining Polish Jews as heroes. Most gentile Poles, on the other hand, harbored a deep hostility toward the Russians, a sentiment that dated back to the time of the czars. (Immediately after the war, few people knew that Poland's fate as a vassal to the Soviet Union was already decided.)

My parents were among those who embraced Marxism as the just path for themselves and their country. They did so

183

despite early signs, such as the emigration ban, that Poland's leadership would not act in good faith. As members of the governing class, they had it easier than ordinary citizens, existing in an insulated sphere, with idealistic, like-minded friends and colleagues. In such a position, they had the luxury of observing their superiors' errors of judgment without having to pay any real price. Understandably, they also saw no contradiction in objecting to individual shortcomings of policy while refusing to admit an overarching flaw in the system. Put simply, they chose to see the forest but not the trees. After all, no one expected communism to work overnight—a long road ahead was assumed. For communists all over Poland, and especially for Adela and other Jews given the anti-Semitic policies of the thirties, Article 69 of the Constitution provided ample reason for patience:

(1) Citizens of the Republic of Poland, irrespective of nationality, race, or religion, shall enjoy equal rights in all fields of public, political, economic, social, and cultural life. Infringement of this principle by any direct or indirect privileges or restrictions of rights by reference to nationality, race, or religion shall be punishable.
(2) The spreading of hatred or contempt, the provocation of discord, or humiliation of man on account of national, racial, or religious differences shall be prohibited.

For those who had endured unceasing discrimination from both the state and next-door neighbors, the idea that discrimination—and with it, religious labels—would now dissolve was an intoxicant. Daily life would be nothing like it had been before the war; Adela's segregated youth would fade into memory. In the new Poland, Adela's children would grow up unburdened by racism in any form. For this reason, postwar Poland was touted by the remaining Jews who shared my parents' mind-set as a sort of Promised Land—a Promised Land based on sounder principles than even the imminent state in Palestine. Adela and her peers could not have known that two decades after the communist government took power they would discover that neither Article 69 of the Polish Constitution nor any related slogan was worth the paper it was printed on. For Polish Jews from across the political spectrum, the impulse answer to the question "Why stay?" was war exhaustion. After six years of fear, hunger, continuous hiding, ghettos, and labor and death camps, these Holocaust survivors wanted simply to start their lives anew: to build families, to enjoy safety and peace.

And for all its miscues, the early Polish government could boast concrete successes. In the areas of health care, access to education, labor policy, and distribution of wealth, it had enacted fixes that few Poles could deny. Yet even as its champions praised the new system, the myth that communism would solve the world's ills was disintegrating steadily. Long before Robert Conquest's *The Great Terror* (1968) and Alexander Solzhenitsyn's memoirs about Stalin's Gulag published in the 1970s, my parents knew that the network of Soviet penal camps accounted for deaths at a rate comparable to Hitler's concentration camps, although most Soviet prisoners died of starvation, disease, and exhaustion. But Stalin's system didn't simply punish opponents at random. Under his rule, entire ethnic groups vanished. In the 1950s, Poland hosted Soviet-style labor camps of its own, administered by the same officials who ran the operations in Russia. In a raw echo of the war years, German shepherds were used at all the Gulag satellites. And though it lacked gas chambers, conditions at the Magadan camp, in the Siberian region of Kolyma, and the sadism of the guards, distinguished it as the Soviet equivalent of Auschwitz-Birkenau.

It is difficult to understand how my parents could have stood by with the knowledge that these crimes were being committed in the name of communism—in Poland or the U.S.S.R. I suppose it was more comfortable to be silent about crimes purportedly committed in the name of equality and justice for all than about the Nazi doctrine of a superior race and the corresponding death camps. They might have been able to explain away imprisonments on a local level. If an "enemy of the proletariat" ended up in the Gulag system, that couldn't be bad for the advancement of a Marxist society. One could also refer to the principle known in Polish as *dla sprawy* (roughly, "for the cause"), whereby, in a communist nation, even a party member might have to endure sacrifice for the greater good of a society. And yes, loyal communists were jailed and murdered. Ultimately, people with my parents' mind-set could only hope that oppressive measures in the short term might give way to fairness over time. The most likely explanation for my parents' passivity was, of course, their anxiety that even the faintest show of dissent would land them in jail or a Gulag camp itself. The question remains, however, why decent people with high moral standards would actively partake in the destructive methods of Soviet or Polish communism. To me, the answer may be found in the title of Paul Hollander's article in the *Washington Post* marking the twentieth anniversary of the fall of the Berlin Wall: "Murderous Idealism":

> The failure of Soviet communism confirms that humans motivated by lofty ideals are capable of inflicting great suffering with a clear conscience.... The embrace and rejection of communism correspond to the spectrum of attitudes ranging from deluded and destructive idealism to the realization that human nature precludes utopian social arrangements and that the careful balancing of ends and means is the essential precondition of creating and preserving a decent society.

At least in spirit, my parents may have given up on the communist system as early as October 1954, following the conference of the Ministry of Public Security, which took place after Józef Światło, one of Poland's highest-ranking secret agents escaped to the United States.[33] A watershed

---

[33] In fact, Józef Światło's escape and the Security Conference that followed marked a critical turning point for many old-guard Marxists, who began to feel disenchanted with the leadership. The speeches they delivered were so blunt that the authorities chose not to keep formal minutes. In the weeks and months after

event for regime operatives, the Public Security conference exposed the corruptive influences of Stalinist policy on Poland, as well as the decaying condition of the economy, which until then had remained hidden from midlevel government employees, along with everyone below them. It was in 1954 that people like my father (though not the general public) learned the extent of the corruption instigated by the Polish Politburo and other ministries, as well as the destructive role of various Soviet advisors or "instructors," as they were officially called. And they now knew it would continue. So outraged was my father by these disclosures that he resigned from his position at the Security Bureau. Only under pressure from his boss, who insisted that people like my father were needed to clean up the corruption, did he resume his job, staying on for another two years. If they hadn't already done so by then, I believe my parents abandoned their illusions once and for all after 1956, when, in a bloodbath, the Soviets crushed the Hungarian uprising. And after the so-called Poznań Events, in June of the same year, when factory workers in the city of Poznań took to the streets calling for "bread and freedom," the authorities labeled the demonstrators criminals and moved to quash this early display of citizen discontent.

When I was growing up, my family lived in the heart of Warsaw at 5b Chopin Street, flat 21, in a complex built in the early 1950s. Chopin Street was a quiet side street lined with majestic *kasztany*, chestnut trees that bloomed in May with stunning flowers. In autumn, glossy, dark-brown chestnuts would fall to the sidewalk. I was not the only one to feel a deep attachment to the chestnut trees of Warsaw—most city

---

the session adjourned, oppression by the Polish government increased steadily; yet at that same historic moment, an opposition movement arose. This opposition gained momentum until, more than three decades later it became known as Solidarity, with Lech Wałęsa as its leader. Not until November 1992 was an informal record of the conference proceedings published in *Kultura*. It had been composed from private notes and illegal recordings.

residents saw the trees as integral to their city and their lives. Even today, when a typical Warsovian is asked about these trees, he or she may well answer: "Yes, they were here before I was born. Each year they bloom in time for the *matura* (final high school exams) and in autumn children will collect the chestnuts and make *ludziki* (doll people) out of them." Every September, I myself would display a few *ludziki* on my windowsill.

Just around the corner from our building, to the right, was the Palermo ice cream shop—Warsaw's best, according to the people in our neighborhood. To the left was a small park, Dolinka Szwajcarska (Swiss Valley), where I would play with my friends for full days and into the night. A large fountain provided the ideal backdrop for our flights of imagination. On occasion, one of us would return home with a black eye or a missing tooth suffered during a fistfight against a group of *żule*, raffish youths who came from homes we neither visited nor cared to know about. Farther down the street was the Romanian embassy, which seemed to me a building of wondrous prestige. I was equally moved by the fine Western-model cars that were usually parked out front. In those few square blocks, one would find several other embassies: Czechoslovakia, Hungary, German Democratic Republic. The U.S. embassy itself was within a few minutes' walk.

Deeper into the city were plentiful mysteries for a kid like myself to behold. My mother's office at PAN was housed in the most prominent building in Warsaw at the time, the Palace of Culture, a gift from the Soviets to the Polish nation. (Why the Soviets, the standard-bearers of communism, would choose the word "palace" for a building is beyond me.) The structure, a typical Soviet-style creation—uninspired and uninspiring—stood as the highest in the city. In order to get to the upper floors, you had to switch elevators. For me as a child, this fact alone gave the building divine status.

Our complex, consisting of buildings 5a and 5b, was occupied by a few high-powered members of the Politburo, one or two Polish army officers, a journalist, several government functionaries, a Soviet "instructor," a saleswoman of movie tickets, and two janitors, one for each building, along with a few other professionals. For us children—and our neighborhood was bursting with children in those postwar years—the Swiss Valley park and the *podwórko*,[34] the parklike area between the two building units, constituted the center of the universe. There, as younger children, we would frequent the playground, which included the usual equipment along with two frames on which adults used to beat the dust off of carpets. On the volleyball court behind one of our buildings (which doubled as a soccer field), we used to play endless contests in both sports. On a quiet afternoon, one of us needed only to bounce a ball twice on the sidewalk, and kids would climb out the windows.

The volleyball court was separated from the street by an iron fence with pointed bars on top. Though you could certainly exit through the gate, we all chose to climb the fence when leaving the *podwórko*. The older kids would joke that several girls had lost their virginity climbing that fence, though the younger of us weren't sure what that meant. Protected from direct view of the apartments, the volleyball court also made for a perfect gathering point for the older kids, where they could share a cigarette or have a sip of whisky, smuggled out of their parents' liquor cabinet.

I am writing about our *podwórko* because it was something of a paradise not only for children but for all residents, including my parents. Everybody knew everybody, and unlike in past generations, appropriate distance was always maintained. My parents' best friends lived near us, and we considered the building's other residents to be close acquaintances. All adults in our building adhered to an unwritten code: if they saw any child engaging in mischief of any kind, they'd make sure our parents "accidentally" found out before the evening was over.

---

[34] Literally a courtyard, though this term does not do justice to that expansive, social space.

I also remember my parents' bridge marathons and how my father would play chess with his friends, so consumed by the game that he was blind to the world around him. Once I had the audacity to smoke a cigarette in his presence during one of these chess games, but he was so caught up in his moves, he didn't even notice.

The immortal personalities of our *podwórko* included Ms. V, a woman probably in her early forties known for her frivolous lifestyle. When I was growing up, she was conducting simultaneous love affairs with two gentlemen: a national heavyweight boxing champion in the daytime, and one of the highest-ranking political figures in the nation, who showed up late at night. Every kid on the block also knew that on summer days, Ms. V neglected to put on underwear.

And then there were the custodians, Cienkus and Rupiński. To this day, I have not located a single resident of those buildings, some of whom are still my close friends, who can tell me the janitors' first names. Once a year, the mayor of center city Warsaw would launch a competition for most attractive *podwórko*. For the occasion, both of our janitors would make an extraordinary effort to turn the place into a jewel of urban landscape. The rest of us, too, got swept up in the competition. We'd chip in by mowing the grass, cleaning the trash area, repainting the benches, and being extra careful not to sabotage our chances in any way. Though we never won that award, had you seen our *podwórko,* and Chopin Street itself, you would have agreed it was the finest in the city, if not all of Poland.

In particular, Mr. Cienkus's magnanimous acts included taking all the kids from the playground across the street to the candy store, where we were allowed to buy as much candy as we could digest. Admittedly, we only cashed in like this on the days when he had drunk too much. (Luckily for us, such days were numerous.) Our hero in the *podwórko,* however, was Rupiński, who in his spare time would carve for us swords, shields, daggers, bows, and other battle paraphernalia out of wood or cardboard. How else could we rise to the rank of Knight of the Round Table, or set an elaborate trap near our building gate for the neighboring Indian tribe. Mr. Rupiński also would daily place two bottles of fresh milk beside our door. I don't remember whether he provided this service in conjunction with the milk distributor or if my parents paid him directly for his work.

To give a true sense of our lives in Warsaw, however, I must tell of the blank canvas we experienced as children. Blank in the sense that we had no ethnicity, no Judaism, no religion, and—most critically—no sense of continuity with our parents' past. This past was simply not discussed. Nor were we made aware of any attachment to our grandparents, aunts, and uncles, who had perished during the war. Not that we asked about our absent relatives. We knew the subject was off limits. And when our teachers taught us of the devastating war of just a generation ago, the inquiring gaze we later directed at adults we knew was met by silence.

My friend Mirek, who, for the record, was not Jewish, was the only kid I can remember who had a grandmother. She lived together with her children and grandchildren in their flat, one floor up from ours. For Mirek, his grandmother was simply a part of life, but I felt strange around her. She seemed to me a ghost from a world passed away, a world that was unfamiliar and inaccessible.

Then there was the blankness of growing up in a communist country, where all culture that originated outside the state was frowned upon. Though religion existed on some level in communist Poland, it was hardly visible, and people didn't really discuss it. A few churches operated in Warsaw, but we knew only a few who attended. And only years into my own exile did I learn that there was an active synagogue in the city. As for our own Jewishness, we knew it as a fact, but this meant virtually nothing in practice, at least through the fifties and early sixties. Through literature alone were we exposed to our buried culture as well as to anti-Semitism. Authors we read included Ilia Erenburg, Sholem Aleichem,

191

Isaac Bashevis Singer, Romain Gary, and Isaac Babel. But these writers' stories did not feel like a part of our ancestry, and we didn't see them against the backdrop of the Holocaust or even Judaism. We were aware that somehow they must hold a connection to our own lives, but we could not guess where, nor did we really try. None of this is to say that anti-Semitism did not exist powerfully in postwar Poland. Even today when I visit, I overhear the occasionally jarring remark despite the almost complete absence of Jews. But perhaps owing to my father's position in the government, our location on Chopin Street, and the social circles in which my family mingled, we did not feel or see bigotry in the early years. Now however, in recollecting my childhood, I am continually astonished at my level of ignorance and naiveté.

At home, Jewish subjects were never raised, except by our neighbor Uncle Adam, who taught us the Hebrew alphabet along with a few words. Adam Wein was not really our uncle, but to this day we think of him as one. And this fact says a great deal. We convinced ourselves that blood relatives could be replaced by people with whom we felt close—and to some extent they could be. Where Adam's Hebrew lessons were concerned, our interest was fueled mainly by the exotic nature of the language and Adam's magnetism, not by any ties we saw to the people who had vanished only a generation ago. During our life in Poland my parents never attended a synagogue, not even during the high Jewish holidays such as Yom Kippur or Rosh Hashana. No religious ceremonies, a Seder or even a festive Sabbath dinner, were held in our home. If the word "Torah" was ever uttered in my presence, it was surely stripped of its content. It wasn't until our attempt at a new life in Israel that I discovered my mother could speak fluent Yiddish. Now and then during our time in Warsaw, she would drop a Yiddish saying or tell a joke, but I still never truly associated her Yiddish with the culture it represented.

I should have known better. I should have asked more questions about her childhood. My brother and I had never been surrounded by so-called Yiddishkeit, or a Jewish way of life. Unlike displaced Jewish families in other countries who created little shtetls for themselves—or, as Ilan Stavans puts it eloquently in his book *On Borrowed Words*, "portable ghettos of Yiddishkeit"—Adela voluntarily stripped herself of almost all connection to her years prior to the war. Though never trying to conceal her origins, she chose not to incorporate the culture of her childhood into her own children's lives. Phrases like "As my father used to say," or "During the Sabbath when I was a young girl," were not a part of her vocabulary. The nostalgic Jewish landscape of Poland, with its shtetls and synagogues, *choolent* and gefilte fish, the omnipresent Torah, and a large family gathered around the table during holiday time, was certainly an integral part of her ethnic heritage, but she chose to withhold it all from us. Ironically, we knew more about Adolf Hitler than about the people he destroyed—our ancestors.

There were also, I recall, stray incidents in which we were reminded of our Judaism. All throughout my childhood, my family employed *gosposia*s (live-in housekeepers). The first of these, starting in my earliest years, was Ursula, a young German woman, who for whatever reason had remained in Poland during the chaos of the German postwar retreat. She left Warsaw when I was just two years old, returning to her family in Germany. After Ursula came Pani (Polish for "Madam") Stasia, whom I adored for most of her time with us. As a child, I would follow her anywhere, and honor her every request. Sometimes I would even go along with her to church, though while she prayed, I would grow impatient to leave the sanctuary. I am not sure if my parents ever knew about those church visits.

One day, after one of Felek's and my physical fights, which could get vicious, Stasia showed her mean streak. As my brother and I were explaining ourselves to our parents, she interjected that I had called my brother a "dirty Jew," and that was why we'd fought. I was stunned at this outright fabrication, and my parents looked at each other in disbelief. As my shock turned to fury, I let forth a string of insults at Stasia, including calling her a "whore." After the incident, I never trusted Pani Stasia again and used every opportunity I could to show my disdain. One morning my parents gave Stasia a hundred-*złoty* note—the equivalent of about $100 in buying power in the United States today—to purchase bread for breakfast. She disappeared, returning six months later without an explanation. By this point, of course, we had hired a replacement for Stasia, a plumpish farmwoman named Zosia, who lasted with us only a few months.

As for our contact with the West at large, it too was severely limited. Only a very few families had travel privileges—and to destinations limited to the Eastern bloc. Though at school we did read some literature from Western authors, the selections were confined to classics that in no way could be construed as anticommunist. Among the American authors we read were Faulkner, Twain, Steinbeck, Hemingway, and Salinger. And sometimes we got to watch foreign movies, including Westerns, suspense films, and certain others, as long as they propagated no overtly political message. All of these movies, I will note, were dubbed with the same voice speaking for all characters and *both* genders.

In the mid-1950s in Warsaw, the era of hushed conversations with trusted friends against a wall of loud music began. And though the Polish censors were hard at work sifting through literature, art, and journalism, they couldn't block all forms of expression that questioned the prevailing authority. Artists and scholars alike found ways of encoding and camouflaging their messages so that the censors would not suspect antigovernment intent. In increasing numbers, such material found its way into our home. A battered copy of *Kultura*, a monthly periodical written by Poles exiled in Paris, would make its appearance on my

194

parents' night table. And there were days when we would listen to Radio Free Europe, the forbidden CIA-sponsored station that transmitted news reports to the communist world. Although these reports came from a capitalist source, many of us appreciated the timely and uncensored broadcasts. And in my mother's communications with family and friends abroad, she frequently relied on innuendo to explain the ever-more-repressive sociopolitical situation in Poland. She was profoundly disappointed for this to be the outcome.

Whether my parents entertained the idea of leaving Poland for good in the 1950s, I do not know. If they did, they surely never communicated their doubts to Felek and me. This may have been because leaving Poland was not a matter of a passport and a ticket. We lived behind the Iron Curtain. Our borders were sealed. Legal emigration simply didn't exist.

Until March of 1968, anti-Semitism did not really enter the mix of frustrations in postwar Poland. Breaking this calm were political events that unleashed a wave of anti-Semitism and prompted my family to leave the country for good, changing our lives irrevocably. Not only my family but most Jews who had made postwar Poland their home were compelled to emigrate. They scattered themselves to lands as diverse as Australia, Germany, France, Italy, Sweden, Switzerland, Denmark, Brazil, Canada, and of course the United States and Israel.

It goes without saying that our family had not practiced Judaism in any way. And though my mother kept in touch with her sister, Hala, who lived in Tel Aviv, for my brother and me, Israel was nothing but another country on the map. We did not associate its Jewish character with our own lives. Even the box of matzos that miraculously landed on our dinner table once a year prompted nothing more than a little bit of curiosity.

In March 1968 we became Jews. The subject of being a Jew quickly found its way into our topics of daily conversation, our thoughts, and our mentality. No longer did we hang around for hours on the volleyball court of our *podwórko*. And Chopin Street became a magnet for secret service agents, who tracked the comings and goings of my father and other residents of Jewish ancestry. We locked the doors to the flat not only as we used to—at night—but also in the daytime. Divisions among friends, neighbors, schoolmates, and my parents' colleagues began to form. Only the chestnut trees stood in their former grace. But by the time the events of 1968 burst forth, we couldn't even be bothered to admire them. Our lives had taken a sudden and surprising turn—a turn for which no one in our family or among our friends could have been prepared.

The flash point for this attack on Polish Jewry was a new production of *Dziady* (*Forefathers' Eve*), a play written by Adam Mickiewicz. Required reading for every Polish high school student, the play was composed long before communism became the official state ideology. Yet it depicted Polish political prisoners struggling against their Russian captors. And in the rich tradition of Polish dramaturgy, the playwright, though dead 113 years, had used sleight of hand to criticize the Russian authorities who ruled at the time. Considering the Russians' influence in Poland, the censors feared the play might incite anti-Soviet expressions, which until now had been mainly dormant. Exuberant ovations from audiences didn't offer officials any reassurance, and the play was pulled from the stage after only a few performances. Almost forty years later, a friend of mine who attended the play recalled, "Never before had I been so electrified by a play. Suddenly I realized that something big was happening onstage, and I was a part of it."

Warsaw's students, sensing their moment, took to the streets in protest. They spoke out against not only the act of censorship but also against the widening gap between true Marxism and the corrupt ideology of the current government. In a short time, the protests spread to other cities. Most student demonstrators refrained from violence, seeking dialogue as their end goal and being careful not to criticize Marxist theory itself, but the Polish authorities showed little restraint. Thugs hired by the secret police beat and arrested the students, who were carted off to jail by the busload. In its growth, the student movement came to represent wholesale opposition to the failed implementation of communism in Poland.

At one student demonstration in early March, I witnessed a scene that took such hold of my psyche that flashbacks of the day still invade my sleep. As I later learned, a considerable number of undercover ZOMO[35] operatives had quietly infiltrated the crowd, carrying concealed nightsticks. On a prearranged signal, they all produced their weapons and proceeded to assault the young demonstrators. In the aftermath, I recall young people doubled over on the pavement, holding their stomachs and faces, coughing up blood. Through the ZOMO actions, the demonstration was dispersed in probably less than an hour, complemented by several arrests. Immediately after the crackdown, I ran to the nearby apartment of a friend. I remember standing at the window and staring down at deserted Marszałkowska Avenue, which evoked a vacated battlefield. The buses, trams, and cars that usually gave life to the thoroughfare were nowhere to be found. All one could see were the possessions left behind by the fleeing students—jackets, shirts, shoes, caps—along with the abandoned backpacks and drifting papers that gave the scene an extra poignancy. The silence was eerie. Just minutes before, the impassioned speeches of protesters had been interrupted by a mayhem of shouting and orders through bullhorns. Now the human voices, of both inspiration and repression, had gone quiet.

Not since the end of the war had dissident activity been so loud and focused. With good reason, the leadership felt threatened and sought a scapegoat on whom to assign blame. With United Workers Party's First Secretary Władysław

---

[35] Zmotoryzowane Odwody Milicji Obywatelskiej (Motorized Reserves of the Citizens' Militia) were paramilitary riot police of the communist era.

Gomułka at the lead, the regime embarked on a crusade designed to pin every state failure on the Jewish presence in Poland. Regrettably, the strategy worked, and public opinion began to turn against the Jews. In his book on the pivotal year 1968, Mark Kurlansky writes of lead student activist Adam Michnik, who remarked: "When I saw anti-Semitic articles, I had never seen such a thing. It was fascism. It wasn't allowed. Until then anti-Semitism was an abstract term. I thought, in Poland after the Holocaust, anti-Semitism was impossible." By doctrine, expressions of anti-Semitism were forbidden in the Eastern bloc (despite Stalin's savagery toward his own Jews).

The anti-Semitic campaign had actually been set in motion a year before, when Poland severed diplomatic relationships with Israel in reaction to the Six-Day War. In televised speeches on June 19, 1967, and March 19, 1968 (Jewish families like my own only began to feel the impact after this latter speech), Gomułka cemented the government's stance by proclaiming that Polish Jews were loyal to a second homeland. Hitler had always referred to Jews as parasites, and the resonance was unmistakable. Jews were suddenly depicted as a fifth column, a lurking threat. As for the term "Zionist," it acquired a slew of meanings: not only that of a Jew but also a student organizer, a dissident, an intellectual, anybody with a Jewish-sounding name, or any undesired member of the administration. Never was "Zionist" used to denote its true meaning. (To this day, I cannot understand why the term should be viewed in a negative light.) Even before Gomułka's second speech had ended, I knew I would never again consider Poland my homeland.

Not since the fall of Nazi Germany had an anti-Semitic word been uttered on the airwaves in Poland or across the Eastern bloc. In his two speeches Gomułka had broken the taboo, and his March 1968 performance prompted almost all the remaining Polish Jews to pack up and flee the country. In his most recent book, *Uchodźcy* (Refugees), Henryk Grynberg cites an exhortation from the newspaper *Głos Młodych* (The Voice of the Young): *"Koniec wasz bliski, pakujcie walizki"*

(Your end is near, pack your suitcases). The author goes on to classify this period in Poland as the "worst racist persecution since Hitler's Reich."

Jews who did not leave voluntarily were fired from every sector of political, academic, cultural, and industrial life. Those dismissed included the last Jewish officers of the Polish armed forces. "Even doctors from small towns, where they were needed most, were fired," writes Grynberg. To show the sweep of the Polish government measures, he points out that "Nazis decided [who belonged in Germany] according to race; for Moczar,[36] supporters' last name was sufficient." That sometimes meant even gentiles were forced to leave their positions if they happened to have a Jewish- or German-sounding name. Grynberg, who himself managed to leave Poland for the United States just before the anti-Semitic barrage, assures the reader that once in America, "I woke up each morning with a relief that I was not waking up in Poland." According to statistics, more than two thousand Jews—among them government ministers, high-ranking party members, editors and journalists, educators, and scientists (including many leading figures at PAN), along with the military officers—were fired based on accusations that ranged from harboring Zionist beliefs to subversion of Polish values through revisionism and the "channeling of foreign influence."[37] My father, who had worked at the National Tourism Bureau since leaving his position at the State Bureau of Security of the Ministry of the Interior in 1956, was forced into early retirement. My mother, acting as she did throughout her life, did not wait for the Jew-bashing to get the best of her. At one of the vitriolic party committee meetings at the Polish Academy of Sciences shortly after Gomułka's speech, she

---

[36] Mieczyslaw Moczar was the leader of a conservative nationalist group known as the Partisans. In 1967–68, using the June 1967 Six-Day War between Israel and its Arab neighbors as a pretext, Moczar and his faction instigated the purge of the remaining two hundred Jewish officers in the Polish People's Army.

[37] "Revisionism" was characterized in official language as a specifically Zionist plot.

turned in her party membership card and later resigned from her job.

For me, too, the ground began to tremble. Having absorbed a de facto Jewish identity overnight, I was assaulted with questions every day at school: Would yesterday's friends remain my friends today? Would the instructor force upon us another lecture about Zionism? Indeed, the most painful blows came from the school's teachers and the principal, figures whom I had respected greatly beforehand. How, I wondered, did they even know I was Jewish? And how could they view me, without any conceivable reason, as a sudden adversary?

By granting my mother, my brother, and me permission to emigrate (officially this happened in July), the Polish government stripped us of our citizenship. This was the ultimate indignity, and we felt as if we had been reduced to a lower life form—a form suddenly undeserving of Polish recognition. I do not know exactly what they had in mind as far as our humanity, but the cruel fact was that where Hitler and the Nazis had failed to wipe out every Jew in Poland, the Poles, and their supposedly egalitarian government, were finishing the job.

For my parents, and probably for every Jew who lived in Poland at that time, the most tragic part of this development was its government sponsorship. Despite all the shortcomings of the Polish regime, until 1968 Jews could still feel they had helped transform their country into a place where they could live without fear of discrimination. But now even that illusion was shattered. I do not exaggerate when I say the anti-Semitism of 1968 hurt my parents more deeply than any event since the war. They were staggered, and it would take decades for me and my brother to realize what they must have been going through.

In later years, Adela seldom discussed her departure from Poland, but she stayed disappointed and embittered by the experience. There were days when nostalgia would pay her a visit. She simply could not erase with the flick of a wrist forty-six years of having lived in and devoted herself to a nation and the Marxist concept upon which it was reinvented. Until her death, Poland would never diminish to merely another place she had lived, an old address. It continued to occupy her life, and her heart. She missed her Polish friends, the games of bridge that sometimes stretched full days and into the night, interrupted only by a sandwich break, a glass of tea, or a shot of vodka. Though Adela made many new friends as an émigré, and the old ones never stopped writing, calling, and visiting, she felt a tremendous loss in leaving Poland permanently. "I too am dreaming about spending time with you, and I miss our nightly conversations in the dense fog of cigarette smoke," wrote Elwira Milewska-Zonn[38] in one of her letters to my mother.

My mother and Elwira worked together at the Polish Academy of Sciences and frequently corresponded after 1968. I remember Elwira and her husband visiting our home in Frankfurt in the early seventies and later too. She knew intimate details about Adela's life, and the closeness of such a friendship is perhaps best shown through personal correspondence. In Elwira's letter of December 1997, she wrote, "So, it is already January 17," alluding to the day of the *Todesmarsch* from Auschwitz-Birkenau in 1945. She made no other comment, except to wish Adela "all the sweetest," as if it were her birthday. In a way, it was.

Until her children became adults, my mother kept her memories from both her childhood and the Holocaust locked away. Only after she left the country of her birth did she begin to speak with any openness on these subjects. On one level, she likely wanted to escape the chaos of her past. (My father, who never opened up throughout his life, probably fit this category too.) On another, it seems certain that she wanted to make room for the new reality she hoped to experience in communist

---

[38] Mrs. Milewska-Zonn and her husband, Włodzimierz, coauthored children's books about astronomy. An internationally known astronomer, Mr. Zonn was director of the Space Observatory at the University of Warsaw. Both husband and wife were also remarkable educators.

Poland. Yet I am finally convinced that she also wished to shield us, her children, from the venom of the Nazi years. She may have done this only partly consciously, because trauma certainly accounted for most of her reticence, but she did it nonetheless. Though I never asked her about this subject explicitly, I know that she did not succeed in protecting Felek and me from her past. Once my brother and I knew more details about her experiences from the war, we adopted them as if they had been our own. I now wonder whether the bond between a child and a parent could leave room for a different reaction.

For the person leaving his or her country behind, certain terms can be applied—immigrant, exile, displaced person, refugee. More come to mind—dissident, political asylum seeker, defector, refusenik. In leaving Poland, Adela became an émigré, an expatriate, an exile, and a refugee all at once. Although she was never officially expelled from her country, the March 1968 government created a peril-filled climate that forced her to buy a one-way ticket elsewhere. When news of the firing of Jewish workers at all levels of employment hit the streets, and the Polish press began to run anti-Semitic content on its front pages, the unease turned to pressure. And when the Polish government began to openly sponsor anti-Semitism, this pressure prompted fear. On August 27, 1968, Adela, my brother, and I—my father stayed behind[39]—would be one of the first Jewish families to leave Poland. I never asked my mother what propelled her to act so swiftly, but today I can

_____

[39] The government explanation for my father's staying behind in Poland is connected to his position as a Bureau of Security official and to his knowledge of state secrets. I know, for example, that he was a chief investigator in a high-profile political case in which the Soviet government played a major role. In addition, he had access to the confidential personal files of various officials. Had he applied to emigrate with us, his request would certainly have been denied, and denial would thus have been extended to his immediate family members. I am compelled to believe that the official explanation was also the real one, given that the Polish authorities continued to turn down his request to leave the country for years to come.

speculate with ease. Most obviously, she knew the lessons of her past. She had been threatened, demeaned, and hunted during the war, and suddenly she had been thrust back to that mindset. The Polish government was nothing like the murderous Nazis, but suddenly the mood of the nation neared that of Poland in the late thirties. Intimidated and disoriented, Adela faced nightmares that evoked those of three decades before. At her core, my mother was a realist. She acted as rapidly as she did out of self-preservation, an instinct that for her had become second nature. As for the Polish government's cleansing of the nation's Jews and the accompanying media circus, this constituted a psychological pogrom unprecedented in postwar Europe.

Perhaps this is the right place to talk about Jews and their suitcases. From the first day of their arrival in Europe, sometime around the turn of the twelfth century, Jews kept a close eye on their suitcases. In virtually every European country, they have had a recurring dread of one day being forced out of their homes. The often repeated phrase "living on suitcases," signifies their transitory life, imposed by others. I myself relate to the theme, having endured the burden of immigration three times as a young man. Documentary photographs and video footage also vividly represent the pathos-filled connection between the Jew and his or her travel bag; recall, for example, the images of immigrants disembarking from ships at Ellis Island. The tattered valises fairly burst, not only with clothing but also with the intangibles: hopes, desires, and ambitions to make good on an uncertain future. But for my parents—and, in my opinion, for other Polish Jews of the postwar era as well—the notion of "living on suitcases" existed merely as a nostalgic reflection, a vestige from childhood and the war years. With communism—and particularly communist Poland, rising from the ashes of war—"living on suitcases" was supposed to be a thing of the past. This is why the phrase was never uttered in our home or in the homes of my parents' Jewish peers. Thus, their generation may have been the first in Europe to sit on something other than their suitcases; to feel entirely grounded. How fallacious their self-certainty turned out to be.

Kasztany at the entrance to the podwórko *at*
5b Chopin Street

Warsaw, circa 1966

Adela's travel document

Sixteen

Frankfurt via Israel

ON THE DAY OF OUR departure from Poland in August 1968, we knew we would never return. My mother was forty-six, my brother was twenty-one, and I was eighteen. On the platform at Warszawa-Gdański Station, numerous friends and family members had assembled to bid us good-bye. The crowd was augmented by Polish secret agents, who snooped around to see who had come, though I cannot imagine what they expected to find: Jewish sympathizers? Enemies of the state? The embraces were especially heartfelt that afternoon, and as the train shunted and began to chug forward, we found ourselves facing a gray, foggy unknown.

On that first leg of the journey bound for Austria, my father had joined us, knowing he would have to disembark before we reached the Czech border. In the compartment, my brother, mother, and I each had one suitcase along with a five-dollar bill in our pocket, the legal maximum permitted to an emigrant. As we rode, my father offered me a cigarette, a gesture that would have been unimaginable the day before, though I did not take him up on it. Once we reached the border, he got off the train and rode back to Warsaw.

The scene in Czechoslovakia made our journey feel all the more uncertain. Just seven days before, Soviet tanks had rolled into Prague, with Moscow looking to quell burgeoning rebellion. We had arrived at night, and with each passing station we saw Soviet soldiers guarding the platform, poised with their Kalashnikovs in firm grip, their eyes fixed on our train and on us. In the dim light, we were astounded to see graffiti on some buildings: "Russkis Go Home!" "Long Live Dubček!" "Freedom!" In Poland, such visible dissent would have been unthinkable, and I recall feeling a chill run down my spine. The next morning, on our arrival in Austria, we were awaited at the station by officials from the Sokhnut (the Israeli organization that helps absorb new immigrants) and my parents' friends.

We remained in Vienna for only a short time before continuing to our final destination, Israel. In those first few days in Austria, and perhaps even longer after that, we still hadn't grasped the fact that we had passed to the other side of the Iron Curtain. We knew only the place we had run away from and could feel no certainty about the place where we were headed. This uncertainty created a strain for us. Though we saw the fancy shops, shelves laden with merchandise, and the clean streets and well-maintained buildings—noting that even the vending machines worked (they never did in Warsaw)—we were too preoccupied with our overturned reality to fully take in this new landscape.

Had my mother had another choice, she would not have chosen Israel as our final destination. She had lived her whole life in Europe and could barely imagine adapting herself to the wilds of a fledgling Middle Eastern nation. Israel seemed to all of us distant and hot, and as Jews in communist Poland, we had come to feel at a remove from Zionism. We also couldn't help wondering if our move to Israel would prove Gomułka's claim that we did hold allegiance to two nations.

I remember our first bus ride together from Tel Aviv to Haifa on a very hot afternoon. My mother and I were standing at the Tel Aviv *Takhanah Mercazit* (central bus station), a noisy bedlam where buses and taxis sped in every which direction and street vendors hawked goods from blankets outstretched on the sidewalk. At the time, the most popular item was the transistor radio. In little rough-hewn shops around the station's perimeter, one could purchase coffee, sweets, sandwiches, and fresh-squeezed juice, still a fixture today in Israeli society.

A line had formed at the platform to board our bus, and there my mother and I waited patiently. But when the driver opened the door, the line splintered instantaneously as the passengers stormed onto the bus. We had no idea about the free-for-all that was Israeli society and continued to wait our turn, seeing from the numbers that there would be plenty of seats. Once we did reach the door, the driver, oblivious, slammed it in our faces, and I had to wave to get him to open up again. Doing so, he howled at us, "What are you waiting here for! Are you in line at the movies! Or would you rather get on the bus!" Disappointment mixed with pity in the look he gave us. Then, with the door ajar behind us, while we still stood on the stairs, he stepped on the gas. For my mother and me, it was a good thing the bus engineers had designed safety grips, or else we might have tumbled down the aisle before we even had a chance to remove our money and pay the fare. We hurried to the first seats available, sighing as we sat down. In 1968, the year after the Six-Day War triumph, young Israeli soldiers were looked upon as icons, and four or five eventually boarded our bus and seated themselves in the back. As they dozed off, their Uzis dropped to the floor. Every time the driver would apply the breaks, the guns would slide raucously on the metal floor to the front of the bus. Few passengers seemed to be bothered by this episode, especially since the guns would simply slide back down the aisle to the soldiers' feet when the driver accelerated.

For all our disorientation, Israel received us hospitably, offering us *ulpan* (an accelerated Hebrew class), a guaranteed spot at the university of our choice and scholarships for me and my brother (a privilege reserved for new immigrants), a financial allotment for an apartment, and even some basic furniture. Newcomers to the country were also entitled to tariff-free purchases of foreign-manufactured products, a point of envy for most Israelis who had to pay full price. And yet it was clear after a few months that my mother would not stay long in Israel.

The first seeds for Adela's return to Europe were actually planted on September 10, 1952, when, citing "unspeakable crimes committed in the name of the German people," German chancellor Konrad Adenauer signed the Luxembourg Agreement, committing Germany to reparations for Jewish Holocaust survivors. His counterpart was Israeli foreign minister Moshe Sharett, who would become Israel's second prime minister. Adenauer knew that if Germany were ever to regain any stature in the international community, the country would have to confront its past. By signing the agreements, he broke a seven-year official silence from his nation on the subject of the Holocaust. Over the next five decades, the Germans would pay a sum of more than 100 billion Deutschmarks (about sixty billion dollars) to some 500,000 Holocaust survivors.

There were, however, conditions for eligibility, including a ban on applications from citizens of communist countries. In any case, no legal representation existed for private claims in the Eastern bloc. This was partly why Adela started thinking about moving back to Europe. And once she began to consider her return, she never really thought again. A middle-aged European exile in Tel Aviv was not exactly an American in Paris. And according to the terms of the Luxembourg Agreement, Holocaust survivors would have to process their claim by the last day of 1969. This helped Adela confirm her plans to leave Israel.

She cleared out her apartment in Holon, where units had been constructed especially for the new immigrants, and settled all her outstanding accounts with the Israeli government. These included the loans granted to all new immigrants for airfare and various social services. On borrowed money, she traveled to

Germany in early spring of 1969 with the intention of settling in Frankfurt.

And here is where the inevitable question comes: Why Germany? Why not France, Italy, Sweden, or the United States? Why not stay in Israel? Adela would be confronted with this question incessantly, both before she left Israel and after she had made her home in Frankfurt, and it always made her uneasy. To move to Germany caused enough internal distress on its own, but to have to deal with the question aloud felt even worse.

Aside from the financial incentive, Adela had specific reasons for choosing Frankfurt. One was her proficiency in German. Another was that she had acquaintances in the city. Frankfurt was a crossroads for travelers—both legal and illegal—en route from Poland and points east, and many people who had been effectively expelled from Poland in 1968 now made their home there. If Adela craved anything, it was some of the contentment she had known in Warsaw just a few years prior.

Immediately upon her arrival in Frankfurt, she rented a small room from an older widow. She did not stay long, though, moving temporarily to the home of Stefan Orlean and his wife, Rózia, whom Adela knew from Niwka. Just after her arrival, Stefan arranged for a job for her as well as a small studio apartment on 151 Raimundstrasse. In 1970, I joined my mother in Frankfurt, and we continued to live in that little room for a full two years.

The job that the Orleans had arranged for Adela, her first in Frankfurt, was as a waitress at an *Imbiss,* a hot dog stand in the heart of Frankfurt's busiest shopping area, known as the Zeil. Later she recounted that, on her first day of work, she returned home so exhausted that she fell to the floor the moment the door closed behind her. The first two nights after working at the *Imbiss,* she slept on that floor, fully clothed, until morning came and she had to rise again. Fortunately for Adela, she was alone in the house during these two days of fatigue because the Orleans had gone on vacation abroad. Eventually she got used to the physical demands of her work routine.

The owner of the stand was a landsman who had immigrated to Germany some twenty years before Adela. A rather simplistic man, he insisted that Adela eat her lunch daily at the stand, offering a 30 percent discount as a perk. At first, she adapted to the owner's crude manner, having no other options for decent work without a permit. It went without saying that she earned a low wage with no benefits of any kind, including health insurance and vacation or sick days. But an incident soon showed the arrangement to be untenable. One day when Adela asked for an hour off from work, the owner began to complain rather volubly, with no regard for the diners around him. According to Stefan Orlean, Adela responded with a volley of pointed retorts that left the owner speechless as she gathered her belongings and headed home. In hearing this story, I realized for the first time that my mother was capable of losing her temper.

After she walked away from the *Imbiss,* Adela took on a string of odd jobs, a reflection of the struggles of any new immigrant. The first was as an inventory assistant at Pelikan's warehouse, a storeroom for office supplies located in a Frankfurt suburb. Unlike her inflexible former supervisor, the boss at this position treated her protectively from the get-go. He forbade her from lifting heavy boxes, even though she worked at a warehouse. But the commute was lengthy and tiring, and six months later she moved to a job as a data-entry clerk at an area bank.

Into the mid-1970s, Frankfurt remained a center, as well as a passage point, for migration from the Eastern bloc countries. The city also attracted a growing influx of foreign guest workers (*Gastarbeiter*) from Turkey, Italy, Greece, and Yugoslavia. From Poland, immigrants both Jewish and gentile included lawyers, journalists, television professionals, writers, movie producers, doctors, poets, hotel managers, and even a restaurant consultant whom I remember in particular. These people had once been respected professionals, comfortable enough

212

economically and enmeshed in their social circles. Many of them had been an active part of the larger wheel that constituted Polish society. But now, like Adela, they all lived at a subsistence level. Sadly, it was not the promise of equality under Polish socialism that placed these people on a common level, but their shared desperation for survival on foreign soil. Among the elite in communist Poland, position, education, and intellectual acumen were valued, material possessions scorned. Now these émigrés had nothing, not even their former status to back them up.

It may well be a European phenomenon that émigrés of the same ethnic community choose a particular café to make their own. In the late sixties and early seventies in Frankfurt, that café for Polish Jews was Café Opera. There, sitting at tables and draped in cigarette smoke, newcomers to the city would seek advice from fellow displaced countrymen who had arrived earlier than they had. The new arrivals were eager for pointers on work opportunities, attorneys, doctors, and places to stay. Just to speak in Polish provided enormous solace, especially in a country where these individuals would have to assimilate by speaking the language of their recent persecutors.

Ultimately such émigrés settled for unmeaningful jobs that paid little, lived in cramped quarters, solicited the help of friends and acquaintances, and "huddled" with fellow exiles. They all knew what the world war had already taught them: there is no darker, more depressing loneliness than that of an exile. (For some, when their state of mind became unendurable, the only answer was suicide.)

Of these newcomers to Frankfurt, a good number passed through Adela's studio apartment. Some even lived with us for a few weeks. During their visits, the place felt crowded and uncomfortable, and my mother and I had little time to ourselves. Sometimes our guest would be a friend of a neighbor from Warsaw, other times a relative of someone who happened to know my mother from an episode of her past. At times entire families stayed the night. Like exiles all over the world, they had no place to go, and often someone new would be waiting in the stairway for hours until Adela returned home. Their needs ranged from a place to stay for the night to advice on getting a lawyer to information on who that month was hiring workers without a permit. Often they needed supper. Before bedtime, we would move our two chairs and the small round table to the corner of the room so that they could sleep on the floor. One night when I got up to use the bathroom, I accidentally stepped on somebody's hand or leg because there was so little space in which to maneuver. Later, when we moved to a two-bedroom apartment near the center of the city, we felt like kings. To us, the place was huge.

At the end of 1971, my mother received her first reparations payment. As she opened the envelope, her hands trembled so violently that I took it away from her and opened it myself, before handing it back.

"What is it?" I asked.
"It's about the money for my parents—your grandmother and grandfather." (She would never say "grandparents." Lumping her mother and father together felt somehow dishonest to her.) "It's the *Wiedergutmachung* [reparations]."

The accompanying note identified the check as compensation for the loss of her parents' fabric shop during World War II, for her own lost years of education, and finally for the death of her parents at the Auschwitz gas chambers. To receive a payoff for the murder of her parents was a sickening thought, explaining why some in the Israeli establishment opposed the premise of the Luxembourg Agreement in the first place. Menachem Begin famously wondered, "Who ever heard of some of the murdered going to the murderer for compensation?" And my mother herself asked me a number of times whether I thought it were right to accept the money. She couldn't help thinking that Fishel and Rózia were worth more to the Germans dead than alive.

What I remember most about that night was how my grandmother and my grandfather came alive like never before. Chaim, Moniek, and Hala were there too. My mother had told me about her family before, but she had always done so sporadically and with unease. But that night she told stories until the morning hours. This was when she told me about her father's buried jar of gold coins and her refusal to try and locate it. And a few tales of how Moniek would fool the Gestapo by dressing up as a wealthy Polish landowner. She told me where Rózia used to keep the herring that she bought for the Sabbath dinner, and about Marcyna, the stern-faced water-carrier who once lost her wits after she dropped the water buckets and tumbled backward down the stairwell. A few stories about Auschwitz entered into that night's conversation too. We did not go to sleep that night. We didn't feel tired. That night, sleeping didn't seem appropriate.

Seventeen

Returns from the East

I REMEMBER MY FATHER as an exceptionally strong man, though one would never deduce this from his slender physique. Born in the town of Kutno, 125 kilometers west of Warsaw, he was the second-youngest sibling of three brothers and four sisters. He hardly knew his mother, who died when he was thirteen. Though Jewish in name, the Jachimowicz family practiced little of the Gutermans' observant ways. Michał's father was a shoemaker more preoccupied with feeding his seven children than passing on Jewish custom and law. That left room for plenty of other influences. Under the guidance of his older brother, Bronek, Michał became riveted by communism in his boyhood. His experience working at a paper mill must also have contributed to his enthusiasm for the proletarian cause. In September of 1938, just as he turned nineteen, he was charged with communist conspiracy and incarcerated at Bereza Kartuska, an internment camp notorious for prisoner mistreatment where most inmates were dubbed

217

enemies of the state. At the time, that designation included communists and antifascists. Michał, one of the youngest political prisoners to serve time at the institution,[40] wasn't the first member of the Jachimowicz family to be locked up there. A few months earlier, his brother had been released after serving a two-year sentence, also for communist conspiracy.

The time Michał spent in the penitentiary would be the most violent in his youth, and perhaps his entire life. This was so in part because the prison housed both political prisoners and common criminals, a combustible mix. In defending himself and his comrades against the nonpolitical inmates, Michał—according to Bronek—would sometimes get embroiled in vicious physical fights. Michał's release came two months before the Germans invaded Poland, when the authorities set all the inmates free.

A few weeks after his release from prison, Michał crossed into Belarus to probe the prospects for survival in the Soviet Union. Judging the situation to be decent, he returned home to Włocławek, where his family had moved from Kutno several years earlier, and he led them on a four-hundred-mile voyage east to the Soviet Union, just as the German forces closed in on Warsaw. His family would remain in the Soviet Union for the duration of the war, though almost never as a unit. All would survive except his father, who died in Tashkent after receiving an overdose of quinine intended to treat a case of malaria. Like Adela, Michał was no novice to hunger or to dehumanization. During his years in the Soviet Union, especially in Uzbekistan, he and the rest of his family faced famine for prolonged periods. As a child, I remember my father at the table, eating rapidly and swallowing large mouthfuls of food without chewing much. Somewhere in his distant memory, the

---

[40] A collection of documents and depositions of former inmates, *Bereziacy* (Książka i Wiedza, Warsaw, 1965), lists Michał Jachimowicz (Prisoner No. 1776) as a member of the KZMP (Polish Communist Youth Organization). His older brother, Bronek Jachimowicz (Prisoner No. 666), is listed as a member of the KPP (Polish Communist Party).

apparition of hunger trailed him; he could never be entirely sure that tomorrow there would be something to eat.

Immediately after the war, Michał returned to Poland with a fellow officer and friend, Leon Winiawski. Together they worked for the Repatriation Bureau in Dziedzice, tracking new entries into the country. It was at the bureau, in spring of 1945, that Michał met Adela for the first time. She was twenty-two, he twenty-five. The war had left Michał with not only the usual psychological baggage that results from combat, but also with two shrapnel fragments, which would remain lodged in his flesh for the rest of his life.

When he met Adela, Michał had already been married once before. That marriage had failed during the war, and almost certainly because of the war. He had also lost an infant daughter to starvation thirty-four days after her birth. At the time, his wife and two sisters were living in Tashkent, a city ravaged by famine. Because her malnourished body had failed to produce breast milk, she fed her daughter water and tea, which led to the child's death. At the time, Michał was working as a *kochiegar*[41] at a sugar plant near Kuybyshev several hundred miles away. If the marriage hadn't been doomed for whatever other wartime reasons, this lack of contact did it in for good.

I am looking at the very first photograph of my parents together, taken in 1945 at the Repatriation Bureau. At the time, they were not yet a couple. In a dimly lit office, my father stands beside Adela, who is seated at a desk. He appears to be dictating a letter, which she types out dutifully. In the pose, they both look slightly tense. Though Michał wears his Polish army uniform, I cannot make out his rank. Around his waist is a broad, menacing gun belt secured by a thinner leather strap that runs diagonally across his shoulder. For all I know, the letter he is dictating outlines progress in securing new Polish borders. Just as likely, it could be a report about the injuries

---

[41] A laborer who shovels coal into a large, industrial oven, usually a boiler.

219

sustained by his comrade Leon Winiawski in fighting Polish insurgents, opponents of communism who supported the government-in-exile in Great Britain. Michał holds something in his right hand, which I can only assume to be a cigarette butt. In the photograph, my father looks very slim, and his cheeks are sunken. Where others might have bags under their eyes, my father's eyes display shallow depressions. If I didn't know his physique better, I might guess that my father, not Adela, had returned from a Nazi concentration camp.

In another of the few post–World War II photographs of my parents, this one taken in 1947, they sit next to each other, with Michał's arm resting on Adela's shoulder. Adela's smile is profound and contains equal parts pride and reassurance. It is one of the rare instances of her smiling in a photograph, and I can only recall a few instances in my life when I saw her exude the joy conveyed in this photograph. Maybe this expression reflected the inner feeling of love—along with respect, affection, security, and most important to her, loyalty—that had been nearly impossible to experience during the war. This peace of mind may have been all the deeper because, a few months before, she had given birth to my brother, Felek. After the war, a doctor had told her no former Auschwitz inmate could conceive a child, a dream Adela had long nurtured. (Hence the formal name Felicjan, "bearer of happiness," though my grandfather's name Fishel may have been part of the inspiration too.)

What attracted Adela to Michał as a life partner? One factor was surely the sincerity of his belief in communism and his vision of a grander world. As Adela's sister, Hala, and her husband stood on the train platform in 1950, set to emigrate to Israel, Michał was beside himself: "You are making a big mistake!" he cried. "The communists will soon be here." In 1952, he made the same plea as Gucia Mandelbaum and her family embarked for the same destination. Michał would tout Lenin's assurance that "Ultimately, the victory of socialism over capitalism on the world's scale [will be] ascertained fully and unconditionally." And he believed with fervor in the central line of the Communist Party anthem, the "Internationale": "He who was nothing will become everything." While survivors of the war from Adela's family were planning to start businesses, earn money, and escape anti-Semitism once and for all, Michał maintained his focus on the virus of materialism, the evils of worker exploitation, and Poland as a true fatherland. Sticking to the communist motto, he argued that in a short time religion would no longer matter. Yet, like Adela, he recognized the imperfections of existing communist regimes and seriously resented figures like Stalin and Poland's postwar leader Bolesław Bierut.

Michał's courageous and masculine sensibility must also have appealed to Adela. Once, at an officers' ball, he even fought to defend her honor. The story goes that Adela had accepted a Soviet officer's offer to dance but that as the dance commenced, the officer's hands crept down into inappropriate positions. Such a crude act was not uncommon at an officers' ball, where most attendees—especially the men—were invariably drunk and getting drunker. But Adela resisted his moves, and attempted to right the course of his hands. During this fateful dance, Michał was having a drink with a colleague on the veranda adjacent to the dance floor. As this fellow officer surveyed the dance floor, he gestured with his eyes to indicate Adela's discomfort. Only a few seconds later, the Soviet officer was on the floor with a bloody nose, and Michał and Adela had been spirited out of the building by Michał's friends. This all happened so quickly that the Soviet casualty could not register who had struck him.

On Michał's part the assault was a bold move. To knock down a Soviet officer carried grave risks, perhaps life-threatening ones. At the close of the war, the Soviets had full control in Poland, and in military circles they were not afraid to exercise their authority. Any attack against an individual could be interpreted as an insult to the entire system. Luckily for Michał, only his friends knew the whole story, and they would never snitch on a fellow comrade. For Adela's part, she was probably half-amused, half-flattered by the incident. Certainly no man had ever gone to physical blows to win her affection. In the end, for better or worse, it seems to have helped his case.

Another trait Adela must have admired in Michał—and which I myself considered his most impressive quality—was his complete detachment from material things. This lack of materialism was complemented by his utter selflessness. Michał's sisters and brothers used to remark that he would take the last shirt from his back to give to someone who did not have one. In this sense, Michał was quite similar to Paweł Jaworski. Had it been my father to spot Adela and Henia on that Kościuszko Park bench in August of 1943, I am sure the story's outcome would have been much the same.

People who socialized with my parents admired Adela, greatly enjoying her company. She was socially adept and made friends with ease. (Some of the male friends felt an attraction to her.) With her remaining family members too, Adela felt an abiding comfort. Those family members treated her adoringly, as if she were royalty. In addition, she was the type of person who had no trouble taking charge of a situation. Michał, on the other hand, could sometimes keep to himself. This inner-directedness tormented him, and Adela considered it a sign of an inferiority complex and a weakness.

I do not know if my father's few affairs with other women constituted his direct answer to living in her shadow, or simply his response to irresistible opportunities. But I do remember an incident from the summer of 1963, when my mother found out about one of his escapades and made quite a scene. Though the fight took place inside their room with the doors closed, I could hear every word. And though I was too young to grasp all the nuances of that eruption, I understood enough to know she was deeply hurt. "What did I do to deserve this?" she kept repeating. Their quarrel upset me deeply too, in part because it represented the first time when my basic sense of security had been shaken. Out of revenge, I even plotted to run away, though I never carried out my plan. Since the day of that blowup, my parents' relationship grew chillier and—apart from a few upswells in warmth—was never the same.

Something must also be said about my father's smoking habit. Though my mother herself smoked, Michał chain-smoked in a way that most of us would find almost repulsive. Adela used to say that my father "doesn't simply smoke cigarettes, he swallows them." (I myself used to feel that every time he inhaled, the cigarette was actually inhaling a piece of him.) My father's smoking habit was so poisonous, neighbors would joke that mosquitoes had piled up a half-meter high outside our windows, having dropped dead on their way to infest our home. That explained why we needed no mosquito flap. And in the mid-seventies, when we lived in Frankfurt, a friend teased my mother that she should replace her white drapes with yellow ones—they would turn yellow anyway from the smoke within a week of being washed.

Józek Krakowski

In 1969, each member of our family was living in a different country. I was studying in Jerusalem, and my brother, having come down with a severe illness, had moved to Basel, Switzerland, where his doctor said the climate would be more suitable for his recovery. Already divorced from my father, Adela had by then moved back to Frankfurt. Though the Polish authorities had imposed the divorce in exchange for my mother's travel document, my parents had wanted it for the obvious personal reasons. (The document, known as a *titre de voyage,* was not a passport and allowed the traveler a single one-way border crossing.)

Józek Krakowski entered the picture in spring of 1970. He and my mother met at the Café Opera in Frankfurt. Like Adela, Józek was a refugee from Poland. But unlike Adela's ex-husband, he was gregarious and outgoing in nature, full of humor and joie de vivre. He had a contagiously open personality that earned him many friends, myself included. He was also generous, always ready to come to the aid of a fellow émigré in need. I remember how he would make the rounds from table to table at the Café Opera soliciting funds—whatever the cafe-goers could contribute—for a fellow émigré who couldn't pay his rent, or who needed money for a lawyer.

Now, like many of his fellow refugees, Józek struggled to make ends meet in Germany, accepting whatever job came his way. But he had once been a person of consequence in the postwar Polish government, and an ardent communist. Before the war, this devotion cost him years in prison, including a stint in 1936 in the same cell as Władysław Gomułka. That relationship with Gomułka, which began as one of mutual brotherhood, would eventually crumble into disharmony. By 1956, Józek, who fought in the war in several Polish units including the Anders Army, had already grown disillusioned with the Polish Politburo when Gomułka offered him the cabinet-level position of transportation minister. Józek declined, accusing Gomułka of "surrounding yourself with disloyal people, the same people who had helped imprison you in 1948." Gomułka, who could be set off by even the minutest expression of dissent, responded with a display of rage.

Later that year, when the person ultimately named transportation minister requested that Józek turn in a list of all Jewish employees at the national tourism agency, ORBIS, which he headed, Józek turned in only his own name, adding, "I don't hire people based on their ethnicity." Gomułka was so infuriated by this act of insubordination that he jailed Józek without being able to produce a charge. For months, government prosecutors tried to dredge up charges against Józek on which to base a trial, but they found only evidence of his impeccable character, and he was ultimately released.

In the time they spent together, Józek's presence helped ease my mother's strain from having returned to a nation where less than thirty years before the Nazis had held power, where the faces of her persecutors never stopped haunting her. He repeatedly proposed that they move in together, and she repeatedly declined.

Michał Jachimowicz, 1972

Life was not easy for Michał after his family left Poland, and daily existence included deflating ironies. One was that, shortly after our departure, Michał had relocated from our apartment on Chopin Street to a one-room flat away from the city center, on Mordechaj Anielewicz Street. It happened to be the site of the Warsaw Ghetto during the Second World War. From his window, he could see the monument to the heroes of the famed ghetto uprising. This provided a blunt reminder, every time he looked out the window, that once again Jews were no longer welcome in Poland. And Michał was not spared. In an article published in the monthly army newspaper, *Żołnierz Wolności* (Soldier of Freedom), under the headline "They Left but Didn't Surrender," my father was accused of "riding roughshod" over the Polish nation. With most of his friends and his immediate family now living elsewhere, Michał felt a cosmic loneliness. In a letter to me in May of 1970, he wrote: "The pain of loneliness is well known to me. I know the meaning of four empty walls."

In autumn of 1971, my mother met with Michał in Budapest. Adela had emigrated from Poland three years before, and in the interim, he had attempted time and again to persuade the Polish government to let him go as well, but all his efforts had been in vain. By early 1971, my father had already known that a legal way out of Poland was not in his near future. Now, he pleaded with her not only to help him leave Poland but also to take him back as her husband once they had succeeded. Adela was ambivalent and apprehensive. To help him out of Poland was one thing, but to restart a life together when so much had marred their former marriage was asking a lot. Was their marriage not over? At the time, they had been separated for a few years, and though adapting to life in Germany hadn't been easy, she had managed in her own way to settle down. While battling poor health, Adela earned enough money even to send financial help to Michał on occasion.

I do not know exactly what prompted her to agree to his offer, but she did. She still must have felt something for her ex-husband and empathized with his loneliness, his melancholy at having to live away from his family. Also, despite the strains in their relationship over the years, my mother and father shared an underlying love for one another, complemented by tolerance and respect, that could be awakened from dormancy. I perceived this affection until their last days, no matter how irritated or angry they might be on the surface.

Michał was prone to depression, and Adela had always been a rescuer of those in need. She herself knew as well as anyone the effects of isolation. When my parents met in Budapest, my father was indeed fighting depression, a case that had begun to affect him not long after we left Poland. In early 1969, Esia (Viola) Wein,[42] Uncle Adam's daughter, had run into Michał in the street in Warsaw. She recalled that he had lost much weight and wore a miserable expression. Together they sat at the Café Bristol, and he attempted to persuade Esia to leave Poland in the following way: "Esia, see how I look? Do you want to look like me? I can promise you that you will be lonely as a dog, and all your friends who promise you miracles today will abandon you to your ill fate, and you will have nobody to talk to."

Our family's dispersion had a disquieting effect on all of us, including my brother and me, but I think it hit my mother hardest—she who had been riven from her family and friends so many times before. Perhaps she felt that the time had come for our family to enjoy a little bit of wholeness, and unity. In one of her letters to Michał, she wrote:

> *I know the weight of your loneliness, but believe me, neither I nor the children enjoy the sweetness of life because of it. I have absolutely no idea how long it will take until you will be together with us—our sons miss you very, very much, and I don't know for whom I should feel sorry first: you, them, or in the end, myself. Forgive me that this letter is a*

---

[42] Today, Viola is a writer living in Israel.

bit sad, but such a long separation doesn't call for a happy disposition.

To forgive and to forget was one of the central qualities of Adela's humanity. Now, out of a sense of righteousness and perhaps also a sense of duty, she once again embarked on a rescue mission.

With the Cold War then at its height, the Berlin Wall would separate the East from the West of Europe for another eighteen years. The security was tight and punishments for illegal trespassers harsh. But smuggling operations had always been Adela's specialty. And once she decided on a course of action, she could not be stopped. As in the years of the German occupation, Adela planned the operation to save Michał on her own. Only this time, she did not begin on the defense—she launched the attack herself. As the manager of a discotheque in Frankfurt (yet another odd job), she was known as Frau Chefin ("Mrs. Boss") or Frau Irene. It was a boisterous club, frequented by members of the Frankfurt underworld. In addition to performing the ordinary duties of a discotheque manager, Adela would break up fights and rein in drunks and teenage hoodlums, with help from the club bouncer. For me and many others, it was bizarre to observe her in such a position, but patrons respected her authority without question. In any dispute, her word was final. Aside from the job's strange points, it made for a decent enough place to meet up with old acquaintances. On many occasions, she would find herself seated at the bar with a friend or relative who had come to visit from Poland, Israel, or the United States. These guests recoiled from the pounding beat of the music and complained constantly, yet they stayed to talk—and they returned without fail.

It was in this discotheque that her plan to rescue Michał was born. From a few of her shadier clients, she enlisted help in drawing up a blueprint. These associates were unsavory enough that they couldn't tell Adela exactly how they earned their living, and she was wise enough not to inquire. Adela had arranged for an agent to provide Michał with falsified documents while she worked out the other details, including finances, which would not be simple. The price tag for the documents plus the operational tasks exceeded what our family could afford. So for the next few weeks, my mother called more or less everyone she knew, family and friends, until she had gathered enough funds to go ahead with the plan.

It was in West Berlin in November 1971 on a gray, rainy day when stage one was enacted. A light wind blew, the type that chills you to the bone long after you return to the warmth of your living room; in other words, a typical early winter day in central Europe. Adela and my brother, Felek, had just crossed the checkpoint to East Berlin at Friedrichsstrasse, better known as Checkpoint Charlie. They were en route to meet Michał to discuss the details of his escape, also to have him sign falsified passport and visa forms and to get his photograph, to be placed in the passport a few months hence. Adela hid the passport against her stomach, secured by the elastic of her underwear, and carried the visa forms in her purse.

During this first stage of the mission, everything proceeded without incident. Having arrived in East Berlin from Warsaw the day before, Michał stood waiting for Adela and Felek at the checkpoint exit. For the entire day the three walked through the streets and talked over every detail of the plan. Fearing they could be overheard, they dared not risk sitting down in a restaurant or coffee house. After all, this was the German Democratic Republic (GDR), with its oppressive and paranoid government that distrusted everything and everybody. Heavily armed border patrol agents were taught to view travelers as belonging to one of two categories: the West or the East. Western travelers were to be treated as potential spies, Eastern travelers as defectors. As a veteran of the Polish Security Bureau, Michał knew the eavesdropping methods used in the Eastern bloc as well as anyone, but the GDR's secret security service was undisputedly the best among those behind the Iron Curtain.

Shortly before Adela and Felek returned to West Berlin (visitors from the West were not allowed to stay overnight in East Berlin), all three of them stopped at the hotel where Michał had spent the previous night. There he gave them a suitcase loaded with Polish delicatessen items, a couple of furniture catalogs, and a leather jacket for Felek. After an emotional good-bye, Adela and Felek reentered the border checkpoint, hoping not to be searched on their way back to the West. As she had done in the morning, Adela held the passport with Michał's signature and his unattached photograph against her stomach, and she carried a signed but otherwise blank Romanian visa application in her purse. In Felek's charge was the suitcase, which now contained the jacket, food, and furniture catalogs.

They entered the checkpoint building and found themselves in a poorly lit room, standing before a long wooden table. Two male border patrol officers in green uniforms conducted the document checks. Although not finding anything of interest in Felek's possession, they ordered Adela into a nearby cabin for a strip search. A female border officer watched as Adela disrobed garment by garment. At the same time, the officer became distracted as she glanced over the emptied contents of Adela's purse, perusing her address book, which had scores of names from all over the globe. Seizing the chance to act, Adela slipped the passport from her underwear into her purse, which sat empty and wide open with all its other contents scattered over the table. By a miracle, the guard didn't notice, nor had she shown interest in the other contents of the purse, including the smuggled documents.

Though my mother was a gentle woman of mild disposition, she could draw upon vast reserves of inner strength in times of peril, and this has always astounded me. Anyone who has read even a little about the passage to and from the Eastern bloc knows that had Adela been caught, she would have spent many years in a German prison. Considering what she had already been through, this was a fate she probably could not have withstood.

Shortly after the Berlin meeting, I was dispatched to Bucharest to scout the train border crossings into Germany, Austria, Yugoslavia, and Romania. I was instructed to check how each country's agents inspected passports, what type of stamps and paperwork were required, how many checkpoints were to be cleared, and other such details. Even today, I am not sure if what I observed prompted my mother and her coconspirators to switch to a plan B. Instead of an escape through Romania, Michał would travel through Budapest. This new plan would also eliminate the need to cross the Yugoslavian border, and it would substantially reduce the need for falsified visas.

On a peaceful morning in Frankfurt in August of 1972, two men and one woman, all of middle age and posing as German tourists, boarded a train bound for Budapest. The three passengers did not let on to knowing each other, and traveled in separate cabins of the same car. When they happened to cross paths in the corridor while taking a break to stretch and have a cigarette, they would exchange pleasantries as if encountering a stranger. In late evening of the next day, each of the three passengers rode a separate taxi to the same hotel. Once they had checked in—still separately of course—the two men left for dinner, both heading to the same restaurant. The woman, Adela, went to a different restaurant, where she found Michał enshrouded in his customary plume of cigarette smoke.

The next evening, Adela and Michał met at the same café. This time, however, the two men also showed up, though they sat at a separate table. Periodically each of the four conspirators would glance at his or her watch as though expecting somebody. After a while, one of the two men rose from his table and headed for the restroom. Immediately after his return, his partner made his own trip to the restroom, where he removed a passport from behind one of the fixtures. From his pocket he took a small metal tool with which he extracted the photograph from the document and replaced it with that of Michał. A perfect fit, Michał's photograph had a matching portion of the stamp on it. When the second agent had returned from the bathroom, having completed his work, it was Michał's cue to rise. Once in the stall, he unfastened an envelope taped to the back face of the toilet and placed it into the side pocket of his jacket. That evening, Adela and Michał were the last couple to leave the restaurant.

The next afternoon, Adela, Michał, and one of the agents met on the train bound for Frankfurt. The second agent stayed behind at the hotel. On the ride, they sat in the same car, but silently, pretending at first not to know one another. For the duration of the trip Michał repeatedly glanced at the passport, and to himself whispered his new name along with every other identifying detail. My mother later told me that on that train ride, he had smoked enough cigarettes "to kill not only one but a whole herd of elephants."

Just before the train reached the Hungarian-Austrian border, the travelers sprinkled vodka onto their clothing and placed three glasses, some food, and the half-empty bottle on the table. The plan was to appear drunk, if not actually to be a little tipsy, the best way they knew to diffuse the palpable tension. Michał sat in the corner seat, feigning a nap. While still on the Hungarian side, the train came to a halt, the door to their compartment swung open, and two Hungarian border officers stretched out their hands for passports. The officers appeared relaxed, even bored, and the travelers hoped to display similar nonchalance. But inside they quaked. As the guards left, taking the passports with them according to regular procedure, all three reached for the vodka bottle in concert, emptying it in little time. When the border officers reentered the cabin, Adela and her agent were talking to each other in German. One guard shined his flashlight at Michał's face, just to make sure the drowsy fellow in the corner matched the photo on the passport. In the end the passports were returned without any questions.

A few minutes had passed when all three passengers felt that gentle lift we all experience when a train has jolted forward. Only for them, this was no fleeting sensation. With every inch traveled, as the train slowly gained speed, their hearts grew lighter and lighter. Ten minutes later the train stopped, but on the Austrian side of the border. Even if his ruse were now to be discovered, Michał knew that he would never return to Poland again.

Almost four years to the day after their farewell in Warsaw, Michał arrived in Frankfurt carrying a German passport. The name of the agent who accompanied them was Ignac G., a regular at Adela's discotheque and a person without whom the plan would never have gone off. A day later, an unfortunate German tourist reported his stolen passport to the German embassy in Budapest. Before heading to make the report, he had placed a phone call to Adela. "It's okay, we arrived safely," I heard her whispering into the handset.

When my father arrived from Poland in 1972, Adela was still working as manager at the discothèque. With saved and partially borrowed money, the two of them took over a small gift shop near the busy central railroad station. It wasn't the fanciest neighborhood in the city, but the steady flow of *Gastarbeiter*, immigrants, and tourists, together with hard work, helped them eke out a living.

In 1975, my brother, Felek, and his wife, Joanna, immigrated with their infant daughter, Tamara, to the United States. Three years later, my wife, Ora, and I followed them, along with our daughter Norah, then seven months old.

After suffering a minor heart attack in 1985, Adela was diagnosed with a serious heart condition, with her doctors recommending at least two bypasses. At the time, open-heart surgery was a new technique in Europe, still under development and very risky. Few hospitals were even equipped to undertake the procedure. But neither the doctors nor Adela saw a better option, and my parents traveled to Genolie, a small town near Geneva, Switzerland, for her to be operated on. By the procedure's conclusion, four bypasses had been performed. Just a few hours after Adela had been moved out of the intensive care unit, she suffered a massive heart attack. Surely she would not have survived had she not already been in the hospital.

As for my father, he used to say, "I'd rather live a few years less than give up the pleasure of smoking." And his life was almost certainly cut short by his habit. In 1987, he was diagnosed with lung cancer, and his doctor gave him half a year to live, at most. On hearing this news, my mother immediately sold the gift shop to tend to him. Under her care, he lived another five years. He was never confined to a bed and didn't even bother to quit smoking. In fact, he died while smoking a cigarette.

On December 30, 1997, in a festively decorated hall near Tel Aviv, Adela celebrated her seventy-fifth birthday. With a glass of champagne in her hand, she was just about to deliver a short speech when she was felled by what would be a fatal heart attack. Her long-standing battle with heart disease had reached its final stage. The next morning as I stood at her bedside, she made an unequivocal gesture that she wanted to die. Her eyes begged for my help. In the days that followed, though half her body was paralyzed, she repeated the gesture a few more times, showing the superhuman resolve that always guided her when any life—her own or someone's else's—was at stake. On the morning of her birthday party, she had already felt her hours to be numbered. "I will be glad if I live to the end of today," she had told Henia.

Adela's condition worsened rapidly, and she died ten minutes before midnight on January 27, 1998, only a short time after a medical transport plane flew her from Tel Aviv to

Frankfurt, and fifty-three years to the day after Auschwitz was liberated.

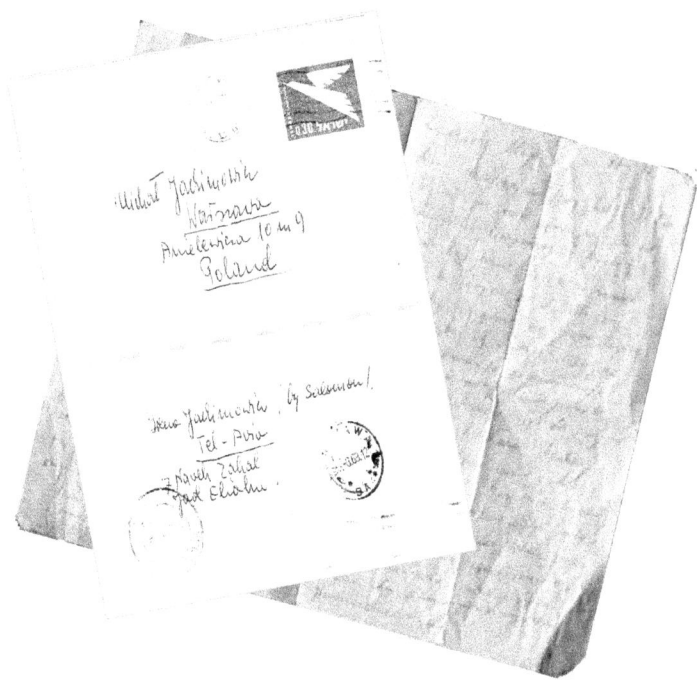

But whoever sees my mother
in a purple smock in a white hospital
trembling
stiffening
with a wooden smile
and white gums

her face is like a large smudged tear
she clasps her hands like a frightened
little girl
her lips are blue

but whoever sees my mother
a hounded little animal
with a bulging eye

—Tadeusz Różewicz

Epiloge

Silence

AMONG THE LONG-TERM responses of Holocaust survivors, the most common has been silence. This was so with my mother, who did not speak to us about her experiences until two decades after they took place. In the public mind, at least a couple of ideas have taken hold to explain this silence. One is that survivors remained silent out of shame over their inability to resist. A second idea has to do with Poland in particular, where Jews were said to accept jobs in the postwar government on the condition that they would not seek revenge on former Nazis or collaborators. While these ideas are strongly believed by many to this day, I believe that both were driven by political agendas of various forces, not truth. The early Israelis, for example, wanted to distance themselves from their supposedly passive European relatives. In doing so, they turned away from meaningful and effective acts of resistance from Jews across Europe, wounding the memory of their brothers in the process.

It is only fair to measure wartime Jewish resistance against the activities of other nations and ethnicities under similar circumstances. In my opinion, Jewish resistance during World War II was remarkable; after all, many Jews in the postwar Polish government did take revenge, often mercilessly.[43] We must not forget that, for Jews, fighting meant choosing how to die, not how to survive. Along these lines, I consider it unfortunate that World War II literature largely omits Jewish soldiers' participation in various Polish units—such as the Anders Army and forces under the command of Wanda Wasilewska[44]—along with the Red Army and armies of other nations. These soldiers, almost exclusively, fought not for the purpose of liberating Poland or any other country but rather to defeat the Nazis. At the cemetery where Polish soldiers who fell at the famed battle of Monte Cassino in Italy are buried, many headstones bear Stars of David. In my view, the poppies at the site drink not only "Polish blood," as the famous song goes, but Jewish blood as well.[45]

I would like to discuss the topic of silence in greater detail, but this book is not the place. I will, however, attribute Adela's silence to two factors. The first, as noted earlier in the book, was to shield Felek and me from her past. If there was one thing she didn't want, it was for her two children to absorb her experience of war and thereby somehow relive it. The second explanation is the more forceful of the two: it took my mother twenty-some years to open up about the Holocaust because she simply had not worked through the trauma that had consumed her psyche. All manner of studies show that it can take decades to process the trauma inflicted by events such as the Holocaust. Indeed many victims never came to terms with it at all. This helps explain why most testimonies from Holocaust survivors, such as those produced by the Shoah Foundation, were recorded decades after the war. This time frame also applies to films, documentary reenactments, monuments, and museums, most of which were

---

[43] For more on this subject, see the chapter "Fire" in Melvin Konner's *Unsettled: An Anthropology of the Jews.*

[44] The First Army of the Polish Armed Forces, aka the Kościuszko Army.

[45] Reference is being made to the famous Polish song "*Czerwone maki pod Monte Cassino*," about the bloody World War II battle also known as the Battle for Rome.

created in the last thirty-five years. And most books about the Holocaust were written after 1965.

The Story Untold

Though many individuals shared a common destiny during the Holocaust, each story is unique to the point that, apart from the obvious suffering, one can identify only a few parallel threads. Two prisoners in the same camp, living in the same block, working in the same group, survived in two different ways, died in two distinct sets of circumstances. By logical extension, each survivor wore his or her memories differently. Truth is nothing but an individual perception of reality. Apart from personal reasons, I wanted to document Adela's story because I saw its complexity and uniqueness—how, in all its details, it would be unlike any other Holocaust narrative and, to be more exact, it would be the story of one turbulent life.

As I reviewed tapes of interviews with my mother and others while writing this book, a related issue caught my attention. Many Holocaust survivors, including Adela, were not telling the whole truth. When confronted about missing parts of stories or certain inconsistencies, they would retort, "I don't remember" or "That is not important," or else respond with silence. In making this observation, I would like to point out a couple of questions that remain unanswered. The first: David Glejcer. Why did Adela never tell me his story? Was it because of the guilt she felt about his death? Second, had her letter to him been necessary? And had she meant to comfort him—or herself? In another example, as we move into the war years, we run into questions about underground workers and their possible ulterior motives. Take the case of Mr. Ostalowski, who sheltered Adela briefly. Few had intentions as pure as Ewald Pradela, Wanda Sitko, and Mrs. Tatarczucha, and according to Adela and other witnesses' reports, Mr. Ostalowski was not one of them. The question remains as to whether Kazik Budniak, the boyfriend of Adela's fellow escapee Eva, paid for Adela's stay without her knowledge, or whether Adela herself paid a price to Ostalowski in return for hiding her and Henia.

I will never know the answers to these questions and many others. Certain stories can barely be told because they happened, as Ka-Tzetnik described it, on "another planet," in a sphere unknown to what we consider humanity. This is not only a function of the degree of suffering but also of excruciating details that have no place in our everyday moral code. Examples outside the scope of this book come to mind: How can someone, with a clear conscience, tell the story of having saved the lives of two children by sacrificing their mother? Or how can a mother explain her decision to throw her infant from a speeding cattle car into the frigid night with the hope that a good soul would find the child and take it under his care?

Other wrenching stories can be and have been told. The Jewish policeman, for example, by freeing his mother from a bunker in the Zawiercie ghetto, delivered twenty others in hiding into the hands of the Gestapo. How to explain such a decision? As for a friend of Adela's in postwar Poland and later Germany, how could she have agreed to become the naturally inseminated surrogate mother to the child of an SS officer and his wife, in exchange for safe shelter? These types of choices, or as I prefer to call them, "situations," were numerous, and they happened over and over again, often multiple times during the course of a single day. Historian Tom Segev reflects on the issue in his book *The Seventh Million*:

> [The Holocaust survivors] did not escape the nightmare of their pasts. Over the years they wrote thousands of books about that "other planet" they had left yet not left, but all they could do was enumerate the atrocities. Those were part of their stories that could be told. The rest remained inside. "Even if you studied all documentation," Elie Wiesel has said, "even if you listened to all the testimonies, visited all the camps and museums and read all the diaries, you would not be able to even approach the portal of the eternal night. That is the tragedy of the survivor's mission. He must tell a story that cannot be told. He must deliver a message that cannot be

delivered."…In this sense the enemy, ironically, realized his goal. Since he extended the crime beyond all bounds, and since there is no way to cross the bounds except through language, it is impossible to tell the full story of this crime.

Here is Charlotte Delbo on her state of mind at Auschwitz:

I thought of nothing. The will to resist was doubtlessly buried in some deep, hidden spring which is now broken, I will never know. And if the women who died had required those who returned to account for what had taken place, they would be unable to do so. I thought of nothing. I felt nothing. I was a skeleton of cold blowing through all the crevices in between a skeleton's ribs.

Roman Frister, a young boy during the Holocaust, presents his thinking:

Anyone not of immediate use to me was filtered immediately out of my consciousness. Before I could file away a face in my memory, it was blurred. I saw the forest, not the trees; mankind, instead of men.

During their time at Auschwitz and afterward, many prisoners lost their grasp of reality along with their ability to assess the world around them. In *I Came Back*, Krystyna Żywulska writes of a hungry female prisoner who expressed her hope for a new "transport to be gassed" to a fellow inmate working at the *Effektenlager,* where she would hoard items to trade for food. Ka-Tzetnik remarked many years after the war that "Where there are people, there is Auschwitz."

What differentiates Holocaust survivors from one another are their individual stories of survival behind the high-voltage fence of the Nazi prison. What unifies them is a story that cannot be told, a story understood only by those who were there, by those whose eyes locked on the same piece of bread that would go to only one of them. Today I am not certain if everything my mother told me was truthful, but I am one hundred percent sure that it was real.

Present Like Past

My mother—and I have noticed this quality in all Holocaust survivors I have met—never really stopped reliving those six years of the Second World War, and this inability to let go showed itself in various habits she kept up through the course of her adulthood. One that comes to mind is that for years she could not leave the house without a bottle of water in her purse. This was a direct consequence of the fear of thirst she developed while hiding with Henia in the shit pool during the liquidation of the Zawiercie ghetto. A second was her skill at "organizing" items, which she had learned well at Auschwitz. In the camp, goods to be snatched included cigarettes, bread, scraps of fabric, any of which might save a prisoner's life, whether in the long or the short run. Several months after the war had ended, when Poland's retail infrastructure had begun to recover, Adela was still unconsciously pilfering cigarettes and other items from street kiosks. In the mind of a recent inmate for whom the war would never completely end, the sight alone of a pack of cigarettes justified stealing it. Once she came to her senses, it was mortifying to return those goods to the shop owner while offering an explanation he couldn't possibly understand. Her manual dexterity worked very much to her advantage during that search at the Berlin border checkpoint, where—in the presence of the East German guard—she transferred my father's falsified documents from her underwear to her purse.

Once I was old enough to accompany my mother to a shop or to visit a friend, we would often walk together. She would insist that I slip my hand under her arm. This was "how a gentleman should accompany a lady on the street," she would instruct; and he should "always stay on the side of the sidewalk closest to the traffic, for you are here to protect her." It was not

242

until we lived together in Frankfurt, and the city blocked off a few streets to motorists to create a pedestrian mall, that I noticed my mother would never walk down the middle of a pedestrian thoroughfare. Instead, she always insisted on staying close to a wall, almost touching it, and giving the appearance that she wanted to pass unnoticed. People coming into and out of shops would bump into us. When I asked my mother for an explanation, she mentioned something about walking the streets of the Aryan side, how if you kept close to the walls at the Auschwitz barracks, when for one reason or another you snuck out, your chances of being spotted by a guard from the *Lagerstrasse*, the main walkway between the barracks, would be greatly reduced.

Then there was Adela's relationship to food. In the two years after she left Auschwitz, she ate compulsively, and her weight gain is noticeable in photographs from this period. "She was unstoppable," remarked her friend Irena Winiawski (Leon's wife), with whom Adela spent time at the Repatriation Bureau. "I tried to warn her about the disservice that she was doing to herself, but it was to no avail, she wouldn't listen. She couldn't listen." Until Adela gave birth to my brother in July of 1947, she could part neither with incessant food nor with her gnawing memory of hunger. In my own lifetime, I never saw my mother carry around excessive weight. I remember her as having a medium build, of defined and proportionate figure.

The war showed its continued hold on Adela through many of her other tendencies. These included her nervousness whenever around a German shepherd, her aversion to words such as "selection" and "sauna," and the mortal fear she always felt in the presence of a haystack. This last phobia originated on the evening in August of 1943, when she and Henia hid in a haystack and noticed a search plane hovering above them in the night sky. For Adela, there was no association of the haystack with the bucolic or the peaceful.

For other war associations, Adela was not beyond turning to humor. When I was young, for example, she created a game called "nothing soup":

Me (cheerfully): Mom! What's for lunch?

Adela (a hardly detectable but mischievous smile): Nothing soup.

Me (pure curiosity): What is nothing soup?

Adela: Well, nothing soup is a special soup made out of nothing.

Me: You mean just water, right?

Adela (faint traces again of a mischievous smile): No! Not water, nothing soup.

Me (growing impatient): I don't understand. How can you make a soup out of nothing?

Adela (perfectly calm): Jacusiu (diminutive for Jacek)! Be patient! If you wait long enough you will discover what I mean by nothing soup. I learned how to prepare it during the war. I memorized the recipe. I will never forget it.

I, of course, never tasted nothing soup and would need to grow a few more years—and better grasp my mother's past—before I had an idea of what nothing soup really meant.

Adela also had almost an obsessive need to throw things away: clothing, household items, furniture, even personal items such as letters or photographs. (This didn't help me any in writing this book.) Though I cannot connect this behavior to a specific event during the war, I will hypothesize that it was her way of breaking with the past and starting fresh. No minimalist, she would often explain her actions by saying, "What was in the past stays in the past."

Adela's worst moments in the postwar years were the flashbacks, when in a subway car or on a crowded street she would recognize a face from the past. Despite all she had been through, my mother was known for having a tranquil personality all her life. But during those flashbacks, her facial muscles would suddenly tighten, and she would lower her eyelids and focus on the floor, then nudge me with her elbow and whisper: "The woman in the brown jacket was the Kapo of my block," or "The man next to the window sipping coffee interrogated me in the Bielsko prison." Certainly her suspicions were unfounded—the people she pointed out were much too young to have taken part in the Holocaust. But they must somehow have resembled the figures who left their imprints in her memory. And to my mother, though the question of age never crossed her mind, those faces were real, irrevocably bound with terror and death.

This would be a good place to finish Adela's story, but my editor advises me that "death" should not be the last word of a book like this one. Of course, he is right. After all, I don't want to remember my mother by her nightmares but by her conduct, her lifestyle, and by all the details that made her who she was.

First I remember her for the unbreakable ties she forged with the people who helped her, as well as with those whom she helped out of dead-end situations, no matter who they were or where they came from. The helped included Janka Pradela, Wanda Sitko, Shmuel Ron, Zofia Klemens,[46] and many others. Right after the war, Adela sought out these people and continued to maintain a connection to them until her last days. Those she helped included Ursula, a young German girl left behind in Poland by her parents, who had fled during the chaos of the Soviet victory. In later years, as mentioned earlier, Ursula lived with us and cared for Felek and me. Only in the mid-fifties did the Polish government answer my parents' plea for Ursula to be allowed to return to Germany to finally reunite with her family.

From her experience in the war, Adela did not discriminate between people of wealth and poverty, of high education and low. For her, only a person's character mattered. And for this

---

[46] Zofia Klemens sheltered Adela during the war. Though not included in this book, her story is included in *The Memories Never Let Go of Me*, by Shmuel Ron.

reason, she never degraded or looked down on her fellow human beings. Often this meant she could tolerate people's failings long after others had lost patience with them. I guess that, as a result, I have doubts about the claim that some have made that suffering invariably hardens its victims and makes them suspicious of others. Adela proved the opposite, her experiences during the Holocaust ennobled her.

Then there are the lighter points. I remember my mother when I think of Gregory Peck, her favorite actor—"the most handsome man on earth," as she used to describe him. I remember her by the vocalists Yves Montand, of France, and Mieczysław Fog, of Poland, whose songs made her pine for love in a way few poets could describe. And, perhaps less loftily though no less fondly, I remember her at the kitchen table; the time, for instance, when I caught her with a huge slice of Polish sausage in one hand and an enormous hunk of bread in the other—how her body language evinced uninhibited joy. I recall thinking to myself, "This is how people must feel in paradise." At family gatherings, I remember her munching on her favorite appetizer: marinated herring with "an accompaniment," slang for a shot of vodka. Nor will I neglect to mention the way she drank down the juice from the herring jar—when nobody was looking, of course.

Finally I remember my mother sipping coffee in a café in Frankfurt, enjoying a cigarette (Marlboro hard box), talking to friends. I see both of us sitting in the kitchen in dim light at opposite sides of a small table recording her story until the early morning hours.

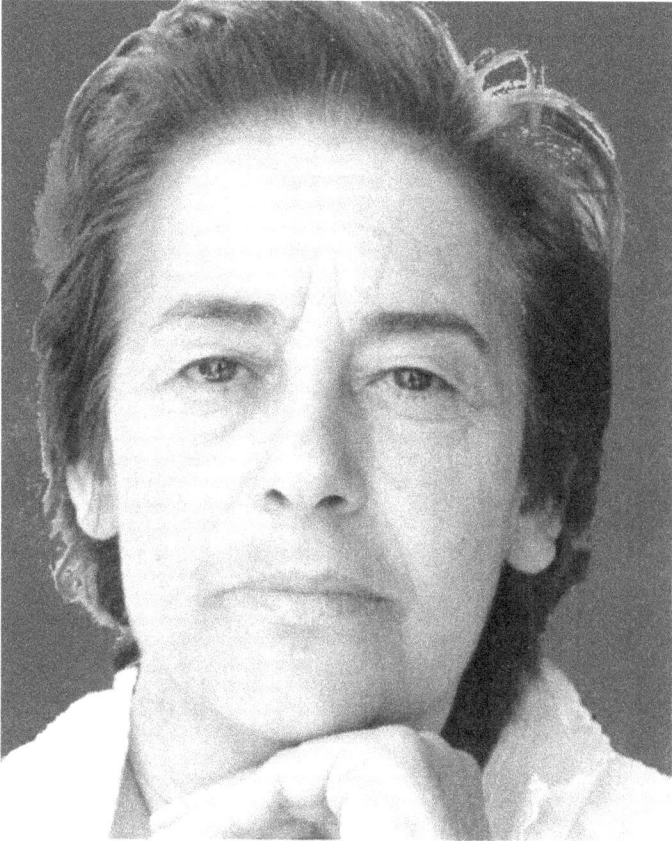

Adela, circa 1992

Adela's People

I DEDICATE THIS CHAPTER to all the people who helped Adela and Henia survive during the Holocaust. For most of them, history will leave neither books nor monuments, not even a recorded mention of their courage and deeds. In a generation or two, nobody will know that they existed, let alone the details of how their actions saved Adela, Henia, and many others. I know that my mother would want me to honor these people in this way.

For some of these stories, I wish the details were more complete. Namely, information available to me about Icio Ryński, Paweł Jaworski, and the Kobylec family was either poor or nonexistent. This is because underground work required utter secrecy, and operatives often used aliases in order to protect their identities. I am not even certain, having said this, if Paweł Jaworski was a real name. I also took the liberty, in this book's reference section, to include a short memoir written by Janka Pradela and two letters by Shmuel Ron. These documents are significant because they shed more light on Adela's and Henia's life during the Holocaust. In no particular order, here are their stories:

Wanda Gelbhard (née Sitko)

Wanda Sitko was born in Sosnowiec on April 2, 1923. During the Second World War, her family, devout Catholics, sheltered Jews in their home, an act punishable by death by the Nazis. Besides Adela and Henia, the Sitkos sheltered many members of the Feder family, including Jerzyk from the Bielsko transport. Shortly after the war, Ms. Sitko married Shmuel Gelbhard. The couple did not have children. Ms. Sitko still lives in Sosnowiec, at 7 Piłsudski Street—oddly, the same address as the Gutermans' in Niwka—apartment 11, her husband having died earlier.

When discussing people who had sheltered Jews during the war, Adela would mention two families and one individual: the Sitko and the Kobylec families, and Zofia Klemens. During my interview with Ms. Sitko on February 22, 2003, in Sosnowiec, she could not recall her first meeting with Adela, though they had met at least once before Adela knocked at her door after escaping the Death March. It is safe to assume, anyway, that Adela learned about Ms. Sitko through her underground contacts, most likely Mietek Kobylec, a member of the Polish resistance movement and a coconspirator with Paweł Jaworski.

Ms. Sitko and I spoke by phone and exchanged letters for more than six months before we met in person. When I arrived in the foyer of her modest, poorly lit apartment, Pani Wanda (this is how I addressed her in Polish) had been expecting me. She was a tall woman with gray hair and piercing blue eyes. Though rather stoic in appearance, she embraced me warmly. With her left hand she held a cane, but she stood so steadfast that at first the cane appeared to be a mere accessory. As she began to walk, I no longer doubted its purpose. Ten years before, her doctor had insisted on a hip replacement, but she had refused, saying she didn't want to risk a possible mishap during the operation. Now I could see the pain in her face with every step she took. After she brought me a glass of hot tea, a custom in a Polish home, we sat down to talk.

In answering my questions, Ms. Sitko spoke with a determined voice but broke down at times, especially when she talked about her younger sister or her mother, both of whom had died. Many times during her testimony, she would gently tap my hand. I believe this was her way of seeking comfort, perhaps of feeling closer to Adela. Little did she know that this contact actually comforted me. My mother used to touch my hand in a similar fashion, and in these moments during the interview I felt very connected both to my mother and to this woman whom I had just met for the first time.

I have read many testimonies about Poles helping Jews in World War II, but I had not until this point met a "hero" in the flesh. For both of us, the encounter was emotional, and our common awareness of Adela made it even more intense. We felt like people who had known each other for a long time—like family. Pani Wanda showed me the secret knock on the window that those in need of shelter used to identify themselves. She also told me about the time in Sosnowiec in 1939 when she had seen Jewish bodies driven on a horse-drawn lorry to be dumped in mass graves. Soon after witnessing this sight, she fell ill with epilepsy, and for the next seventeen years epileptic attacks robbed her of her speech for various intervals. Pani Wanda also confirmed all I had read and heard about the Germans' brutality during their occupation of Sosnowiec. In August of 1943, the Germans had forced her to work in a "cleaning commando" after the liquidation of the Środula ghetto. She remembered finding Jews still hiding in a few buildings, and she marched one young woman out of the ghetto as if she were a member of the cleaning crew. She also met a young mother who had smothered her baby out of fear that its crying might give away the hideout of the others in the same basement.

251

Shmuel Ron (Rozencwajg), alias Edward Klemens

Shmuel grew up in Katowice and became an active resistance fighter during World War II, in which his parents and younger sister were murdered by the Germans. In 1948, he emigrated to Israel, where he met his wife, Katrit, with whom he later had two sons. In Israel, Shmuel worked for many years as a family therapist, while devoting much of his spare time to painting and writing. His book, *Die Erinnerungen haben mich nie losgelassen* (*The Memories Never Let Go of Me*), was published in German in 1988.

After corresponding with Shmuel for about a year, I interviewed him in 1992. I noted at the time that his recollections did not always match Adela's, a reminder of the imprecision—and sometimes selectivity—of memory where war is concerned.

Among his clique of resistance fighters during the war, Shmuel was one of the boldest and most courageous, and he showed terrific ingenuity during sting operations against the German occupiers. Of the stories Adela told me about Shmuel, perhaps the most captivating were those that involved his "antennae" when it came to survival, and his magnificent capacity for dramatic getaways. I do not know how many times he avoided the *Blockmeister*s, *szmalcownicy*, and the Gestapo, but his reputation suggests he did so often. Certainly Adela was aware of this when she made her plea to him "with burning eyes" in the Bielsko prison. Even from Bielsko, Shmuel accomplished an escape, though he injured himself on a barbed wire fence severely enough to land him in a hospital. At his hospital ward, he was eventually arrested and transferred to Auschwitz.

Shmuel was an active and well-connected member of HaShomer HaTzair, a Zionist group that initiated resistance work during World War II. The organization would ultimately produce leadership for the uprisings in the ghettos of Warsaw, Vilna, and Białystok. Shmuel also had personal encounters with members of the Yishuv (Jewish community of prestatehood Palestine). Of the controversies associated with the Yishuv, one involves the leadership's sometimes opportunistic refusal to aid European Jews during Hitler's time. Wrote Shmuel, "The question of what the Yishuv leaders knew about our fate and what they could have done to destroy the machinery of extermination has never ceased to trouble me." Throughout Shmuel's book, the reader senses an underlying disappointment in the Yishuv leadership. In my conversations with Shmuel, I learned that some of this disappointment resulted from letdowns on a personal level—sometimes during his moments of greatest need. Once, long after the war, when he tried to give voice to his frustrations, one of his closest collaborators threatened Shmuel that, as he told me, "unless I shut up, they would break my bones."

Shmuel Ron is one of the more colorful figures to have been a part of Adela's life during the war, and she remained in touch with him in the following decades. I have translated Shmuel's letters to me and my brother from Polish into English, and printed them in the reference section of this book. Shmuel passed away in 2001 in Jerusalem.

Janka Pradela
(Shopa, Knosala[47])

When I met Janka for the first time, I was still a child. She had come from Silesia to visit us at our apartment in Warsaw. Later, I met her a few times in Frankfurt, where she had emigrated in the early eighties. A simple woman with a big heart, she married four times, the last time in Frankfurt.

When we talked in 1985, Janka remembered Marysia (the name given to Henia during the war) very well. This was no surprise, because of her extensive involvement in keeping Henia hidden during the latter part of the war. First, she had sheltered Henia in her own home near Katowice after Ewald, her first husband, had brought her there. Over time, Henia would be sent back to Bronka, Paweł Jaworski's ex-wife, and then returned again to Janka by Paweł. Since the Gestapo and the neighbors raised questions about the little girl, Janka decided to move Henia to her aunt's house in Herby. Janka then visited the child periodically and made sure she was looked after. For several years after the war, Janka stayed in contact with Henia.

In early 1992, during one of her visits to my parents' home in Frankfurt, Janka gave me a handwritten five-page essay, "My Memoir of the Times of Hitler's Occupation." She was not well educated and for her to compose even a short memoir would have taken great effort and determination, accompanied by a strong urge to tell her story. I translated the piece from Polish into English, and it is printed in this book's reference section in

---

[47] Subsequent surnames taken by Janka upon remarrying.

its entirety. Janka's memoir gives added perspective to the experiences of Ewald Pradela, Paweł Jaworski, Regina Guterman, and Henia. Janka passed away in 2000 in Frankfurt.

Ewald Pradela

An inevitable question about narratives from the Holocaust involves the reliability of survivors' memory. Often two survivors, or resistance members, will recollect the same event in entirely different ways, either because the trauma has impeded clear thinking or out of some form of self-protection. Considering the risk that they might be misunder-stood or unfairly judged by posterity, some Holocaust survivors, and their children, would prefer that their story not be told. What was an instinct of self-preservation or act of desperation in a murderous time could be misconstrued today as an act of evil.

Stories about Ewald Pradela told to me by his wife, Janka, and her family, my mother, and Regina Guterman were so disparate that I am unable to combine them into a unified picture. In the end, I have decided to use only the information related to me by his wife. This is because, though only remotely connected to his resistance activities, she knew him best out of all the witnesses. And based on what I know about her personally, I am convinced that neither self-interest nor other ulterior motives would have influenced her story. I cannot say the same about the other interviewees, including my mother. The reader will therefore notice some discrepancy with information presented earlier about Ewald. I consider this a necessary consequence of recording stories of underground work, where the truth often lies buried with those who are no longer among the living.

Ewald was a Volksdeutsche deeply involved in resistance against the Germans during World War II. He worked for the same organization as his close friend Paweł Jaworski, though in a different cell. In the spring of 1944, acting on a tip from one of the members of his group, the Gestapo arrested Ewald and charged him with *Rassenschande,* a "shame to the race" in literal translation but referring in practice to illegal sexual relations between a gentile and a Jew. He was imprisoned in the Katowice jail. After a series of lengthy and bloody interrogations, the SS staged a sham trial and sentenced him to time in a concentration camp. This was the trial at which Regina Guterman served as a witness, having been led by armed escort out of Auschwitz just to testify. It was during the prosecutor's arguments that Ewald, via facial expressions, made clear to Regina that Henia was alive and well. Ewald survived his stay at the camp and returned home a few days after liberation. Janka recalled in her testimony as follows: "In November 1945, my husband returned from the camp. He was already very sick.[48] First, after his return, I found out that he was in a [concentration] camp called Rosenheim."

From an interview with a member of Janka's family who knew Ewald well, I learned that he apparently did not die a natural death. In 1948, he was stabbed in the chest while waiting at a tram stop in Zatęż. The assailant was one of his old enemies, a Silesian fascist. At first glance, Ewald's wound appeared not too deep, with little bleeding. He was so certain that it was only a flesh wound that he treated it himself and didn't bother to tell anybody. But after neglecting the wound for a few days, the area around his heart became infected, ultimately leading to a massive burst of his aorta. Ewald Pradela died within a week after the stabbing.

---

[48] I was unable to find out the specifics of this illness.

Ewald's death did not ensure an end to his difficulties. Because of his membership in the Polish Socialist Party, the church refused him a Catholic burial. So under the cover of night, and with the assistance of local police, Ewald's family put him to rest near the fence of the cemetery at St. Joseph's church in Zatęż.

The Marciniak Family

The Marciniak family hosted Henia at their farm in Herby, near Częstochowa, for more than a year during the German occupation of Poland. They successfully hid her from the roving eye of the SS, claiming she was one of their children. The Marciniaks lived in great poverty, and for them, going to bed hungry was nothing unusual.

Because she was just four years old, Henia remembers almost nothing of the time she spent at the Marciniaks' home. But she does recall a scene that seems to have occurred every Sunday after church, during which the whole family would relax on the bench in front of the house. They would be lined up according to age—from the father, to his wife, to the oldest son, and so on down the line, with Henia sitting somewhere in the middle.

Itzhak (Iciek, Icio) Ryński

Iciek Ryński was born in Modrzejów in 1923, and everyone I spoke with empha-sized his physical strength and immense courage. Though not a close friend of Adela's, I am sure that through the Środula rescue he earned her admiration.

Once he had escaped to the Aryan side, Iciek disguised himself well as a gentile and worked as a train engineer. Sometimes he would sneak into the Środula ghetto to visit Adela. When he learned of the Zawiercie ghetto liquidation, and knew Adela and Henia were among those being cleared out, he entered the fray in an attempt to rescue them once again. He did not succeed even in finding them, and the SS stopped him from returning to the Aryan side, placing him and a friend on a transport to Auschwitz. Though they managed to escape by cutting a hole in the floor of the cattle car and jumping out when the train stopped at Mysłowice, the Gestapo caught up with them on the platform and shot them both dead. Adela reminisced about Iciek in this way:

> If he had not come to visit me in Zawiercie, he would probably be alive today. He was a very courageous and a very smart man. [I think that] he came to Zawiercie because he had heard about the liquidation and wanted to help me escape. I was told the circumstances of his death by Ms. Horońka, with whom I had stayed for a short time after we escaped from the Środula ghetto. She was an acquaintance of Iciek's. Iciek was just a friend. He was a year younger than I, but he was madly in love with me.

Mrs. Tatarczucha

In the Silesian dialect, the name "Tatarczucha" indicates a woman with a husband of the last name "Tatarczuch." Except for this last name and Bór, the village where Mrs. Tatarczucha lived, Adela left no further reference to this woman. I later learned that Mrs. Tatarczucha and Mr. Tatarczuch were not actually married—that she was only his lover—and that her real name was likely Anna Litewka. Immediately after the war's end, she left Bór, and I could find no trace of her subsequent life. As for the village of Bór itself, today it no longer even exists, having been replaced by a series of massive apartment complexes.

Paweł Jaworski

Aside from Adela's firsthand accounts, I could find very little concrete information about Paweł Jaworski, except that he was a Volksdeutsche category II and that he was originally from Czechoslovakia. A few years older than Adela, at the time their paths crossed he had already separated from his wife, Bronka, though the terms were amicable. He belonged to the PPS, an organization with numerous active resistance cells throughout Poland, particularly in the south. Adela later described the momentous role he played in her life:

> I stayed with Paweł, I lived with Paweł—I shared my bed with him. Paweł was an exceptionally decent human being. We were very close. He had some excellent contacts, but he never revealed them to me. It had to be a powerful organization helping him. He would bring firearms for me to hide, and he would smuggle things. Paweł never told me what he was really doing, where, and why. Until today, I have no idea about these details.

Eventually Adela requested that Paweł help her collaborate with Shmuel Ron's underground group. To participate on her own struck her as too great a burden. Though at first reluctant to involve himself with the transports to Slovakia, Paweł eventually acceded to her requests and, as I mention in the text, became a friend to Shmuel.

A side story gives a final sense of Paweł's character, along with some additional details about Henia's whereabouts during the war. After Paweł's ex-wife, Bronka, learned that Adela had been deported to Auschwitz, she tried in vain to win Paweł back. She did not quit easily. Having learned that Henia was staying with Janka Prade-la, she visited Janka, and using the pretext that Paweł wanted Henia back, took the child to her home, where she lived with her mother. Bronka's intention was only to gain Paweł's affection once again, and she and her mother took good care of Henia. But Paweł did not trust her and placing Henia in peril was the last thing he wanted to do. Afraid she might resort to blackmail—or that she might even turn the child over to the Gestapo should anything happen to him—he kidnapped Henia from Bronka's home and returned her to Janka.

Paweł Jaworski wasn't remarkable only for saving Adela's and Henia's lives. Outside the scope of his PPS activities, he also utilized his underground connections to attempt to rescue Hala, and to aid Adela's and Shmuel Ron's smuggling operations through HaShomer HaTzair. These activities not only strained PPS resources, they also substantially increased the danger to Paweł himself. At the time of Paweł's death, Adela was already in Auschwitz.

Ignac G.

Ignac G. does not belong in this chapter, and he had nothing to do with Adela's or Henia's survival during World War II. But I must mention him here anyway.

The first time I met Ignac G. was at our apartment in Frankfurt, when he and my mother were planning to smuggle my father out of Poland. He appeared to me not only cold but also cold-hearted. There was a certain frosty air about him that announced a detachment from all human emotion. I was afraid of him but at the same time intrigued. During his visits, Ignac talked strictly business, and he clearly felt uncomfortable in my presence. This showed in his body language, his uncertain glances, the physical distance he kept, the reluctance with which he addressed me, and what I interpreted as a general attempt to ignore my presence altogether. Maybe he felt I knew too much about his work, I thought at the time. But that would turn out to be an incorrect explanation.

A gangster of the Frankfurt underworld, Ignac G. was skinny, of medium height, with dark brown eyes and equally dark gleaming hair. He was always well dressed and soft-spoken. Appearing to know his profession expertly, he inspired instant trust from those who retained his services. As a gangster, his demeanor struck me as the opposite of Al Capone's—that of an understated professional.

Yet like my mother, Ignac G. was a Holocaust survivor from Poland. A few years younger than she, at the time the Wehrmacht tanks rolled into Poland on that September day in 1939, he must have been between eight and twelve years of age. I know nothing of the details of his life during the war, but as with every Holocaust survivor, and based on what my mother knew about him, he had suffered abysmally. Finally the Holocaust had left him an orphan.

More than thirty years after that first meeting, I realized that Ignac's coldness reflected nothing more than the internal torment that must have eaten him alive every time he looked at me and my mother. In the years after the war, his profession had allowed no room for the warmth of a family, including a bond between siblings or even close friends. In our home, he must have felt this warmth in a form he hadn't known in a long while, and at first he recoiled from it. But in time, Ignac began to show vulnerability. Sometimes my mother and I would be joined by my brother, Felek, and his wife, Joanna. With us, he spoke Polish for the first time since childhood.

Along with my mother and the "German tourist" whom Ignac had arranged to join the mission, he traveled to Budapest to rescue my father. Felek and I waited for them at Frankfurt's *Hauptbahnhof* (central rail station) when the train finally rolled in from Budapest. On a few later occasions he visited our home and was always greeted with warmth and gratitude, especially by my father. Over the course of these visits, he was increasingly moved by human feelings that surely had been foreign to him for decades. Once I noticed a genuine smile on his face.

I will not claim today that my mother was single-handedly responsible for Ignac's emotional thaw, but it would be inaccurate to deny her influence. One day, he showed up at my parents' gift shop near the railroad station with a small, tightly wrapped package in his hand. Inside was a neat stack of seemingly countless one-hundred-Deutschmark notes, amounting to the sum my mother had paid for Michał's transfer from Poland. He turned to Adela and said: "Please take it back."

REFERENCE MATERIAL

A rare document, certifying the repatriation of Irena Winiawska (b. Celewicz), who became a close friend of Adela's in the town of Dziedzice beginning in July of 1945. The document bears Adela's handwriting in the signature area.

Ban on Changes of Place of Residence by Jews within the Area of the Government-General, December 11, 1939

DECEMBER 11, 1939
Implementation Order No. 1 for the Regulation of October 26, 1939, for the Introduction of Forced Labor for the Jewish Population in the Government-General, December 11, 1939.

Pursuant to § 2 of the Regulation for the introduction of Forced Labor for the Jewish population of October 26, 1939 (*Verordnungsbl.* G.G.P., p.6), I order the following:

1. As from January 1, 1940, it is forbidden for all Jews within the Government-General of the Occupied Polish Territories to move their place of residence or lodging, without the written permission of the local German Administrative Authority, beyond the limits of the community of their place of residence, or to cross the border of this community and to move away after giving up their permanent residence or lodging.

2. All Jews moving into, or transferred into, the Government-General are required to register immediately with the mayor of the locality when they have taken up residence, but no later than 24 hours after entering the Government-General, and to inform the local Judenrat of their presence. The Judenrat will record this information in writing and submit it to the Mayor on the Monday of each week, against written acknowledgment.

3. After having obtained accommodation, all Jews referred to in § 2 must comply with the requirements of § 1.

4. All Jews within the Government-General are forbidden to enter or use pathways, streets and public squares between the hours of 9:00 P.M. and 5:00 A.M. without written authority specifying the times and places, issued by the local German authorities. Orders by local German authorities containing more severe restrictions are not affected by this regulation.

5. The restrictions of § 4 do not apply in cases of public or personal emergency.

6. Jews contravening the regulations under §§ 1 through 4 will be sent immediately to prolonged hard forced labor. This does not affect punishment provided by other orders.

7. The orders under §§ 1 through 6 do not apply to Jews who have moved under the provisions permitting them to do so in accordance with the law setting out an "Agreement between the German Reich Government and the Government of the U.S.S.R. concerning the transfer of the Ukrainian and Byelorussian population out of the area belonging to the Zone of Interest of the German Reich."

8. The public announcement of these instructions will be carried out by the Mayors according to orders by the sub-district Commander (*Kreishauptmann)* or the City commander (*Stadthauptmann*). The Judenraete will be instructed by the Mayors.

9. These orders are effective immediately.
Cracow, December 11, 1939

Higher SS and Police Leader (Hoeherer SS- und Polizeifuehrer)
in the Government-General
of the Occupied Polish Territories
Krueger

My Memoir of the Times of Hitler's Occupation
(Spring 1992)

Janka Pradela

In the year of 1940, I lived with my older sister, Józefa, and with my younger sister, Gertrud, in Katowice-Zatęż at Knapenweg 1, in a flat on the third floor. The flat consisted of a kitchen and one room. In December 1940, I married Ewald Pradela. He was unemployed at that time. We had a son, Werner, who was being raised by my husband's parents. I was working as a hairdresser in Zatęż.

One day, I was informed by the Gestapo that my sister Gertrud had been arrested at her workplace, the Beldon Steel Mill, in Zatęż. The reason for her arrest: She was sharing bread with war prisoners who worked with her in the same place. She ignored two official warnings that she allegedly received prior to her arrest.

One day, my husband took me to a meeting. I did not know where, why, and with whom. At that time, I had no idea that my husband was doing underground work, and that he was helping other people to hide from Nazi authorities. The meeting took place in a small room in the attic at Warszawska Street. There, I met Adela (Jachimowicz) and Paweł (Jaworski). I did not know their last names or their nationality. Neither did I try to find out.

One day, in February or March of 1944, my husband came home with a four-year-old girl, Marysia (Henia). He claimed to have found her alone on the street. He told me that I should not register her with the authorities, and that I should tell anybody asking about her that she is my niece. Marysia was a beautiful child with lots of intelligence.

Paweł, Hela (Regina Guterman), and Zygmunt (Stankiewicz) were paying for Marysia. I do not remember when, but one day Paweł brought a number of Swiss watches, a seal fur, and 10,000 Deutschmarks for safekeeping. Hela lived with us for a couple of days. At that time she allegedly was doing kitchen work in a restaurant in Nysa. A few days later, Hela left and never came back. She said that she was going to work. Hela gave me a ring with a large ruby, and said to sell it if I had to pay for Marysia.

I knew from my husband that the Katowice Gestapo arrested a man named Wolski. He was supposed to be freed against a bribe. The bribe was the things that Paweł left in our house for safekeeping. The exchange was supposed to take place on the first day of the holidays. One night in 1944, Paweł and Zygmunt left our place carrying the goods for Wolski's release. The exchange was supposed to take place in the Kościuszko Park in Katowice. The meeting did not materialize as I found out later, for the meeting turned out to be a Gestapo trap. Paweł started to run away but he was shot and killed.

On the second day of the holidays in 1944, I went to buy some milk for the children and I saw my husband being taken by a Gestapo officer. As I returned home, there was another Gestapo officer waiting for me already. He informed me that my husband had been arrested. Knowing the German language, I asked him for the reason for this arrest. He answered that I knew the reason very well. This Gestapo man ordered me to open the drawer to the wardrobe. I don't know what he was looking for. He found 900 Deutschmarks there. I told him that I was saving up the money for furniture because the furniture I have now was worn out.

The Gestapo man asked why I am lying. He said that he will not take my money away. I became angry and started shouting that I am a hairdresser, and that I earned this money with my own hands and I will not let anybody take it away from me.

He was on his way out through the kitchen when he stopped and asked me how many children do I have?

"One," I answered.

"Whose is the other one?" he asked.

"My neighbor's," I said.

He left.

I did not have to think much. I had to bring Marysia (Henia) to safety. I decided to bring her over to my mother's sister, who was living in a village called Herby. I told my aunt that my husband had been arrested but I had to go to work. My aunt had five children. My uncle did not have any work. They lived in a modest hut on a small piece of land. They wanted to help me, so they took Marysia into their home. Every Saturday I would bring them food. The whole family lived from this. Shortly after my return from Herby I went to Nysa with one of my friends to look for Hela to tell her the whereabouts of Marysia. We looked through all the restaurants in Nysa but we could not find her. I did not know her last name. A couple of days later I decided to go to the Gestapo to ask for a visit with my husband. I prepared a suitcase full of food, things to drink, and fresh clothing. I took my son, Werner, with me. He was only four years old then. I was not sure if my husband was still being held at this location. I entered the building. From the first floor I was able to see small cellar windows with the prisoners behind them. I asked my son to call loudly:

"Papa Ewald! Papa Ewald!"

My husband's voice came from somewhere: "*Kommt über!*"

In order to receive permission to visit, I had to go to the fifth floor. I entered room no. 518. There, I noticed a woman huddled in the corner. I could see that she was badly beaten.[49] On the wall hung seven leather whips [used by farmers on cattle]. My son was crying and calling; "*Ich will den Papa sehen!*" The Gestapo man asked me for my last name.

"Pradela," I said.

"Oh, so you are Pradela!"

The whole conversation was in German. He asked me about the woman: "Do you know this woman?"

"No, I don't know her," I replied in Polish.

The Gestapo man went over to his desk and pulled out Paweł's [Jaworski] ID card.

"Do you know him?" he asked. I don't remember how, but I knew that Paweł was dead. "No, I don't know him," I replied.

Then he pulled out the ID of Zygmunt. "I have seen him once or twice," I said.

---

[49] It is impossible to determine the identity of the woman with absolute certainty, but through examining the circumstances I can guess that she was most likely a member of Ewald's resistance cell beaten beyond recognition.

I did not receive permission to see my husband in room no. 518. Without thinking much, I went with my crying son to room no. 520. An older gentleman patted my son on his head and told him that he will see his father. In my presence he called to the guard station and ordered that I will see my husband. I thanked him, and Werner and I took the elevator down to the cellar. The guard brought my husband and allowed us to greet each other with a kiss. Through the kiss, my husband transferred to me a ring from Hela. The guard ordered us to go to another room. We were left alone. There my husband told me everything about his, Hela's, and Zygmunt's arrest. Ewald took the suitcase with food, drinks, and tobacco to the cell. All seven prisoners in Ewald's cell had something to eat that day. The guard was convinced that my suitcase had already been checked in room no. 518, and the person from room no. 520 thought that the guard at the entrance searched it.

This was the last time that I saw Ewald. The Germans staged a trial but I was not allowed to be present in the courtroom. The process took place in Katowice. After the verdict my husband was taken to a camp.

In November or December (I don't remember exactly), two women came to me asking if I knew that Marysia was Jewish, and if I was not afraid of that. I told them that I don't know any Marysia. The two women left.

Shortly after the liberation in January 1945, I was hiding in a bomb shelter (Katowice was not liberated yet), when two women came and asked me to come out. It was Adela and another woman. We went to my apartment, where they asked me about the whereabouts of Marysia. I told them that she was alive and that she lives on my aunt's farm in Herby.

Right after the liberation of Katowice, Irena [Adela] came to me and we both took a train to Herby. It was a freight train carrying ammunition. We were virtually sitting on explosives. Of course, the train was not supposed to stop in Herby. We had to jump out. We stayed in Herby one or two nights. In the meantime, the passenger train had been

273

reinstated and we all returned to Katowice happy and safe. Irena took Marysia immediately under her care.

I am so happy that Marysia, today fifty-two years old, is alive and resides in Israel with her mother, husband, and her sons.

In November 1945 my husband returned from the camp. He was already very sick. He died in 1948. After his return, I found out that he was in a camp called Rosenheim.

I was in contact with Irena and her husband, Michał, until they left Poland. Then our communication stopped. One day I received a note from Irena that she is in West Germany. She was helping me by sending food and clothing packages to Poland. Once she arranged for an invitation to West Germany. I was already a widow then, after my second husband, Wróbel. After I came back from Irena, I decided to emigrate to West Germany.

The Jachimowicz family surrounded me with care and took me into their family circle. In West Germany, I was able to meet with Marysia and her mother, Hala, who came to visit after so many years. Marysia and Hala brought me lots of gifts and financial help, which I was sending to my son, Werner, in Poland.

One day, when my son was visiting in West Germany from Poland, Marysia came from Israel. The reunion was full of happiness. Lots of tears. It was their first reunion after forty-five years.

I returned the gold ring to Hela after she came back from the concentration camp. Irena gave me another golden ring, which I gave to my grandson (Werner's son) as a gift.

With great sadness I accepted the recent death of Irena's husband, Michał, who was like a brother to me. But there is still a sister, Irena, who for me is a priceless friend. A friend for life. A sincere confidante who always is ready to help and advise, and her home is my home.

Correspondence with Shmuel Ron

The following letter is addressed to my brother, Felek, and me.

September 1991, Jerusalem
Greetings,

It is clear to me that we do not know each other and for this reason I do not address you by your first names. This is who I am, and maybe this [letter] will give you a clue why the thought of writing to you was born. I was with Adela, your mother, in the underground between 1943 and 1944, long before you came into this world. I have sons too, more or less your age, and that is why I suppose that Adela did not tell you much (if anything at all) about her past, because I myself did not speak to my sons about my own experiences for many years. There were sufficient reasons for that. However, a few years ago I sat down and did my homework. I wrote a sort of book dedicated to my sons. There is very little history in this work, rather my personal life stories. During your mother's (and your father's) visit here, a thought was presented that today it would be permissible and desirable for the sons to know more about the war experiences of their parents.

I met Adela for the first time in 1942. She was a nurse in a hospital.[50] We did not establish closer contact with each other until the latter part of 1943. I met her again in Katowice holding hands with a four-year-old girl [Henia], the daughter of your aunt [Hala] (today in Israel), and it was an unbelievable sight. At that time, there were almost no more Jews left in Poland, and rarely could one see a young Jewish woman on the Aryan side holding a child's hand. A Jewess with such eyes! Have you ever noticed that in [your] mother's eyes is immortalized the entire history of the Jews. Yes, I saw it especially against the background of those awful times. I myself was on the Aryan side, quasi-German, quasi-Pole. I too having "such eyes" and "such a

---

[50] Mr. Ron is referring to the Jewish Hospital in Sosnowiec, where Adela worked as a nurse under the supervision of Dr. Dreifus.

nose" had problems hiding among a rather inimical population. Being a member of the Jewish resistance, I was able to value—yes, there is no other word for it—the heroism of Adela-Irena [which] enabled her to save her own life and the life of this child. Please notice that at every given moment she had to save her own life and at the same time protect a small child against this wolf pack, a [wolf pack] on two legs. Even from the perspective of time, [her heroism] is not an exaggeration. I know that such cases were extremely rare. At that time [late 1943], Adela was already an advanced agent of the Polish resistance who had contacts with a noble human being, Paweł Jaworski, and also with Zygmunt Stankiewicz. It was a time when a handful (and during those times it was a substantial handful) of remaining members formed the uprising (an unsuccessful uprising) which took place in Sosnowiec and Będzin, and entered the Aryan side, without money, without handguns, and without documents. We were engaged in a rescue mission, and everybody who had the courage to leave his hideout (where each of us felt relatively safe) was obligated to participate in this action. Until then, Adela had not been a member of any organized resistance. Nevertheless, there was not even the slightest doubt that having met her, my contacts [became] her contacts and hers [became] mine. It was extremely important [to us] because Paweł J. and Zygmunt S. were members of the Polish underground and their contacts branched out to others, who were placed in various [municipal] offices such as the Employment Office, Health Department, etc. Via Adela, their contacts served our rescue mission well. I would like to stress the fact that Adela did not have to do anything to help our mission. She had her own hideout and she had help from others, but any work for the rescue mission carried substantial risks. She did it only from her own will. Are you aware that such behavior was not only courageous and noble, but [in those conditions] it was almost unprecedented?

There is a Hebrew saying: "The one who rescues the life of one soul, rescues the whole world." Adela had a stake in rescuing more than one soul.

Another activity: People who had evaded the Będzin and Sosnowiec ghetto liquidations were smuggled over the border to Slovakia and from there to Hungary. One of the legs was Katowice-Bielsko. To smuggle frightened, suspected, and suspicious people with "various noses" was no picnic. Without being recruited or asked, Adela became the connecting agent [taking care of the] convoys, risking her own life continuously. In fact, during one such mission she [and I] was arrested. Until the last moment she did not neglect her duty to her niece [Henia], bringing [and hiding] her against stormy currents on the Aryan side, where people willing to help were a rarity. Each day, and sometimes each hour, was a fight for survival.

There are certain episodes that are anchored in my memory. For example, in January 1944 I was supposed to accompany a group to Bielsko, near the border with Slovakia. Adela [a member of the same conspiracy] had a bad feeling [in her gut], and she insisted that we should go together. [During the ride], almost at each railroad station I begged her to get out of the train. So [to make a long story short], we both got arrested.

I witnessed how [the Germans] interrogated Adela, I was interrogated in her presence as well. I remember how one of the Gestapo commended himself:

"Where my fist reaches, no grass will ever grow!"

And when the fist [landed, and landed mercilessly], Adela retained her dignity; she never broke her silence. After that...Auschwitz.

For some time Adela was to organize letter exchanges between my camp and hers. I don't know if your mother ever mentioned [that even in Auschwitz she participated in the resistance]. She was taking part in preparations to blow up the crematorium. A few participants in this mission were arrested and hanged. Lately, historians are looking into these events. I doubt if Adela's name will be mentioned because it is a typical trait of her character—she was often on the front line of action but would step aside when credit was being distributed. This made her different.

I am not sure if I depicted the true profile of Adela.
However, I hope my words should do her justice.

The following letter is Mr. Ron's response to my letter asking about details of the war encounters between himself and Adela.

From Shmuel Ron
January 29, 1992, Jerusalem

Greetings,

I received your letter, and I must admit that apart from being touched, I became "frightened" in the face of the mission before me. Am I going to be able to fulfill it? I am "frightened" because many memories already belong to archeology, and one needs to do a solid amount of work in order to uncover and bring to light many details. It appears that even real archeologists have no clue where something, anything may be found. So, at this very moment, I don't know where to systematically start and what my spontaneity will uncover. But I will start. We will see.

I am convinced that historians, biographers, writers of memoirs, etc., have failed to a certain extent in their work: There is no novel, no research paper, no memorial to the anonymous Jewish mothers, who were able to show so many acts of heroism rescuing children. If I were a sculptor, I would endeavor on such a great mission. (Again, I'd probably be "frightened." Would I be able to do it?) Adela was such a mother, maybe even greater than that, because biologically she was not. I met Adela in 1942 when she was a nurse in a hospital.[51] Later, after a long time, I met her again in Katowice under a railroad bridge facing the direction of Kościuszko Street. She was holding a little girl, maybe four years old, just like a mother. I knew that Adela did not have a child of her own, so who was this girl?

Adela told me when she was hiding in the attic during the liquidation action[52] how she was able to keep the child quiet during the time of horror, fear, and uncertainty as to what the next hour might bring. I felt that this child

---

[51] Mr. Ron is referring to the Jewish Hospital in Sosnowiec. He came there under the pretext of being ill. In reality, he used the hospital as a hideout.

[52] Reference is being made to the liquidation of the Zawiercie ghetto, when Adela and Henia hid for several days in the attic of an abandoned house.

understood her role, that she must not cry, she must not talk, she must not be noticed. My God, how much strength one had to have to achieve such cooperation from a four-year-old girl. And here [under the bridge] began the dual confession: mine about the work on the Aryan side engaged [illegible] in a rescue action, hers about Paweł Jaworski and his nobility, his courage, and his connections to the Polish underground.

Was Adela recruited [by the Polish underground]? Who could think in those categories? It was clear that whatever concerned my work, and everything in Adela's disposition, also her connections to the Polish underground (with the help of Paweł Jaworski), led to the same result without recruitment, without secret declarations [vows] of loyalty, duty, and [illegible].

I introduced Adela to the host of my hideout [Zofia Klemens], which coincidentally was located in the NSDAP [Nazi Party] building, and Adela introduced me to Paweł Jaworski, and he in turn [introduced me] to other members of the Polish underground. There was [also] Zygmunt Stankiewicz from Vilnius. Thanks to him, we made connections to the Arbeitsamt [Department of Labor] and Dr. Jares. Here and there, we were able to use the contacts for many causes, in general achieving [illegible] help—unfortunately, on a small scale. Because how one could help others to fight was by giving them valid papers [IDs]. Sometimes, they were a great help indeed. Anyway, I don't want to exaggerate—we did not have many IDs to give away; in addition, we did not know many people in hiding and in need of papers. Sometimes we had to find those who were hiding, most of the time without substantial results. I don't remember if Adela was an agent of the Polish underground. I remember only that once she had such a mission from Katowice to Bielsko. I accompanied her and both of us met with a certain young woman. Thanks to Adela's contacts with Paweł Jaworski, we were able to renew the contact with the National Jewish Committee in Warsaw. We received a list from "Celina" (it was Celina

Zivia Lubetkin[53]) and, I believe, from "Adolf" (Abram Berman). They asked for or gave quasi-directives [specifying] who should be rescued. They did not know that the Sosnowiec and Będzin ghettos were almost completely destroyed and no one from these communities was alive anymore. I remember one name from those to be rescued, Dr. Liberman,[54] a known doctor and a civic activist. He was not alive then, in winter of 1943.

The contacts with the Polish underground were a little bit strange: they were offering money, but we did not need it then; they were offering papers [IDs], but one of our people was a specialist in falsifying papers and stamps. Actually, as far as I can remember, we offered them help with falsifying stamps, and I believe that they accepted it. I even remember in which apartment I met with the delegate from Warsaw. It was an apartment on Powstańców Street, on the corner of Kościuszko Street, a ground-level apartment. I had a meeting there twice. If my memory does not fail me, Adela was there only once. Either way, these contacts were only possible thanks to Adela via Paweł Jaworski.

Adela had an "ugly" habit of being stubborn, and she insisted on accompanying me by train to Bielsko on the Slovakia-Hungary Eretz Israel route. I wasn't too thrilled with her stubbornness, but who could have known what is certain and what makes sense. In January 1944,[55] almost everybody from our group who was being hidden by the Kobylec family in Michałkowice, and by Zofia Klemens in Katowice, had already crossed the Slovakia-Hungary border.

---

[53] Zivia (Celina) Lubtkin, born in 1914 in Byten, Poland, was a leader in the Labor Zionist Youth Movement (DROR), among the organizers of the pioneering underground in occupied Poland. She was also among the founders of Ż.O.B. [Żydowska Organizacja Bojowa], Jewish Combat Organization, serving at its headquarters, and was a representative of her chapter of the Jewish National Committee as well as of the underground's coordination committee of the Warsaw ghetto.

[54] Dr. Liberman was a famous physician in Silesia. For a brief period, he was the chief doctor of the Jewish Hospital in Sosnowiec.

[55] Actually, the transport from Katowice to Bielsko took place on December 31, 1943.

I remember one such group.[56] *There was an older lady, a young boy six or seven years old, a young man my age, and two to three other persons whom I don't remember. Adela insisted that she must accompany them to the designated location, to a smuggler in Bielsko. The smuggler—an SOB—Roman Brzuchański turned out to be a traitor. His deception cost the lives of a few of "our people." [From the beginning], Adela and I had an uncomfortable feeling about this trip. At each stop, I was trying to convince her that there was no reason for both of us to take the risk. Nothing helped.*

At one moment, two huge guys came up to me from the back and grabbed my arm. They introduced themselves as Gestapo, and warned me that any attempt to flee would end fatally. They took me to their office and after a while presented me with Adela. They would beat me quite hard in Adela's presence, hoping for her to break down and start to "sing." But it did not happen. She was holding on strong. I remember that they dressed Adela in a ridiculous-looking nightgown, so that she would be easily recognized in case of escape. In turn, they dressed me in Adela's ski suit for the same reason. After interrogations by the Gestapo (I don't remember if Adela was beaten too), we were taken to a police station, where from time to time transports were leaving for Auschwitz. It was a large station, one could actually call it a prison building. It had separate wings for male and female prisoners. My cell was extremely crowded.

I am not going to write about all the details of this prison. It was not a spa. I am not going to describe my escape either. For the price of a good pair of shoes (exchanged for rags), a Kapo who was going from cell to cell enabled me to meet with Adela. I remember her eyes piercing through a small opening in the door. They were like flames. She was begging me to flee. "Remember Marysia," she said. (I believe that was the name of her sister's daughter [Henia].)

Perhaps it was a coincidence, but thanks to those glowing eyes I escaped. The rest is only a coincidence, luck, or maybe a miracle. My mission will not be fulfilled without

---

[56] The group is portrayed in greater detail in the chapter "Eighteen Days."

mentioning Auschwitz. Adela found out that I was there too. (In March of 1944, I was arrested again and subsequently brought to Auschwitz.) Somehow, it was possible to smuggle letters between Adela and me.

IMPORTANT MESSAGE:

I don't know the details, but I know that [in Auschwitz] Adela was involved in a smuggling operation involving explosives. There was a conspiracy to blow up the crematoria. My cousin, who was with Adela in Auschwitz, knows all the details. She lives in San Antonio, Texas, and she will gladly report on the details of Adela's stay in Auschwitz. You can call her and tell her that I sent you. A friendly reception is guaranteed. Her phone number is....

I have not answered all the questions that you asked: For example, I did not sleep on a bunk, but directly on the floor. How Adela was sleeping—I don't know....

I did not put too much effort into accurately describing facts, nor was I consistent in methods and style: And my illegible writing, chaotic, without discipline. The price of a better letter would not be small for me and it would take long months and maybe even longer. So, I hope that you were able to cope with my writing style, and if not, I don't know what to do.

If you were able to translate my letter into English, anything that concerns Adela, I would like to show to my sons. They do not know Polish but they speak English.

Greetings, Shmuel Ron

P.S. After I read my letter, I am not sure anymore as to the accuracy of the events. For example, after my escape from the [Bielsko] prison, I kept working in the underground, taking advantage of cooperation with Paweł Jaworski and Zygmunt Stankiewicz, and others from Adela's circle. That is why one can have the impression that Adela was present during those operations. The fact is that she was already a prisoner in Auschwitz. So, I was not accurate in my recounting by associating certain events with the physical presence of Adela, when her presence was only symbolical. The fact remains that many of those contacts [with the underground] were possible only thanks

283

to Adela. In this case, the symbolical presence is (for me) equivalent to a physical one.

If occasion allows, please greet your mother, father, and your brother. Shmuel Ron

Books and Articles

Anissimov, Myriam. *Primo Levi: The Tragedy of an Optimist.* New York: Overlook Hardcover, 1999.

Bartov, Omer. *Mirrors of Destruction: War, Genocide, and Modern Identity.* New York: Oxford University Press, 2002.

Bartov, Omer. *Murder in Our Midst: The Holocaust, Industrial Killing, and Representation.* New York: Oxford University Press, 1996

Browning, Christopher. *Ordinary Men: Reserve Police Battalion 101 and the Final Solution in Poland.* New York: Harper Perennial, 1993.

Chęciński, Michael Moshe. *My Father's Watch.* New York: Gefen Books, 1994.

Cohen, Judy. *Women of Valor: Partisans and Resistance Fighters.* 2001. http://www.theverylongview.com/WATH/valor/anna.htm.

Czech, Danuta. *Auschwitz Chronicle: From the Archives of the Auschwitz Memorial and the German Federal Archives.* New York: Owl Books, 1997.

Delbo, Charlotte. *Auschwitz and After.* New Haven: Yale University Press, 1995.

Ficowski, Jerzy. *Rodzynki z Migdałami (Raisins with Almonds).* Warsaw: Ossolineum, 1964.

Frister, Roman. *The Cap: The Price of a Life.* Translated by Hillel Halkin. New York: Grove Books, 1999.

Goldkorn, Joseph. *Unbelievable but True* [original in Yiddish]. Tel Aviv: H. Leivik Publishing House.

Gross, Jan T. *Fear: Anti-Semitism in Poland after Auschwitz.* New York: Random House Trade Paperbacks, 2007.

Grynberg, Henryk. *Monolog Polsko-Żydowski (Polish-Jewish Monologue).* Wołowiec: 2003.

Grynberg, Henryk. *Uchodźcy (Refugees).* Warsaw: Świat Ksiązki, 2004.

Heller, Celia S. *On the Edge of Destruction: Jews of Poland between the Two World Wars.* Detroit: Wayne State University Press, 1994.

Hollander, Paul. "Murderous Idealism," op-ed, *Washington Post,* November 2, 2009.

Konner, Melvin. *Unsettled: An Anthropology of the Jews.* New York: Penguin, 2004.

Krall, Hanna. *Sublokatorka (Subtenant).* Warsaw: Świat Ksiązki, 2008.

Langer, Lawrence. *Holocaust Testimonies: The Ruins of Memory.* New Haven: Yale University Press, 1991.

Oz, Amos. *A Tale of Love and Darkness.* Orlando: Harcourt Inc., 2004.

Polonsky, Antony. *From Shtetl to Socialism: Studies from Polin.* Oxford: Littman Library of Jewish Civilization, 1993.

Ron, Shmuel. *Die Erinnerungen haben mich nie losgelassen (The Memories Never Let Go of Me)*. Frankfurt am Main: Verlag Neue Kritik, 1998.

Różewicz, Tadeusz. *Selected Poems*. Krakow: Wydawnictwo Literackie, 1997.

Sack, John. *An Eye for an Eye: The Untold Story of Jewish Revenge against Germans in 1945*. New York: Basic Books, 1995.

Segev, Tom. *The Seventh Million: The Israelis and the Holocaust*. New York: Picador, 2000.

Śmiałowski, M. *Wspomnienia (Memoirs)*. Warsaw: Spółka Wydawniczo-Księgarska, 1995.

Spector, Shmuel, and Robert Rozett. *Encyclopedia of the Holocaust*. Yad Vashem: The Jerusalem Publishing House Ltd., 2000.

Stavans, Ilan. *On Borrowed Words: A Memoir of Language*. New York: Penguin Books, 2002.

Szternfinkel, Natan E. *Żydzi w Zagłębiu (The Jews of Zagłębie)*. Sosnowiec: Sowa Press, 1993.

Wiesel, Elie. "What Really Makes Us Free," *Washington Post*, Parade, December 6, 1987.

Żywulska, Krystyna. *I Came Back*. London: Dennis Dobson Ltd., 1951.

Websites and Periodicals

The Nizkor Project (www.nizkor.org)

PolishJews.org

Żołnierz Wolności (*Soldier of Freedom*), a periodical of the People's Army of Poland

www.ingramcontent.com/pod-product-compliance
Lightning Source LLC
Chambersburg PA
CBHW031827090426

42741CB00005B/156